The Jesus Workbook:
A Self-Guided Study of a Chronological Harmony of the Gospels

Copyright © 2018 by Andrew Jackson

Published by IEB Publishing

Cover design: Orlen Stauffer

The Gospel quotations are from The International English Bible®
translated by Dr. Andrew Jackson.

Email - JesusWorkbook@DrAndrewJackson.com

978-0-9976758-8-7

THE JESUS WORKBOOK

A SELF-GUIDED STUDY OF A
CHRONOLOGICAL HARMONY OF THE GOSPELS

DR. ANDREW JACKSON

THE JESUS WORKBOOK

TABLE OF CONTENTS

28 - The Prophet John Begins His Public Ministry (Matthew 3:1, Mark 3:1-3, Luke 3:1-2, John 1:6-13)

29 - Prophet John's Message and Baptism (Matthew 3:2-10, Mark 1:4-6, Luke 3:3-14, 18)

30 - Religious Leaders Question John (John 1:19-28)

31 - Jesus Will Baptize With the Holy Spirit and Fire (Matthew 3:11-12, Mark 3:7-8, Luke 3:15-17)

32 - The Baptism of Jesus (Matthew 3:13-17, Mark 1:9-11, Luke 3:21-23)

33 - Satan Tests Jesus (Matthew 4:1-2, Mark 1:12-13, Luke 4:1-2)

34 - Jesus' First Temptation (Matthew 4:3-4, Luke 4:3-4)

35 - Jesus' Second Temptation (Matthew 4:5-7, Luke 4:9-12)

36 - Jesus' Third Temptation (Matthew 4:8-10, Luke 4:5-8)

37 - The Devil Leaves Jesus (Matthew 4:11, Luke 4:13)

38 - Jesus is the Lamb of God (John 1:29-34)

39 - Andrew and Peter Follow Jesus (John 1:35-42)

40 - Philip and Nathanael Follow Jesus (John 1:43-51)

41 - A Wedding at Cana in Galilee (John 2:1-11)

42 - Jesus Visits Capernaum (John 2:12)

43 - Jesus Attends the Passover Feast in Jerusalem (John 2:13)

44 - Jesus Clears Out the Jerusalem Temple (John 2:14-22)

45 - Many People See Jesus' Miraculous Signs (John 2:23-25)

46 - Jesus Teaches Nicodemus (John 3:1-15)

47 - God Loves the World (John 3:16-21)

48 - Jesus' Ministry in Judea at the Jordan River (John 3:22-24)

49 - John's Testimony About Jesus (John 3:25-36)

50 - Herod Antipas Arrests John (Matthew 14:3-5, Mark 6:17-20, Luke 3:19-20)

51 - Jesus Leaves Judea for Galilee (Matthew 4:12, John 4:1-3)

52 - Jesus Ministers to a Samaritan Woman (John 4:4-26)

53 - Jesus' Disciples Return (John 4:27-38)

54 - Many Samaritans Believe (John 4:39-42)

55 - Jesus is Welcomed in Galilee (John 4:43-45)

56 - Jesus Moves from Nazareth to Capernaum (Matthew 4:13-16)

57 - Jesus Heals Non-Jewish Official's Son (John 4:46-54)

58 - Jesus' Message and Ministry in Galilee (Matthew 4:17, Mark 1:14-15, Luke 4:14-15)

336 - Jesus Returns to Bethany (Matthew 21:17, Mark 11:19)

337 - Jesus on Faith in God (Mark 11:20-26)

338 - Jesus' Authority Is Questioned (Matthew 21:23-27, Mark 11:27-33, Luke 20:1-8)

339 - The Parable of Two Sons (Matthew 21:28-32)

340 - The Parable of a Landowner (Matthew 21:33-44, Mark 12:1-11, Luke 20:9-18)

341 - Religious Leaders Try to Arrest Jesus (Matthew 21:45-46, Mark 12:12, Luke 20:19)

342 - The Parable of a Wedding Banquet (Matthew 22:1-14, Luke 14:16-24)

343 - Paying Taxes to the Roman Emperor (Matthew 22:15-22, Mark 12:13-17, Luke 20:20-26)

344 - Marriage After the Resurrection (Matthew 22:23-33, Mark 12:18-27, Luke 20:27-40)

345 - The Greatest Commandments (Matthew 22:34-40, Mark 12:28-34, Luke 10:25-28)

346 - Is the Messiah the Son of David? (Matthew 22:41-46, Mark 12:35-37, Luke 20:41-44)

347 - Jesus Condemns the Religious Leaders (Matthew 23:1-36, Mark 12:38-40, Luke 20:45-47)

348 - Jesus Condemns the Religious Leaders (Luke 11:37-54)

349 - Jesus Condemns Jerusalem (Matthew 23:37-39, Luke 13:34-35)

350 - Jesus on True Giving (Mark 12:41-44, Luke 21:1-4)

351 - The Disciples Praise the Jerusalem Temple (Matthew 24:1, Mark 13:1, Luke 21:5)

352 - Jesus Prophecies the Destruction of the Jerusalem Temple (Matthew 24:2, Mark 13:2, Luke 21:6)

353 - The Disciples Question Jesus (Matthew 24:3: Mark 13:3-4; Luke 21:7)

354 - False Messiahs, Wars, Earthquakes, and Famines (Matthew 24:4-8, Mark 13:5-8, Luke 21:8-11)

355 - Global Mission and Persecution (Matthew 24:9-14, Mark 13:9-13, Luke 21:12-18)

356 - Jesus Prophesies the Roman Destruction of Jerusalem (Matthew 24:15-22, Mark 13:14-20, Luke 21:20-24)

357 - False Christs and Prophets (Matthew 24:23-26, Mark 13:21-23, Luke 21:8)

358 - The Second Coming of Jesus Christ (Matthew 24:27-44, Mark 13:24-37, Luke 21:25-36)

359 - The Parable of a Faithful Servant (Matthew 24:45-51, Luke 12:41-48)

360 - The Parable of Ten Young Girls (Matthew 25:1-13)

361 - The Parable of Faithful Stewardship (Matthew 25:14-30; Luke 19:11-27)

362 - God's Final Judgment (Matthew 25:31-46)

363 - Jesus Predicts His Crucifixion (Matthew 26:1-2)

364 - The Plan to Kill Jesus (Matthew 26:3-5, Mark 14:1-2, Luke 22:1-2, John 11:45-53)

365 - Judas' Plan to Betray Jesus (Matthew 26:14-16, Mark 14:10-11, Luke 22:3-6)

397 - Jesus Arrested in Gethsemane (Matthew 26:47-56, Mark 14:43-49, Luke 22:47-53, John 18:2-11)

398 - All the Disciples Desert Jesus (Matthew 26:56, Mark 14:50-52)

399 - Jesus Taken to High Priest Annas (John 18:12-14)

400 - Peter's First Denial of Jesus (John 18:15-17)

401 - Jesus Questioned by High Priest Annas (John 18:19-23)

402 - Jesus Taken to High Priest Caiaphas (Matthew 26:57-58, Mark 14:53-54, Luke 22:54, John 18:18, 24)

403 - Peter's Second Denial of Jesus (Matthew 26:69-72, Mark 14:66-70, Luke 22:55-58, John 18:25)

404 - Jesus Questioned by High Priest Caiaphas (Matthew 26:59-66, Mark 14:55-60, Luke 22:63-64)

405 - Jesus is Mocked and Beat (Matthew 26:67-68, Mark 14:65, Luke 22:63-65)

406 - Peter's Third Denial of Jesus (Matthew 26:73-75, Mark 14:70-72, Luke 22:59-62, John 18:26-27)

407 - The Jewish Sanhedrin Condemns Jesus (Matthew 27:1, Mark 15:1, Luke 22: 66-71)

408 - Judas Commits Suicide (Matthew 27:3-10)

409 - Jesus Sent to Pontius Pilate (Matthew 27:1-2, Mark 15:1, Luke 23:1, John 18:28)

410 - Pilate Hears the Charges Against Jesus (Luke 23:2, John 18:29-32)

411 - Pilate Questions Jesus the First Time (Matthew 27:11, Mark 15:2, Luke 23:3, John 18:33-38)

412 - Pilate Speaks to the Jews (Luke 23:4, John 18:38)

413 - Pilate Questions Jesus the Second Time (Matthew 27:12-14, Mark 15:3-5)

414 - Pilate Sends Jesus to Herod Antipas (Luke 23:5-7)

415 - Herod Antipas Questions Jesus (Luke 23:8-10)

416 - Jesus is Mocked and Sent Back to Pilate (Luke 23:11-12)

417 - Pilate's Wife Pleads for Jesus' Freedom (Matthew 27:19)

418 - Pilate Finds Jesus Innocent (Luke 23:13-17)

419 - Jews Chose Barabbas Over Jesus (Matthew 27:15-21, Mark 15:6-11, John 18:39-40)

420 - The Jews Demanded That Jesus Be Crucified (Matthew 27:22-23, Mark 15:12-14, Luke 23:18-24)

421 - Pilate Sentences Jesus to Crucifixion (Matthew 27:26, Mark 15:15, Luke 23:25, John 19:1,16)

422 - Roman Soldiers Mock and Beat Jesus (Matthew 27:27-31, Mark 15:16-20, Luke 22:63-65, John 19:2-3)

423 - Pilate Presents Jesus to the Jews the First Time (John 19:4-8)

424 - Pilate Questions Jesus the Third Time (John 19:9-11)

425 - Pilate Presents Jesus to the Jews the Second Time (John 19:12-15)

426 - Pilate Washes His Hands (Matthew 27:24-25)

427 - Simon Carries Jesus' Cross (Matthew 27:32, Mark 15:21, Luke 23:26)

428 - Women Weep (Luke 23:27-31)

429 - Golgatha, the Place of the Skull (Matthew 27:33, Mark 15:22, Luke 23:33, John 19:17)

430 - Roman Soldiers Mock Jesus and Offer Him Mixed Wine (Matthew 27:34, Mark 15:23, Luke 23:36-37)

431 - Jesus was Crucified at 9 a.m. (Matthew 27:35, Mark 15:24-25)

432 - Roman Soldiers Divide Jesus' Clothes (Matthew 27:35-36, Mark 15:24, Luke 23:34, John 19:23-24)

433 - Jesus' Prayer of Forgiveness (Luke 23:34)

434 - Written Charge: The King of the Jews (Matthew 27:37, Mark 15:26, Luke 23:38. John 19:19-22)

435 - The Two Thieves (Matthew 27:38, Mark 15:27-28, Luke 23:33, John 19:18)

436 - The People Yell Insults at Jesus (Matthew 27:39-40, Mark 15:29-30, Luke 23:35)

437 - The Religious Leaders Yell Insults at Jesus (Matthew 27:41-43, Mark 15:31-32)

438 - The Thieves Yell Insults at Jesus (Matthew 27:44, Mark 15:32, Luke 23:39)

439 - Thief Receives Forgiveness (Luke 23:40-43)

440 - Mary and the Women Disciples of Jesus (John 19:25-27)

441 - Darkness From Noon to 3 p.m. (Matthew 27:45, Mark 15:33, Luke 23:44-45)

442 - Jesus Cries Out Psalm 22:1 (Matthew 27:46-49, Mark 15:34-36)

443 - It is Finished! (John 19:28-30)

444 - Jesus Gives Up His Spirit (Matthew 27:50, Mark 15:47, Luke 23:46, John 19:30)

445 - Temple's Curtain Torn in Two (Matthew 27:51, Mark 15:38, Luke 23:44)

446 - Earthquake and Tombs Open (Matthew 27:51-52)

447 - Roman Soldiers Praise Jesus (Matthew 27:54, Mark 15:39, Luke 23:47)

448 - Women Disciples Watch Jesus' Crucifixion (Matthew 27:55-56, Mark 15:40-41, Luke 23:48-49)

449 - Roman Soldier Pierces Jesus' Side (John 19:31-34)

450 - The Testimony of the Apostle John (John 19:35-37)

451 - Joseph of Arimathea Takes Jesus' Body (Matthew 27:57-58, Mark 15:42-45, Luke 23:50-51, John 19:38)

452 - Jesus' Body Wrapped in Linen and Oils (Matthew 27:59, Mark 15:46, Luke 23:53, John 19:39-40)

453 - Jesus' Body Put in a New Tomb (Matthew 27:60, Mark 15:46, Luke 23:53, John 19:41-42)

454 - Women Disciples See Jesus' Tomb (Matthew 27:61, Mark 15:47, Luke 23:54-56)

455 - Roman Soldiers Guard Jesus' Tomb (Matthew 27:62-66)

456 - Women Disciples Go to Jesus' Tomb on Sunday Morning (Matthew 28:1-8, Mark 16:1-8, Luke 24:1-8, John 20:1-2)

INTRODUCTION

Gospel Quotations: All the Gospel quotations in the Jesus Workbook are from my English New Testament translation, the International English Bible (available on Amazon).

A Devotional Study Workbook: The Jesus Workbook is not a commentary, but is a personalized devotional study "workbook" that you can read, reflect on, and write your own notes and comments in.

What is a Chronological Harmony of the Gospels? A chronological harmony of the Gospels is an attempt to create a single, merged narrative of the life and teaching of Jesus out of the common and diverse material recorded in Matthew, Mark, Luke, and John. Because the Gospel of John contains unique material from the other three Gospels, its material is the most challenging to locate in a chronological harmony.

Tatian's Harmony of the Gospels in AD 170: Tatian was probably born in Edessa (modern Urfa in Turkey). He traveled to Rome and became a student of Justin Martyr. Following Justin's death in 165, Tatian left Rome and started a school in Mesopotamia. He engaged in mission journeys through the lands around the Euphrates River and his teaching had a major impact on the region of Syria. Around 170, Tatian wrote a harmony of the four New Testament Gospels combined into a single narrative of the life and teaching of Jesus, called the Diatessaron. Tatian's harmony of the Gospels provides a very early witness to the existence of the four biblical Gospels.

A Biography of the Biblical Jesus: Because Jesus has been misused and repackaged in our modern, faddish pop-culture world, it is crucial for Christians (and Churches) to engage in a thorough reexamination of the life and teaching of the biblical Jesus. Although a chronological harmony of the Gospels is not a modern biography, it is nonetheless an inspired biographical narrative that is authoritative in understanding the overall unity of the life and teaching of Jesus Christ.

The Formatting of Traditional Gospel Harmonies: Several Gospel harmonies are available today. However, many of them are academically formatted in horizontal parallel columns in an attempt to provide side-by-side word comparisons of the teaching and events in Jesus' life and ministry. As a result, these harmony formats are very difficult to read as a single narrative.

Numbered Sections, No Chapters: The Jesus Workbook has no chapters. Its layout is intended to be user-friendly and its sections are numbered from 1 to 475 with subtitles and cross-references, which provides an easy reading and flowing narrative.

The Chronological Priority of Luke's Gospel: The Jesus Workbook is primarily structured around the narrative sequence of the Gospel of Luke. Luke is the only Gospel that intentionally provides us with a clearer chronological order to the life of Jesus.

The Geography of the Gospels: I studied historical-geography of the Bible for one year at the Jerusalem University College, and I found knowing the geography of Israel to be an important guide in creating a chronological harmony of the Gospels.

Small Groups: The Jesus Workbook is also a great discipleship tool for small groups to go through together.

No Book is Perfect: All authors know that when they engage in the research it takes to write a book that he or she will make some factual mistakes. No book is perfect, that includes this one. Please help out by emailing me any factual mistakes that you find so that these mistakes can be corrected in future updated editions.

THE JESUS WORKBOOK
A SELF-GUIDED STUDY
OF A CHRONOLOGICAL
HARMONY OF THE GOSPELS

1 - The Word Was God
(John 1:1-5)

John 1:1-5 - (1) In the beginning *(before the creation of the universe)* was the Word *(Logos)*, and the Word was with *(toward)* God, and the Word was God. (2) He was with God in the beginning. (3) Everything was created through the Word, and without him nothing was created that has been created. (4) In him was life, and that life was the light of all people. (5) The light shines in the darkness of this world, and the darkness has not put out *(overcome)* the light.

2 - The Word Became Human
(John 1:14-18)

John 1:14-18 - (14) The Word *(Logos)* became human (flesh) and lived among us. We saw his glory—the glory of the one and only Son, who came from the Father, full of grace and truth. (15) John told the people about Jesus and shouted, "This is the one I spoke to you about when I said, 'He who comes after me is much greater than me, because he existed before me.'" (16) And flowing from his fullness, we have all received never-ending grace—grace upon grace. (17) For the law was given through Moses, but God's grace and truth came to us through Jesus Christ. (18) No human has ever seen God, but the one and only God the Son, who is one with *(at the side of)* God the Father, has revealed him to us.

3 - The Genealogies of Jesus Christ
(Matthew 1:1-17, Luke 3:23-38)

Matthew 1:1-17 - (1) This is the book of the genealogy of Jesus the Messiah *(Christ)*, the son of David, the son of Abraham. (2) Abraham became the father of Isaac, Isaac of Jacob, Jacob of Judah and his brothers, (3) Judah of Perez and Zerah by Tamar, Perez of Hezron, Hezron of Ram, (4) Ram of Amminadab, Amminadab of Nahshon, Nahshon of Salmon, (5) Salmon of Boaz *(whose mother was Rahab)*, Boaz of Obed *(whose mother was Ruth)*, Obed of Jesse, (6) and Jesse of King David. David was the father of Solomon *(by the wife of Uriah)*, (7) Solomon of Rehoboam, Rehoboam of Abijah, Abijah of Asah, (8) Asah of Jehoshaphat, Jehoshaphat of Jehoram, Jehoram of Uzziah, (9) Uzziah of Jotham, Jotham of Ahaz, Ahaz of Hezekiah, (10) Hezekiah of Manasseh, Manasseh of Amon, Amon of Josiah, (11) Josiah of Jechoniah and his brothers, at the time of the Babylonian exile. (12) After the exile to Babylon: Jechoniah became the father of Shealtiel, Shealtiel of Zerubbabel, (13) Zerubbabel of Abiud, Abiud of Eliakim, Eliakim of Azor, (14) Azor of Zadok, Zadok of Achim, Achim of Eliud, (15) Eliud of Eleazar, Eleazar of Matthan, Matthan of Jacob, (16) and Jacob of Joseph the husband of Mary, the mother of Jesus, who is called Messiah *(Christ)*. (17) So there were 14 generations in all from Abraham to David, 14 generations from David to the exile to Babylon, and 14 generations from the Babylonian exile to the Messiah *(Christ)*.

Luke 3:23-38 - This is the genealogy of Jesus: He was recognized as the son of Joseph, son of Heli, (24) son of Matthat, son of Levi, son of Melchi, son of Jannai, son of Joseph, (25) son of Mattathias, son of Amos, son of Nahum, son of Esli, son of Naggai, (26) son of Maath, son of Mattathias, son of Semein, son of Josech, son of Joda, (27) son of Joanan, son of Rhesa, son of Zerubbabel, son of Shealtiel, son of Neri, (28) son of Melchi, son of Addi, son of Cosam, son of Elmadam, son of Er, (29) son of Joshua, son of Eliezer, son of Jorim, son of Matthat, son of Levi, (30) son of Simeon, son of Judah, son of Joseph, son of Jonam, son of Eliakim, (31) son of Melea, son of Menna, son of Mattatha, son of Nathan, son of David, (32) son of Jesse, son of Obed, son of Boaz, son of Salmon, son of Nahshon, (33) son of Amminadab, son of Admin, son of Arni, son of Hezron, son of Perez, son of Judah, (34) son of Jacob, son of Isaac, son of Abraham, son of Terah, son of Nahor, (35) son of Serug, son of Reu, son of Peleg, son of Eber, son of Shelah, (36) son of Cainan, son of Arphaxad, son of Shem, son of Noah, son of Lamech, (37) son of Methuselah, son of Enoch, son of Jared, son of Mahalaleel, son of Kenan, (38) son of Enosh, son of Seth, son of Adam, and the son of God.

4 - Luke's Gospel Based on Eyewitness Testimony
(Luke 1:1-4)

Luke 1:1-4 - (1) Many people have undertaken to compile a narrative account of the things that have been fulfilled among us (2) just as they were handed down to us by those who from the beginning (*from Jesus' water baptism and the start of his public ministry*) were eyewitnesses and ministers (*servants*) of God's word. (3) With this in mind, since I have also carefully investigated (researched) everything from the beginning, I too decided to write an orderly narrative account for you, most honorable Theophilus, (4) so that you will know that what you have been taught is certain and true.

---

5 - Angel Gabriel Visits Priest Zechariah in the Temple
(Luke 1:5-22)

Luke 1:5-22 - (5) During the time of Herod the Great, king of Judea, there lived a temple priest named Zechariah, who belonged to the priestly division of Abijah (*there were 24 divisions of priests in Israel*)—his wife Elizabeth was also a descendant of Aaron (*of priestly lineage*). (6) They both lived righteous lives before God, blamelessly obeying all the Lord's commandments and regulations. (7) But they had no children because Elizabeth could not conceive, and they were both now very old. (8) One day when Zechariah's division was on temple duty and he was serving as a priest before God, (9) he was chosen by the throwing of dice (*lots*), according to the priestly custom, to go into the Lord's temple and burn incense on the altar before the Most Holy Place. (10) And during the time of the burning of the incense, a large group of worshipers was praying outside. (11) Then an angel of the Lord (*Gabriel*) appeared to Zechariah, standing at the right side of the altar of incense. (12) When Zechariah saw the angel, he became startled and was gripped with fear. (13) But the angel said to him, "Zechariah, do not be afraid, for your prayer request has been heard by God. Your wife Elizabeth will give birth to a son, and you are to name him John. (14) He will be a joy and delight to you, and many people will rejoice because of his birth, (15) because he will be great in the sight of the Lord. He will never drink alcohol, and he will be filled with the Holy Spirit even before he is born. (16) He will bring back many people of Israel to the Lord their God. (17) And he will go before the Lord and fulfill what is written in Malachi 4:5-6, 'He will minister in the spirit and power of Elijah, to turn the hearts of the parents to their children, and the disobedient to the wisdom of the righteous—to make ready a people prepared for the Lord.' "

(18) Zechariah asked the angel, "How do I know this will come true? For my wife and I are very old." (19) The angel said to him, "I am the archangel Gabriel! I stand in God's presence, and he sent me to tell you this wonderful good news. (20) And now you will not be able to speak until John's birth, because you did not believe my message, which will be fulfilled in the right time." (21) Meanwhile, the people praying outside were waiting for Zechariah, wondering why he stayed so long in the temple. (22) When Zechariah finally came out, he could not talk to them. Then the people realized that he had seen a vision in the temple, because he was making hand signs to them and he could not talk.

6 - Elizabeth Becomes Pregnant
(Luke 1:23-25)

Luke 1:23-25 - (23) When Zechariah's service as a priest was finished, he returned home (*priests served in the temple only twice a year*). (24) Soon after this his wife Elizabeth became pregnant, and she stayed secluded in her house for five months. (25) She declared, "The Lord has done this for me. In these days he has shown his grace to me and has taken away my shame from among the people.

7 - Angel Gabriel Visits Mary
(Luke 1:26-38)

Luke 1:26-38 - (26) Now in the sixth month of Elizabeth's pregnancy, God sent the archangel Gabriel to the town of Nazareth in Galilee, (27) to visit a young virgin girl named Mary, who was legally engaged to be married to a man named Joseph, a descendant of David. (28) The angel Gabriel went to her and said, "Greetings, you who have been greatly blessed! The Lord God is with you!" (29) Mary was very troubled by Gabriel's words and wondered what kind of greeting this was. (30) But Gabriel said to her, "Mary, do not be afraid, because you have found favor with God. (31) You will conceive in your womb and give birth to a son, and you are to give him the name Jesus (*a name that means "the Lord saves"*). (32) He will be great and will be called the Son of the Most High God! The Lord God will give him the throne of his father David, (33) and he will reign over Jacob's descendants forever—his kingdom will have no end (*will be everlasting*)." (34) Mary asked Gabriel, "How can this happen, since I am a virgin?" (35) Gabriel said to her, "The Holy Spirit will come on you, and the power of the Most High God will overshadow you. Therefore the one to be born will be called the Son of God. (36) Believe me, because even your relative Elizabeth is going to have a son in her old age, although she was unable to give birth. She is now six months pregnant. (37) For nothing is impossible with God!" (38) Mary said, "I am the Lord's servant, so let your message to me be fulfilled." Then the angel Gabriel left her.

8 - Mary is Pregnant
(Matthew 1:18-19)

Matthew 1:18-19 - (18) Now this is the story of the birth of Jesus the Messiah (*Christ*): While Mary was legally engaged to be married to Joseph, but before they were married, she was found to be with a child by the Holy Spirit. (19) Because Joseph—Mary's husband-to-be—lived a righteous life and did not want to disgrace her in public, he decided to end his engagement with Mary in secret.

9 - Mary Visits Elizabeth in Judea
(Luke 1:39-56)

Luke 1:39-56 - (39) Immediately Mary got ready and hurried to a town in the hill country of Judea. (*The hill country of Judea was one of the heartland regions of ancient Israel, around 40 miles/64 km, stretching from Jerusalem in the north to Beersheba in the south*). (40) She entered Zechariah's house and greeted Elizabeth. (41) When Elizabeth heard Mary's greeting, the baby leaped in her womb, and Elizabeth was filled with the Holy Spirit. (42) In a loud voice she declared, "Blessed are you among women, and blessed is the son in your womb! (43) But why am I so blessed, that the mother of my Lord has come to visit me? (44) As soon as the sound of your greeting reached my ears, the baby in my womb jumped for joy. (45) Blessed is she who has believed that the Lord would fulfill his promises to her!" (46) And Mary declared, "My soul magnifies the Lord, (47) and my spirit rejoices in God my Savior, (48) because he has seen the humble heart of his servant. From now on all generations will call me blessed, (49) for the Mighty One has done great things for me—holy is his name! (50) His mercy goes out to all who fear him—from generation to generation. (51) He has done mighty acts with his arm. He has scattered those who are proud in their inner thoughts. (52) He has brought down proud dynasties from their thrones, but has exalted the humble. (53) He has filled the hungry with good things, but has sent the rich away empty. (54) He has helped his servant Israel, remembering to be merciful (55) to Abraham and his descendants forever, just as he promised our ancestors." (56) Mary stayed with Elizabeth for about three months and then returned to her home in Nazareth of Galilee.

10 - The Birth of Prophet John
Luke 1:57-79

Luke 1:57-79 - (57) Now when it was time for Elizabeth to have her baby, she gave birth to a son. (58) Her neighbors and relatives heard that the Lord had shown his great mercy to her, and they rejoiced with her. (59) On the eighth day they came to circumcise the baby boy, and they were going to name him Zechariah after his father, (60) but Elizabeth spoke up and said, "No! His name must be John." (61) They said to her, "There is no one in your family who has the name John." (62) And then they made hand signs to Zechariah, because they wanted to know what he wanted to name his son. (63) Zechariah asked for a writing tablet, and to everyone's surprise he wrote, "His name is to be John." (64) Immediately Zechariah could speak again, and he began praising God. (65) All their neighbors were filled with amazement, and throughout the hill country of Judea people were talking about all these things. (66) Everyone who heard what had happened was puzzled and asked each other, "Who is this boy going to be?" For the Lord's hand was with him. (67) John's father Zechariah was filled with the Holy Spirit and prophesied: (68) "Blessed be the Lord, the God of Israel, because he has come and redeemed his people. (69) He has raised up the king of salvation for us in the house of his servant David. (70) As he said through the (*Old Testament*) prophets long ago: Salvation from our enemies and from all those who hate us—(72) to show mercy to our ancestors and to remember his holy covenant, (73) the oath of promise he swore to our father Abraham; (74) to rescue us from the hand of our enemies, and to enable us to serve him without fear (75), in holiness and righteousness before him all our days. (76) "And you, my son John, will be called a prophet of the Most High God, for you will go before the Lord to prepare the way for him, (77) to give his people the knowledge of salvation through the forgiveness of their sins, (78) because of the compassionate mercy of our God, by which the rising sun will come to us from heaven, (79) to shine on those living in darkness and in the shadow of death, to guide our feet into the path of peace."

11 - John Lives in the Wilderness of Judea
(Luke 1:80)

Luke 1:80 - And John grew up in the strength of the Holy Spirit, and he lived in the wilderness of Judea (*east of Jerusalem, in the lower Jordan River Valley*) until he started his public ministry to the people of Israel.

12 - Angel Appears to Joseph
(Matthew 1:20-23)

Matthew 1:20-23 - (20) But while Joseph was thinking about how to end his engagement with Mary, an angel of the Lord appeared to him in a dream and said, "Joseph, son of David, do not be afraid to take Mary home as your wife, because the baby in her womb is from the Holy Spirit. (21) Mary's first child will be a son, and you are to name him Jesus (*a name that means "the Lord saves"*), for he will save his people from their sins." (22) All this took place to fulfill what is written in Isaiah 7:14, (23) "The virgin will conceive and give birth to a son, and they will call him Immanuel," which means "God with us."

13 - Joseph Marries Mary
(Matthew 1:24-25)

Matthew 1:24-25 - (24) When Joseph woke up from his sleep, he did what the angel of the Lord had told him. He took Mary home as his wife, (25) but he did not have sexual intercourse with her before she gave birth to a son. And he gave him the name Jesus.

14 - Joseph and Mary Go to Bethlehem
(Luke 2:1-5)

Luke 2:1-5 - (1) In those days the emperor Caesar Augustus gave a command that a population census must be taken of the entire Roman empire. (2) This was the first census that took place while Quirinius was governor of the Roman province of Syria. (3) And everyone went to their home town to register their name. (4) So Joseph also traveled from Nazareth in Galilee to Judea, to Bethlehem the town of David, because he belonged to the house and lineage of David. (5) He went there to register his pregnant wife Mary.

15 - The Birth of Jesus in Bethlehem
(Matthew 2:1; Luke 2:6-7)

Matthew 2:1 - Jesus was born about six miles (9 km) south of Jerusalem in the town of Bethlehem (*which had a population of around 1,000*), in the region of Judea in southern Israel, during the rule of King Herod the Great. (*Jesus was born before the death of Herod the Great in 4 BC*).

Luke 2:6-7 - (6) While they were in Bethlehem, the time came for Mary to give birth to her baby (7) and she gave birth to her first baby, a son. She wrapped him in strips of cloth and laid him in an animal's feeding trough (*a manger*) located in a lower room of the house (*traditionally understood as a public inn, but houses at this time often had a section on the lower floor for their animals*), because there was no place for them in the upper guest room.

16 - Angel Visits Shepherds in Bethlehem
(Luke 2:8-12)

Luke 2:8-12 - And there were shepherds living out in the fields near Bethlehem, keeping guard over their flocks at night. (*Shepherds usually lived outside during the warmer months, from March to November*). (9) An angel of the Lord appeared to them, and the majestic glory of God's presence shone around them. They were terrified. (10) But the angel said to them, "Do not be afraid, because I bring you good news of great joy for all the people. (11) Today in Bethlehem—the town of David—a Savior has been born to you; he is the Messiah (*Christ*), the Lord. (12) This will be a sign to you: You will find a baby boy wrapped in cloths and lying in an animal's feeding trough (*a manger*)."

17 - Shepherds Visit Joseph, Mary, and Jesus
(Luke 2:13-20)

Luke 2:13-20 - (13) Suddenly a great army of heavenly angels appeared with the angel, worshiping God and saying, (14) "Glory to God in heaven, and on earth peace to all people on whom his grace rests!" (15) After the angels went back to heaven, the shepherds said to one another, "Let's go to Bethlehem and see what the Lord has made known to us." (16) So the shepherds hurried to Bethlehem and found Mary, Joseph, and baby Jesus, who was lying in an animal's feeding trough (*a manger*). (17) When the shepherds saw the baby, they told everyone what they had been told about baby Jesus (18) and everyone was amazed at what they heard the shepherds tell them. (19) But Mary remembered all these things and pondered them in her heart. (20) The shepherds went back to their flocks, glorifying and praising God for all the things they had heard and had seen, which were just as they had been told by the angel.

18 - The Circumcision and Naming of Jesus
(Matthew 1:25, Luke 2:21)

Matthew 1:25 - And he gave him the name Jesus.

Luke 2:21 - At the end of eight days, when it was time to circumcise the baby boy, he was named Jesus (*which means "the Lord saves"*), the name the angel had given him before he was born.

19 - Jesus Dedicated in the Jerusalem Temple
(Luke 2:22-24)

Luke 2:22-24 - (22) When the time of the purification rites required by the law of Moses (*after 40 days*) came, Joseph and Mary took Jesus up to the Jerusalem temple to dedicate him to the Lord, (23) as it is written by Moses in Exodus 13:2, "Every firstborn male is to be consecrated to the Lord." Luke 2:24 - And they offered a sacrifice in keeping with what is written in Leviticus 12:8, "a pair of doves or two young pigeons." (*This type of sacrifice suggests that Joseph and Mary were from the lower class of society*).

20 - Simeon in the Jerusalem Temple
(Luke 2:25-35)

Luke 2:25-35 - (25) Now there was a man living in Jerusalem named Simeon. He was holy and righteous before God, and was waiting for the restoration of Israel. The Holy Spirit was on him, (26) and it had been revealed to him by the Spirit that he would not die before he saw the Lord's Messiah (*Christ*). (27) And Simeon was led by the Holy Spirit into the temple courts at the same time that Joseph and Mary brought baby Jesus to perform for him the custom required by the law of Moses. (28) Simeon took Jesus in his arms and praised God, saying, (29) "Sovereign Lord, as you have promised; you can now dismiss your servant in peace. (30) For my eyes have seen your salvation, (31) which you have prepared in the sight of all peoples—(32) a light for revelation to the nations, and the glory of your people Israel." (33) Joseph and Mary marveled at what Simeon said about Jesus. (34) Then Simeon blessed them and said to Mary his mother, "Jesus will cause the falling and rising of many people in Israel, and he will be a sign that people will speak against, (35) so the thoughts of many hearts will be revealed. And a sword will even pierce your soul, Mary (*which likely refers to Mary's witness of the crucifixion of Jesus*)."

21 - Anna in the Jerusalem Temple
(Luke 2:36-38)

Luke 2:36-38 - (36) There was also a prophetess named Anna, who was the daughter of Phanuel, of the tribe of Asher. She was very old. She had been married seven years (37) before her husband died, and then she remained a widow until she was 84 years old. She never left the temple courts but worshiped God day and night (*from morning to evening*) through fasting and prayer. (38) Coming up to Joseph and Mary at that very moment, she gave thanks to God and spoke about the child Jesus to everyone who was looking for the redemption of Jerusalem.

22 - Wise Men From the East
(Matthew 2:1-12)

Matthew 2:1-12 - (1) Some time after Jesus' birth (*probably around two years*), wise men (*Magi*) traveled from the east to Jerusalem. (2) They asked, "Where is the one who has been born king of the Jews? We saw his star rising in the east, and we have come to worship him." (3) When King Herod the Great heard this, he and all in Jerusalem were greatly troubled. (4) Herod gathered together all the Jewish chief priests and teachers of the law of Moses and asked them where the Messiah (*Christ*) was to be born. (5) They told him, "In Bethlehem of Judea, for it is written in Micah 5:2, (6) 'But you, Bethlehem, in the land of Judah, are by no means least among the rulers of Judah; for out of you will come a ruler who will shepherd my people Israel.' " (7) Then Herod met with the wise men in private and found out from them the exact time the star had appeared to them. (8) Herod sent the wise men to Bethlehem, saying, "Go and search carefully for the child. And as soon as you find him, immediately report back to me, so that I too can go and worship him." (9) After they had heard from King Herod, the wise men went on their way, and the star they had seen in the east led them to the house where the child Jesus was. (10) They were filled with joy when they saw the star. (11) They went into the house and saw the child Jesus with his mother Mary, and they bowed down in prostration and worshiped Jesus. Then they opened their treasures and gave him gifts of gold, incense, and myrrh (*a fragrant resin extracted from a special tree and used for perfume, incense, and medicine*). (12) And the wise men were warned in a dream not to return to Herod, so they went back to their own country by another route.

23 - Jesus' Family Escapes to Egypt
(Matthew 2:13-15)

Matthew 2:13-15 - (13) When the wise men had left, an angel of the Lord appeared to Joseph in a dream and said, "Get up! Take Mary and the child Jesus and escape to Egypt, for Herod will search for Jesus to kill him. Stay in Egypt until I tell you when to return to Israel." (14) So Joseph got ready and took Mary and Jesus and left that night. They traveled to the Roman province of Egypt (*probably a journey of about 300 miles/483 km to the large Jewish community in the city of Alexandria*). (15) They lived there until the death of King Herod the Great, fulfilling what is written in Hosea 11:1, "Out of Egypt I called my son."

24 - King Herod Tries to Kill Jesus
(Matthew 2:16-18)

Matthew 2:16-18 - (16) Herod the Great was furious when he realized that the wise men had fooled him. So he ordered his soldiers to kill every boy in the village of Bethlehem and its surrounding area. He commanded them to kill every boy two years old or younger, based on the time he had learned from the wise men. (17) This fulfilled what is written in Jeremiah 31:15, (18) "A voice is heard in Ramah, weeping and great mourning, Rachel weeping for her children and refusing to be comforted, for they are no more."

- -

- -

- -

- -

- -

25 - Jesus' Family Returns to Nazareth
(Matthew 2:19-23, Luke 2:39-40)

Matthew 2:19-23 - (19) After Herod the Great died (*in March/April 5 or 4 BC*), an angel of the Lord appeared in a dream to Joseph in Egypt, and said, (20) "Get up, take Mary and the child Jesus and go to the land of Israel, because those who were trying to kill Jesus are dead." (*Jesus' family had probably been living in Egypt for at least one year or possibly two*).(21) So Joseph got up, and took Mary and the child Jesus and traveled to the land of Israel. (22) But he was afraid to go into the region of Judea in southern Israel for Herod Archelaus (*a son of King Herod the Great*) was reigning there. Having been warned in a dream, Joseph traveled to the region of Galilee in northern Israel (23) and lived in the town of Nazareth. So this fulfilled what was said through the prophets, that he would be called a Nazarene.

Luke 2:39-40 - (39) When Joseph and Mary had done everything that was required by the Lord's law, they left Jerusalem and returned to their own town of Nazareth in Galilee. (40) And Jesus grew and became strong; he was filled with wisdom and God's grace was on him.

(*Israel experienced significant political changes following the death of Herod the Great when his kingdom was divided into three sections that were ruled by his three sons. Herod Archelaus ruled over the regions of Judea, Idumaea and Samaria. Herod Philip ruled over the regions of Gaulanitis and Trachonitis northeast of Lake Galilee. And Herod Antipas ruled over the regions of Galilee and Perea. Herod Antipas governed Galilee and Perea for around 40 years, from 4 BC to AD 39, during the entire life and ministry of Jesus*).

(*In Jesus' day Galilee was divided into three regions: Upper Galilee was the mountainous region northwest of Lake Galilee, lower Galilee was approximately between Lake Galilee and the Mediterranean Sea, and the valley was the region of Lake Galilee and the Jordan River, which flowed into and out of Lake Galilee. Galilee was surrounded by Greek principalities and Greek city-states. Built by Herod Antipas on a high hill, Sepphoris was the capital Greek city of Galilee that was located only four miles from Nazareth.)*

(Nazareth was located in lower Galilee and was about 12 miles/19 km southwest of Lake Galilee, with a population of around 500).

26 - Boy Jesus at the Jerusalem Temple
(Luke 2:41-50)

Luke 2:41-50 - (41) Every year Joseph and Mary went to Jerusalem for the Passover Feast (*held in the spring, around late March/early April*). (42) According to the custom of the feast, they went up to Jerusalem when Jesus was 12 years old. (43) When the festival was over, Joseph and Mary returned to Nazareth, but they did not realize that the boy Jesus had stayed in Jerusalem. (44) They thought he was traveling in the caravan of their family and friends. After a day's journey (*about 20 miles/32 km*), they asked their family and friends where Jesus was. (45) When they could not find him, they went back to Jerusalem to look for him. (46) After three days they found Jesus sitting among the teachers in the temple courts, listening to them and asking them questions. (47) Everyone who heard Jesus was amazed at his understanding and his answers. (48) Joseph and Mary were shocked when they saw him. Mary said to Jesus, "Son, why have you scared us like this? We have been frantically searching for you everywhere." (49) Jesus said, "Why were you searching for me? Didn't you know that it is necessary for me to be in my Father's house (*doing my Father's affairs*)?" (50) But Joseph and Mary did not understand what Jesus was talking about.

27 - Jesus Grows Up in Nazareth
(Luke 2:51-52)

Luke 2:51-52 - (51) Then Jesus went down to Nazareth with Joseph and Mary, and he was obedient to his parents. But Mary remembered all these things in her heart. (52) And Jesus grew in wisdom and in body (*years*), and in favor with God and the people.

28 - The Prophet John Begins His Public Ministry
(Matthew 3:1, Mark 3:1-3, Luke 3:1-2, John 1:6-13)

Matthew 3:1 - In those days the prophet John, the Baptizer, went preaching into the wilderness of Judea.

Mark 3:1-3 - (1) This is the beginning of the gospel (*good news*) about Jesus the Messiah (*Christ*), the Son of God, (2) as it is written in Malachi 3:1, "I will send my messenger ahead of you, who will prepare your way," (3) and in Isaiah 40:3, "A voice of one calling in the wilderness, 'Prepare the way for the Lord, make straight paths for him.' "

Luke 3:1-2 - (1) In the fifteenth year of the reign of the Roman emperor Tiberius Caesar—when Pontius Pilate was governor of Judea, Herod Antipas the tetrarch (*a tetrarch was a governor of one of the four divisions of a country*) governed Galilee, his brother Herod Philip was tetrarch governor of Iturea and Traconitis (*the northern Transjordan*), and Lysanias the tetrarch governed Abilene (*the region around Damascus*)—(2) during the rule of the high priesthood of Annas and Caiaphas, the word of God came to the prophet John, son of Zechariah, in the wilderness of Judea.

John 1:6-13 - (6) God sent a man whose name was John. (7) He came as a witness to tell the people about the light, so that through him all people might believe. (8) John was not the light, but he came only as a witness to the light. (9) The true light that gives light to everyone was coming into the world. (10) He was in the world, and even though the world was created through him, the world did not know him. (11) He came to his own people, but his own people did not receive him. (12) But whoever did receive him—whoever believed in his name—he gave the right to become children of God—(13) children who were born not of human blood (*natural descent*), nor of human will, but of God.

29 - Prophet John's Message and Baptism
(Matthew 3:2-10, Mark 1:4-6, Luke 3:3-14, 18)

Matthew 3:2-10 - (2) He proclaimed, "Repent and turn to God! The kingdom of heaven (*God*) has come near (*is at hand*)!" (3) This is the one who was spoken of in Isaiah 40:3, "A voice of one calling in the wilderness: 'Prepare the way for the Lord. Make straight paths for him.' " (4) John wore clothes made of camel's hair, with a leather belt around his waist (*a similar description to that of Elijah in 2 Kings 1:8*), and he ate locusts and wild honey. (5) People went out to him from Jerusalem, Judea, and the whole region of the Jordan. (6) They confessed their sins and were baptized by him in the Jordan River.(7) But when John saw some Jewish religious leaders—Pharisees and Sadducees—coming to him to be baptized, he shouted to them, "You are a generation of snakes! Who told you to escape the coming wrath of God? (8) Live a life that shows that you have repented of your sins. (9) And stop saying that Abraham is your father. For I tell you the truth: God is able to raise up children for Abraham from the rocks on the ground. (10) Even now the ax is ready to cut the root of the trees, and every tree that does not produce good fruit will be cut down and thrown into the fire.

Mark 1:4-6 - (4) And so John the Baptizer came into the wilderness of Judea proclaiming a baptism of repentance for the forgiveness of sins. (*The Judean wilderness was the desert region located east of Jerusalem in the hill country of Judea and the Jordan Valley, measuring about 75 miles north-south and about 10 miles east-west*). (5) All the people of Jerusalem and the whole region of Judea went out to him, confessing their sins, and being baptized by him in the Jordan River. (6) John wore clothes made of camel's hair, with a leather belt around his waist (*a similar description to that of Elijah in 2 Kings 1:8*), and he ate locusts and wild honey.

Luke 3:3-14,18 - (3) The prophet John went into all the wilderness region of the Jordan River, proclaiming a baptism of repentance for the forgiveness of sins. (*The Jordan River is around 156 miles/251 km long and flows north-south through the Sea of Galilee and on to the Dead Sea*). (4) As it is written in Isaiah 40:3-5, "A voice of one calling in the wilderness, 'Prepare the way for the Lord, make straight paths for him. (5) Every valley will be filled in, and every mountain and hill made low. The crooked roads will become straight, and the rough ways smooth. (6) And all people will see the salvation of God.' " (7) John said to the crowds of people coming out to be baptized by him, "You are a group of snakes! Who warned you to flee from the coming wrath of God? (8) You must turn to God and live a life that produces fruit worthy of repentance. And do not say to yourselves, 'We have Abraham as our father.' For I tell you the truth: God can raise up children for Abraham out of these rocks on the ground. (9) The ax is already at the root of the trees, and every tree that does not produce good fruit will be cut down and thrown into the fire." (10) The people asked John, "What should we do?" (11) John said, "Anyone who has two shirts (*inner tunics*) should share with a person who does not have one, and anyone who has food should share with the person who has nothing to eat." (12) Even tax collectors came to John to be baptized and asked, "Teacher, what should we do?" (13) John told them, "Don't collect any more taxes than you are required to collect." (14) Then some soldiers asked him, "And what should we do?" John said, "Don't take money by force and don't accuse people falsely—be content with what you are paid.

Luke 3:18 - And with many other words John exhorted the people and proclaimed the gospel (*good news*) to them.

30 - Religious Leaders Question John
(John 1:19-28)

John 1:19-28 - (19) Now this is the testimony of John, when the Jewish religious leaders sent priests and Levites from Jerusalem to ask him who he was. (20) Without hesitating, John confessed openly, "I am not the Messiah (*Christ*)." (21) They asked him, "Are you Elijah?" John said, "No, I am not." They asked, "Are you the Prophet (*that Moses wrote about in Deuteronomy 18:15-18*)?" John said, "No" (22) Finally they said, "Who are you? Tell us! We must give an answer to those who sent us. Tell us who you are." (23) John answered them by quoting Isaiah 40:3, " 'I am the voice of one calling in the wilderness. Make straight the way of the Lord.' " (24) Now the Pharisees who had been sent (25) asked him, "Why then are you baptizing if you are not the Messiah (*Christ*), nor Elijah, nor the Prophet?" (26) John said to them, "I baptize with water, but one is living among you that you do not know. (27) He is the one coming after me, and I am not worthy to untie the straps of his `sandals." (28) These things took place in Bethany on the other side of the Jordan River (*in the region of Perea east of the Jordan River, located in modern Jordan*).

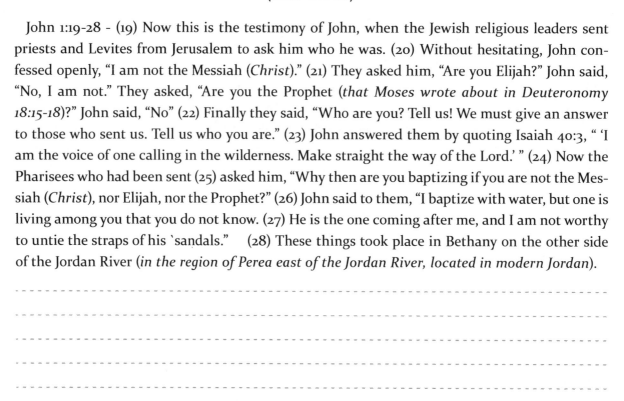

31 - Jesus Will Baptize With the Holy Spirit and Fire
(Matthew 3:11-12, Mark 3:7-8, Luke 3:15-17)

Matthew 3:11-12 - (11) "I baptize you with water for repentance, but the one coming after me is more powerful than me. I am not worthy even to carry his sandals. He will baptize you with the Holy Spirit and fire (*probably refers to the judgment of God*). (12) His pitchfork is in his hand, and he will separate the wheat from the waste. He will gather his wheat into his barn, and burn up the waste with a fire that never goes out."

Mark 3:7-8 - (7) And John proclaimed this message: "After me comes the one who is much greater than me. I am not worthy to stoop down and untie the straps of his sandals. (8) I baptize you with water, but he will baptize you with the Holy Spirit."

Luke 3:15-17 - (15) The people were waiting with great expectancy, because they were thinking in their hearts that John might be the Messiah (*Christ*). (16) John said to them all, "I baptize you with water, but one who is much more powerful than I am will come. I am not worthy enough to untie the straps of his sandals. He will baptize you with the Holy Spirit and fire (*probably refer-*

ring to judgment). (17) His pitchfork is in his hand to clear his threshing floor and to gather the wheat into his barn, and he will burn up the waste with unending fire."

32 - The Baptism of Jesus
(Matthew 3:13-17, Mark 1:9-11, Luke 3:21-23)

Matthew 3:13-17 - (13) Then Jesus traveled from Galilee to the Judean wilderness to be water-baptized by John in the Jordan River. (14) But John tried to stop Jesus from being baptized, and said to him, "Why do you come to me? I need to be baptized by you." (15) Jesus said to him, "Let me be baptized by you now, because it is good for us to fulfill all righteousness." Then John did as Jesus asked. (16) Jesus was baptized. As soon as Jesus came up out of the water, John immediately saw heaven open, and the Spirit of God come down like a dove, staying on Jesus. (17) And a voice from heaven said, "This is my Son, whom I love; with him I am very pleased."

Mark 1:9-11 - (9) At that time Jesus traveled from Nazareth in Galilee to Judea and was baptized by John in the Jordan River. (10) As soon as Jesus came up out of the water, John saw heaven open and the Holy Spirit came down on Jesus like a dove. (11) And a voice came from heaven and said, "You are my Son, whom I love; with you I am very pleased."

Luke 3:21-23 - (21) When all the people were being baptized by John, Jesus was also baptized in the Jordan River. (21) And as he was praying, heaven was opened (22) and the Holy Spirit came down upon him in the physical form of a dove. And a voice from heaven said, "You are my Son, whom I love; with you I am very pleased." (23) Now Jesus was about 30 years old when he began his public ministry.

33 - Satan Tests Jesus
(Matthew 4:1-2, Mark 1:12-13, Luke 4:1-2)

Matthew 4:1-2 - (1) After Jesus' baptism, the Holy Spirit led him into the Judean wilderness (*possibly in the region of Jericho*) to be tested (*tempted*) by the devil. (2) Jesus fasted about six weeks—40 days and nights—and became very hungry.

Mark 1:12-13 - (12) After Jesus' baptism, the Holy Spirit immediately sent him out into the Judean wilderness (*possibly in the region of Jericho*),and he was tested (*tempted*) by Satan for 40 days. (13) He lived with wild animals around him, and angels came and ministered to him.

Luke 4:1-2 - (1) Jesus was full of the Holy Spirit, and the Spirit led him from the Jordan River into the wildernessw of Judea (*possibly in the region of Jericho*), (2) where for 40 days he was tested (*tempted*) by the devil. He did not eat anything during that time, and when those days ended, he was very hungry.

----

34 - Jesus' First Temptation
(Matthew 4:3-4, Luke 4:3-4)

Matthew 4:3-4 - (3) Then the devil—the tempter—approached and said to Jesus, "If you are the Son of God, tell these rocks to become bread." (4) Jesus said, "It is written in Deuteronomy 8:3, 'Humans do not live on bread alone, but on every word that comes from the mouth of God.' "

Luke 4:3-4 - (3) The devil said to Jesus, "If you are the Son of God, tell this rock to become bread." (4) Jesus answered, "It is written in Deuteronomy 8:3, 'Man shall not live on bread alone.' "

----

35 - Jesus' Second Temptation
(Matthew 4:5-7, Luke 4:9-12)

Matthew 4:5-7 - (5) Then the devil took Jesus to the holy city of Jerusalem and had him stand on the highest point of the temple. (6) He said, "If you are the Son of God, throw yourself down, for it is written in Psalm 91:11-12, 'He will command his angels concerning you. They will lift you up in their hands so that you will not strike your foot against a rock.' " (7) Jesus said to him, "It is also written in Deuteronomy 6:16, 'Do not put the Lord your God to the test.' "

Luke 4:9-12 - (9) Finally, the devil led Jesus into Jerusalem and had him stand on the highest point of the temple, saying to him, "If you are the Son of God, throw yourself down from here, (10) for it is written in Psalm 91:11-12, 'God will command his angels concerning you to protect you. (11) They will lift you up in their hands, and you will not even strike your foot against a rock.' " (12) Jesus said, "It is written in Deuteronomy 6:16, 'Do not test the Lord your God.' "

36 - Jesus' Third Temptation
(Matthew 4:8-10, Luke 4:5-8)

Matthew 4:8-10 - (8) Then the devil took Jesus to a very high mountain and showed him the glory of all the kingdoms of this world (*possibly referring to the Roman empire*). (9) The devil said to him, "I will give you all the kingdoms of this world if you will bow down and worship me." (10) Jesus said, "Satan, away from me! For it is written in Deuteronomy 6:13, 'Worship the Lord your God and serve him only.' "

Luke 4:5-8 - (5) The devil led Jesus up to a high place and showed him all the kingdoms of the world (*possibly referring to the Roman empire*). (6) And the devil said to him, "I will give you all their power and glory, because it has been given to me, and I can give it to anyone I want to. (7) All you have to do is worship me, and you can have it all." (8) Jesus said, "It is written in Deuteronomy 6:13, 'Worship the Lord your God and serve him only!'"

37 - The Devil Leaves Jesus
(Matthew 4:11, Luke 4:13)

Matthew 4:11 - Then the devil left Jesus, and angels came and ministered to him.

Luke 4:13 - After the devil had finished testing Jesus, he left him until another opportune time.

38 - Jesus is the Lamb of God
(John 1:29-34)

John 1:29-34 - (29) The next day John saw Jesus walking toward him, and said, "Look! The Lamb of God, who takes away the sin of the world! (30) This is the one I told you about when I said, 'The one who comes after me is much greater than me because he existed before me.' (31) I did not know him, but the reason I came baptizing with water was so that he would be revealed to Israel." (32) Then John declared: "I saw the Holy Spirit descend from heaven like a dove and remain on him. (33) And I did not know him, but God who sent me to baptize with water told me, 'The one on whom you see the Holy Spirit descend from heaven and remain, this is the one who will baptize with the Holy Spirit.' (34) I am an eyewitness to what has happened and I tell you that this is the Son of God, God's Chosen One!"

---

39 - Andrew and Peter Follow Jesus
(John 1:35-42)

John 1:35-42 - (35) The next day John was with two of his disciples. (36) He saw Jesus walking by, and he said to his disciples, "Look! The Lamb of God!" (37) When the two disciples heard John say this, they followed Jesus. (38) Jesus turned around and saw them following him and said, "What do you want?" They said to him, "Teacher (*Rabbi*), where are you staying?" (39) Jesus said, "Come and you will see." So they went and saw where Jesus was staying, and they spent that day with him. It was about 4 p.m. (40) Andrew, Simon Peter's brother, was one of the two who heard what John had said and followed Jesus. (41) The first thing Andrew did was to find his brother Simon and said to him, "We have found the Messiah (*Christ*)." (42) Andrew took him to meet Jesus. Jesus looked at him and said, "You are Simon son of John, but now you will be called Cephas" (*in Aramaic*), which means Peter (*in Greek*). (*The names Cephas and Peter mean "rock"*).

---

40 - Philip and Nathanael Follow Jesus
(John 1:43-51)

John 1:43-51 - (43) The next day Jesus decided to walk to Galilee in northern Israel. When he arrived, he found Philip and said to him, "Follow me!" (44) Now Philip—like Andrew and Peter—was from the town of Bethsaida (*located around 6 miles/10 km from Capernaum on the northeastern shore of the Sea of Galilee*). (45) Philip found Nathanael, and said to him, "We have found the one Moses wrote about in the law, and about whom the prophets also wrote—Jesus of Nazareth, the son of Joseph." (46) Nathanael said to Philip, "Nazareth! Can anything good come from there?" Philip said to him, "Come and see for yourself." (47) When Jesus saw Nathanael walking toward him, he said, "Look! Here is an Israelite with a clean heart (*having no deceit*)!"

(48) Nathanael said to Jesus, "How do you know me?" Jesus said, "I saw you under a fig tree before Philip called you." (49) Then Nathanael declared, "Teacher (*Rabbi*), you are the Son of God! You are the king of Israel!" (50) Jesus said to him, "You believe in me because I told you I saw you under the fig tree? You will see greater acts of God than that. (51) I tell you the truth: You will see heaven open, and God's angels ascending and descending on the Son of Man (*see Daniel 7:13-14*)."

41 - A Wedding at Cana in Galilee
(John 2:1-11)

John 2:1-11 - (1) On the third day (probably two days after Jesus called Nathanael to follow him) a wedding took place in the town of Cana in Galilee. (*Cana was around 8 miles/13 km north of Nazareth*). Jesus' mother was there, (2) and Jesus and his disciples had also been invited to the wedding. (3) When there was no more wine, Jesus' mother said to him, "They have no more wine!" (4) Jesus said, "Mother (*Woman*), what does this have to do with me? For my time has not yet come." (5) Jesus' mother said to the servants, "Do whatever he tells you." (6) Now nearby there were six stone water jars that were used by the Jews for purification (*ceremonial*) washings, each could hold about 20 to 30 gallons. (7) Jesus told the servants, "Fill these jars with water." So they filled the jars. (8) Then he told them, "Now take some of the water to the wedding master." So they took it to him. (9) Although the servants knew where the water came from, the wedding master did not. After he tasted the water that had been turned into wine, he called the bridegroom aside (10) and said to him, "Everyone serves the best wine first and then he serves the cheaper wine after the guests are drunk, but you have saved the best wine until now!" (11) Turning water into wine at Cana was the first miraculous sign through which Jesus revealed his glory; and his disciples believed in him.

42 - Jesus Visits Capernaum
(John 2:12)

John 2:12 - After the wedding in Cana, Jesus walked about 16 miles/25 km to the town of Capernaum (*located on the northwestern shore of Lake Galilee*), along with his mother, brothers, sisters and disciples. And they stayed there for a few days.

_____

_____

_____

_____

_____

43 - Jesus Attends the Passover Feast in Jerusalem
(John 2:13)

John 2:13 - When the time of the Jewish Passover was near, Jesus walked about 85 miles/137 km up to Jerusalem.

_____

_____

_____

_____

_____

44 - Jesus Clears Out the Jerusalem Temple
(John 2:14-22)

John 2:14-22 - (14) He went into the temple courts (*probably the court of the non-Jews*) and saw people selling cattle, sheep, and pigeons for sacrifices, and moneychangers sitting at tables exchanging money to make a profit. (15) So Jesus made a whip out of rope and drove everyone out of the temple courts, along with the sheep and oxen. And he scattered the coins of the moneychangers and turned over their tables. (16) Jesus shouted to the pigeon sellers, "Get out of here! Stop turning my Father's house into a public market!" (17) His disciples remembered that it is written in Psalm 69:9, "Zeal for your house will consume me." (18) Then some Jews said to Jesus, "Show us a miraculous sign to prove to us that you have the authority to do these things!" (19) Jesus said to them, "Destroy this temple, and I will raise it again in three days." (20) The Jews then said, "It took 46 years to build our temple, how are you going to raise it up in three days?" (21) But Jesus was talking about the temple of his body. (22) After Jesus was raised from the dead, his disciples remembered his prediction. Then they believed God's word and all the things Jesus said.

_____

_____

_____

_____

_____

_____

_____

45 - Many People See Jesus' Miraculous Signs
(John 2:23-25)

John 2:23-25 - (23) Now while Jesus was in Jerusalem at the Passover Festival, many people saw the miraculous signs that he was doing and believed in his name. (24) But Jesus would not entrust himself to them for he knew the hearts of all people. (25) He did not need anyone to tell him about the human condition, because he knew what was in the heart of each person.

46 - Jesus Teaches Nicodemus
(John 3:1-15)

John 3:1-15 - (1) Now there was a Pharisee named Nicodemus in Jerusalem, who was a member of the Jewish governing council (*the Sanhedrin*). (2) He came to Jesus under the darkness of night and said, "Teacher (*Rabbi*), we know that you are a teacher who has come from God, because no one could do the miraculous signs you are doing unless God was with him." (3) Jesus said to him, "I tell you the truth: No one can see the kingdom of God unless they are born again (*from above or from God*)." (4) Nicodemus was puzzled and asked Jesus, "It is impossible for an adult to reenter his mother's womb and be born again?" (5) Jesus said, "I tell you the truth: No one can enter the kingdom of God unless they are born of water and the Holy Spirit. (6) Those born of the flesh are flesh, but those born of the Holy Spirit (*spirit*) are spirit. (7) You should not be surprised that I said, 'You must be born again.' (8) For the wind blows wherever it wants and you hear its sound, but you do not know where it comes from or where it is going. So it is with everyone who is born by the Holy Spirit." (9) Nicodemus asked Jesus, "How can this be possible?" (10) Jesus said, "You are a teacher of Israel, and you do not understand my teaching? (11) I tell you the truth: We speak about what we know and have seen, but still you do not believe our testimony. (12) I have told you earthly things and you do not believe me, so how can you believe if I tell you heavenly things? (13) "No one has ever gone into heaven except the Son of Man (*see Daniel 7:13-14*) who has come from heaven. (14) Just as Moses lifted up the snake in the wilderness (*see Numbers 21:9*), so the Son of Man must be lifted up, (15) and everyone who believes in him will have eternal life."

47 - God Loves the World
(John 3:16-21)

John 3:16-21 - Jesus said, (16) "For God so loved the world that he gave his one and only Son, so that whoever believes in him will not perish but have eternal life. (17) For God did not send his Son into the world to condemn the world, but to save the world through him. (18) Whoever believes in him is not condemned, but whoever does not believe is condemned already, because he has not believed in the name of the one and only Son of God. (19) This is my verdict: The light has come into the world, but people loved the world's darkness instead of God's light because their works were evil. (20) For whoever does evil hates God's light, and will not come into the light for fear that their evil deeds will be exposed. (21) But whoever lives a life of truth comes into God's light, so that it will be seen clearly that what they have done, has been done in the sight of God."

48 - Jesus' Ministry in Judea at the Jordan River
(John 3:22-24)

John 3:22-24 - (22) After this, Jesus and his disciples walked into the Judean countryside of the Jordan River Valley, where he stayed some time with them, baptizing people in the Jordan River. (23) Now John was also baptizing people at Aenon (*meaning springs*) near Salim, because there was plenty of water there, and people were coming to be baptized. (24) This happened before John was put in prison.

49 - John's Testimony About Jesus
(John 3:25-36)

John 3:25-36 - (25) At that time, an argument erupted between some of John's disciples and a certain Jew over the issue of purification (*ceremonial*) washings. (26) John's disciples went to John and said to him, "Teacher (*Rabbi*), that man who was with you on the other side of the Jordan River—the one you testified about—look, he is baptizing and everyone is going to him." (27) John said to them, "No one receives anything unless it is given to him from God in heaven. (28) You know that I have already told you that I am not the Messiah (*Christ*), but I was sent ahead of him. (29) The bride belongs to the bridegroom, but the friend of the bridegroom waits and listens for his coming, and is full of joy when he hears the bridegroom's voice. I tell you, my heart is full of joy, because the time has come (*is complete*). (30) Jesus must increase; and I must decrease (*become less*). (31) The one who comes from heaven is above all. The one who is from the earth belongs to the earth, and speaks as one from the earth. (32) He tells us what he has seen and heard, but no one accepts his testimony. (33) Whoever believes his testimony confirms that God is true. (34) For the one whom God has sent into this world speaks the words of God, because he gives the Holy Spirit in all its fullness (*without limit*). (35) The Father loves the Son and has placed all things under his authority. (36) Whoever believes in the Son has eternal life, but whoever rejects the Son will not see eternal life, because the just wrath of God remains on them."

50 - Herod Antipas Arrests John
(Matthew 14:3-5, Mark 6:17-20, Luke 3:19-20)

Matthew 14:3-5 - (3) Now Herod Antipas had arrested John and put him in prison because of Herodias, the wife of Herod's brother Philip (*who lived in Rome*)—(4) for John had told Herod, "It is not lawful for you to marry your brother's wife." (5) Herod wanted to kill John, but he was afraid of the people because they believed that he was a prophet.

Mark 6:17-20 - (17) For Herod Antipas had given orders to arrest John, and he had him bound and put in prison. Herod did this for Herodias, his brother Philip's wife, whom he had married. (18) For John had been telling Herod, "It is not lawful for you to marry your brother's wife." (19) So Herodias became angry with John and wanted to kill him. But she was not able to, (20) because Herod feared John and protected him, knowing that he was a righteous and holy man. When Herod heard John speak, he was greatly perplexed, but he enjoyed listening to him.

Luke 3:19-20 - (19) And John also spoke against Herod Antipas because he had married Herodias, the wife of his brother Philip, and against all the other evil things that he had done. (20) Then Herod did another evil thing by arresting John and putting him in prison.

(*Herod Antipas was the son of Herod the Great and the Roman governor of Galilee and Perea. He arrested John and put him in the prison at the Machaerus fortress in Perea, in modern Jordan*).

51 - Jesus Leaves Judea for Galilee
(Matthew 4:12; John 4:1-3)

Matthew 4:12- When Jesus heard that John had been put in prison, he left Judea and traveled to Galilee.

John 4:1-3 - (1) Now when Jesus learned that the Pharisees had heard that he was gaining and baptizing more disciples than John—(2) although it was not Jesus who was baptizing, but his disciples—(3) he left Judea and returned back to Galilee in northern Israel.

52 - Jesus Ministers to a Samaritan Woman
(John 4:4-26)

John 4:4-26 - (4) Now on his way to Galilee, Jesus had to walk through the region of Samaria. (5) So he entered the Samaritan town called Sychar (*on the slope of Mount Ebal*), near the field that Jacob had given to his son Joseph. (6) It was about noon, and Jesus sat down at Jacob's well because he was tired from his journey. (*Jesus had probably been walking for about six hours*). (7) When a Samaritan woman came to draw water from the well, Jesus said to her, "Can you give me a drink of water?" (8) (*Jesus was alone because his disciples had gone into town to buy food*). (9) The Samaritan woman said to him, "You are a Jew and I am a Samaritan woman. Why do you ask me for a drink of water?" For Jews would not associate with Samaritans. (10) Jesus said to her, "If you only knew the gift of God and who it is that asks you for a drink, you would have asked him and he would have given you living water." (11) The woman said to him, "Sir, the well is deep, and you do not have a bucket to draw water. Where are you going to get this living water? (12) Are you greater than our father Jacob, who gave us this well and drank from it himself, as did his sons and animals?" (13) Jesus said to her, "Whoever drinks this water will be thirsty again, (14) but whoever drinks the water that I will give them will never be thirsty again. The water that I will give him will become a spring of water gushing up to eternal life." (15) The woman said to Jesus, "Sir, give me this water so that I won't be thirsty, and I will not have to draw water from this well ever again." (16) Jesus said to her, "Go and bring your husband to me." (17) The woman said, "I don't have a husband." Jesus said to her, "You are right in saying 'I do not have a husband.' (18) The truth is, you have had five husbands, and the man you now live with is not your husband. What you have just said to me is true." (19) The woman said to him, "Sir, I can see that you are a prophet. (20) Our Samaritan ancestors worshiped on this mountain (*Mount Gerizim*), but you Jews say that we must worship in Jerusalem (*at the Jerusalem temple*)." (21) Jesus said to her, "Woman, believe me, the time is coming when you will not worship the Father on your mountain nor in Jerusalem. (22) You Samaritans worship what you do not know, but we worship what we know, because salvation is from the Jews. (23) But the time is coming and has now come, when the true worshipers of God will worship the Father in the Holy Spirit (*spirit*) and truth, because the Father seeks these kind of worshipers. (24) God is Spirit, and his worshipers must worship in the Holy Spirit (*spirit*) and in truth." (25) The woman said to him, "I know that the Messiah (*Christ*) is coming. When he comes, he will explain everything we need to know." (26) Then Jesus said to her, "The one who is speaking to you is the Messiah—I am he!"

(*The Samaritans were the offspring of Israelites left behind from the Assyrian exile of the northern kings and non-Jews. Because of this, there was hostility between the Jews and Samaritans*).

53 - Jesus' Disciples Return
(John 4:27-38)

John 4:27-38 - (27) Just then Jesus' disciples returned. They were amazed that he was talking with a Samaritan woman, but no one said, "What do you want?" or, "Why are you talking with her?" (28) Then, the woman left her water jar and hurried into town and told the people, (29) "Come with me, meet a man who told me everything I ever did. Do you think he could be the Messiah v?" (30) Many Samaritans rushed out of the town to meet Jesus. (31) Meanwhile Jesus' disciples said to him, "Teacher (*Rabbi*), you need to eat something." (32) But Jesus said to them, "I have food to eat that you do not know about." (33) Then his disciples said to each other, "Has someone given him food?" (34) Jesus said, "My food is to do the will of of him who sent me into this world and to finish his work. (35) You often say, 'There are still four months until the harvest.' Look! I tell you the truth: Lift up your eyes and see that the fields are already ripe for harvest. (36) Even now the one who reaps receives pay and gathers a harvest for eternal life, so that the sower and gatherer rejoice together. (37) This is a true saying, 'One sows and another harvests.' (38) I sent you to gather a harvest that you did not work for. Others have done the hard work, and you have reaped the benefits of their labor."

54 - Many Samaritans Believe
(John 4:39-42)

John 4:39-42 - (39) Many of the Samaritans from that town believed in Jesus because the woman said, "He told me everything I ever did." (40) So when the Samaritans came to Jesus, they asked him to stay with them, and he stayed there for two more days. (41) And during those two days, many more Samaritans believed in Jesus because of his teaching. (42) They said to the woman, "We first believed because of what you told us, but now we have heard for ourselves, and we know that this man is truly the Savior of the world!"

- -

- -

- -

- -

- -

55 - Jesus is Welcomed in Galilee
(John 4:43-45)

John 4:43-45 - (43) After the two days Jesus left Samaria and walked north into Galilee. (44) (*Now Jesus had said that a prophet has no honor in his own country*). (45) So when Jesus arrived in Galilee, the people there welcomed him, because they had seen the miraculous signs (*miracles*) that he had done at the Passover Feast in Jerusalem, because they also had been there.

(*The region of Galilee in northern Israel was around 45 miles/72 km north-south and 25 miles/40 km east-west, with a population of around 300,000 living in about 200 villages and towns. There were only two Greco-Roman cities in Galilee, Sepphoris and Tiberius, both built by Herod Antipas. Sepphoris served as Herod Antipas' initial Galilean capital, located about 4 miles/6 km northwest of Nazareth. Tiberius became his new Galilean capital, named after the Roman emperor Tiberius. It was located on the western shore of Lake Galilee around 10 miles/16 km south of Capernaum. The Gospels do not record Jesus ever ministering in the cities of Tiberius or Sepphoris, although we do know that citizens of these cities went out to Jesus*).

- -

- -

- -

- -

- -

56 - Jesus Moves from Nazareth to Capernaum
(Matthew 4:13-16)

Matthew 4:13-16 - (13) Jesus left Nazareth and went to live in the town of Capernaum, which was located on the northwestern shore of Lake Galilee in the region of the tribes of Zebulun and Naphtali. (*Capernaum was a fishing town located on the northwestern shore of Lake Galilee; it had a population of around 1,500*). (14) This fulfilled what is written in Isaiah 9:1-2, (15) "Land of Zebulun and land of Naphtali, the Way to the Sea, east of the Jordan River (*the region of Perea, modern Jordan*), Galilee of the non-Jews—(16) the people living in darkness have seen a great light; on those living in the land of the shadow of death a light has risen." (*Refers to the trade route that ran through this region to the Mediterranean Sea that was called the "Via Maris," or "Way of the Sea." The northern tribes of Israel were surrounded on three sides by non-Jewish populations).*

57 - Jesus' Message and Ministry in Galilee
(Matthew 4:17, Mark 1:14-15, Luke 4:14-15)

Matthew 4:17 - From that time on Jesus began to proclaim, "Repent and turn to God, for the kingdom of heaven has come near (*is at hand*)!"

Mark 1:14-15 - (14) After John was put in prison by Herod Antipas, Jesus walked into Galilee proclaiming the gospel (*good news*) of God. (15) He declared, "The time has been fulfilled! The kingdom of God has come near! Repent and believe the gospel!"

Luke 4:14-15 - (14) Jesus returned to Galilee in the power of the Holy Spirit, and news about him spread throughout the whole region. (15) He taught in their synagogues and was praised by everyone.

58 - Jesus Heals Non-Jewish Official's Son
(John 4:46-54)

John 4:46-54 - (46) Once again Jesus walked to Cana in Galilee (*about 20 miles/32 km from Capernaum*), where he had turned water into wine. And in Capernaum there was an official whose son was very sick. (47) When this man heard that Jesus had returned to Galilee from Judea, he hurried to meet Jesus and begged him to come and heal his dying son. (48) Jesus said to him, "Unless you people see miraculous signs and wonders (*miracles*) you will never believe." (49) The official said to him, "Sir, come down before my son dies." (50) Jesus said, "Go; your son will live." The man believed what Jesus said and left for his home. (51) While he was walking there, his servants met him and said, "Your son is living!" (52) The man asked them, "What time did he begin to get better?" They said, "Yesterday around 1 p.m." (53) Then the father realized that it was the exact time that Jesus had said to him, "Your son will live." So, the official and his whole household believed in Jesus. (54) This was the second miraculous sign (*miracle*) that Jesus did after coming from Judea to Galilee.

59 - Jesus Rejected in Nazareth
(Luke 4:16-30)

Luke 4:16-30 - (16) Jesus traveled to his hometown of Nazareth, where he grew up. (*The village of Nazareth was located about 12 miles/19 km southwest of Lake Galilee; it had a population of around 500*). (16) On the Sabbath day he went into the synagogue, as was his normal practice. When he stood up to read, (17) Jesus was given the scroll of the prophet Isaiah. Jesus opened it and read Isaiah 61:1-2, (18) "The Spirit of the Lord has come upon me because he has anointed me to proclaim the gospel (*good news*) to the poor. The Lord has sent me to proclaim freedom for the prisoners and to give sight to the blind, to free everyone who is oppressed, (19) and to declare the year of the Lord's favor.' " (20) Then Jesus rolled up the scroll, handed it back to the synagogue attendant and sat down. Everyone in the synagogue was staring at him. (21) Then Jesus said to them, "Today, this passage in Isaiah is fulfilled in your hearing." (22) All the people began saying good things about Jesus and were amazed at the gracious words that he spoke. They asked, "Isn't this Joseph's son?" (23) Jesus said to them, "Surely you will quote this proverb to me, 'Doctor, first heal yourself!' And you will tell me to do the miraculous signs (*miracles*) here in my hometown of Nazareth that you have heard I did in Capernaum. (24) "But I tell you the truth: No prophet is accepted by the people of his hometown. (25) I assure you that there were many widows in Israel during the time of Elijah, when there was no rain for three and one half years and there was a severe famine throughout the land. (26) Yet Elijah was not sent to any of the widows of Israel, but to a widow in the town of Zarephath in the non-Jewish region of Sidon. (27) And many people in Israel had leprosy (*various skin diseases*) during the time of the prophet Elisha, but none of them were healed except Naaman the Syrian." (28) When the people in the synagogue heard Jesus say this, they became very angry. (29) They got up, drove Jesus out of the town, and took him to the edge of the cliff on which Nazareth was built to throw him over. (30) But Jesus walked right through the crowd and went on his way.

60 - Many People Press to Hear Jesus Teach
(Luke 5:1)

Luke 5:1 - One day Jesus was standing on the northwestern shore of Lake Galilee, also called Lake Gennesaret. Many people pressed around him to listen to the word of God.(*The heart-*

shaped, freshwater Lake Galilee was around 60 miles north of Jerusalem and around 13 miles/21 km long and 7 miles/11 km wide).

61 - Jesus Teaches in Capernaum's Synagogue
(Mark 1:21-22, Luke 4:31-32)

Mark 1:21-22 - (21) They went to Capernaum, and when the Sabbath day came Jesus entered the synagogue and began to teach. (22) The people were amazed at his teaching, because he taught them as one who had God's authority and not like the teachers of the law of Moses.

Luke 4:31-32 - (31) Jesus walked back into the town of Capernaum in Galilee, and he taught the people in the synagogue on the Sabbath day. (32) The people were amazed at his teaching, because he spoke with authority.

62 - Jesus Frees a Man From a Demon
(Mark 1:23-26; Luke 4:33-35)

Mark 1:23-26 - (23) Suddenly, a demon-possessed (*demonized*) man in the synagogue screamed out, (24) "Jesus of Nazareth, what do you want with us? Have you come to destroy us? I know you are—the Holy One of God!" (25) Jesus said with authority, "Be quiet! Come out of him!" (26) The demon shook the man violently and came out of him with a loud shriek.

Luke 4:33-35 - (33) There was a demon-possessed (*demonized*) man in the synagogue. The demon screamed through the man, (34) "Go away, Jesus of Nazareth! Why are you bothering us? Have you come to destroy us? I know you are—the Holy One of God!" (35) Jesus ordered the demon to be quiet and to come out of him. Then the demon threw the man to the ground in front of everyone and left without hurting him.

63 - News About Jesus Spreads Through Galilee
(Mark 1:27-28, Luke 4:36-37)

Mark 1:27-28 - (27) The people were all so amazed that they asked each other, "What is this? Is this a new teaching with God's authority? Jesus even commands demons and they obey him." (28) Because of this, news about Jesus spread quickly through the whole region of Galilee.

Luke 4:36-37 - (36) All the people were amazed and said to each other, "What kind of teaching is this? He has God's authority and power to order demons to come out of people." (37) And the news about Jesus spread throughout the surrounding region of Galilee.

----

64 - Jesus Heals Peter's Mother-in-Law
(Matthew 8:14-15, Mark 1:29-31, Luke 4:38-39)

Matthew 8:14-15 - (14) When Jesus entered Peter's house in Capernaum, he saw Peter's mother-in-law lying in bed with a fever. (15) He touched her hand and the fever left her, and she got up and began to serve him.

Mark 1:29-31 - (29) As soon as they left the Capernaum synagogue, they went with James and John into the house of Simon (*Peter*) and Andrew. (30) They found Peter's mother-in-law lying in bed with a fever, and they told Jesus about her. (31) So Jesus went and took her hand and helped her up from her bed. The fever left her and she began to serve them.

Luke 4:38-39 - (38) Jesus left the synagogue and went to the house of Simon (*Peter*) in Capernaum. When he arrived, Simon's mother-in-law was suffering with a high fever, and they asked Jesus to help her. (39) So Jesus bent over her and ordered the fever to leave her, and it did. She immediately got up and began to serve them.

----

65 - Jesus Heals Many People
(Matthew 8:16-17, Mark 1:32-34, Luke 4:40-41)

Matthew 8:16-17 - (16) That evening, people brought to Jesus many who were demon-possessed (*the demonized*), and he drove out the demons with a command and healed all who were sick. (17)

This fulfilled what is written in Isaiah 53:4, "He took up our infirmities and carried our diseases."

Mark 1:32-34 - (32) That evening, after sunset, the people brought to Jesus all who were sick and demon-possessed (*the demonized*). (33) The whole town of Capernaum gathered at the door of the house, (34) and Jesus healed many people of all kinds of diseases. He cast out many demons, but he would not let them speak because they knew who he was.

Luke 4:40-41 - (40) After the sun had gone down that evening, the people brought people with all kinds of sickness to Jesus, and he healed each one by placing his hands on them. (41) Demons came out of many people, shouting, "You are the Son of God!" But Jesus rebuked them and ordered them not to speak, because they knew he was the Messiah (*Christ*).

66 - Jesus Withdraws to Pray Alone
(Mark 1:35-37, Luke 4:42)

Mark 1:35-37 - Jesus got up very early the next morning, while it was still dark. He left the house and walked to an isolated place (*probably in the hills west of Capernaum*) where he could pray alone. (36) Simon (*Peter*) and his companions went out to search for him, (37) and when they found him, they said to Jesus, "Everyone is looking for you!"

Luke 4:42 - At daybreak the next morning, Jesus went out to an isolated place to be alone. The people came looking for him and when they found him, they tried to stop him from leaving them.

67 - Jesus' Ministry Tour Through Galilee
(Matthew 4:23-25, Mark 1:38-39, Luke 4:43-44)

Matthew 4:23-25 - (23) Jesus walked throughout Galilee teaching in their synagogues, proclaiming the gospel (*good news*) of the kingdom of God, and healing every kind of disease and sickness among the people. News about Jesus spread north of Galilee throughout the whole region of Syria. People brought to Jesus all who were sick with various diseases, those suffering severe pain, those tormented by demons (*the demonized*), those having seizures (*epileptics*), and those who were paralyzed. Jesus healed them all! (25) Large crowds of people followed Jesus from

Galilee, the Decapolis (*the southeastern region of Lake Galilee that included a group of ten non-Jewish cities*), Jerusalem, Judea, and the region east of the Jordan River (*Perea*).

Mark 1:38-39 - (38) Jesus said, "Let us leave here and walk through the nearby towns of Galilee, so that I can proclaim the gospel (*good news*) of God there also, because this is the reason that I came into this world." (39) So they walked throughout Galilee, preaching in their synagogues and casting demons out of people.

Luke 4:43-44 - (43) But Jesus said to them, "I must proclaim the gospel (*good news*) of the kingdom of God to those living in other towns also, because that is why I was sent into this world." (44) And Jesus kept on preaching in the synagogues of Galilee (*some manuscripts say Judea*).

68 - Jesus Heals a Man's Skin Disease
(Matthew 8:1-4, Mark 1:40-44, Luke 5:12-14)

Matthew 8:1-4 - (1) When Jesus came down from the mountainside (*probably in the hills west of Capernaum*), large crowds of people followed him. (2) A man with a severe skin disease (*leprosy*) came and fell on his knees before Jesus and said, "Lord, if you are willing, you can heal me." (3) Jesus reached out his hand and touched the man saying, "I am willing. Be clean!" Immediately his skin disease was healed. (4) Then Jesus said to him, "Make sure you don't tell anyone. But go and show yourself to the priest and offer the gift according to the law of Moses, because this will be a witness to him." (*Leviticus 13-14 provided guidelines for the examination of skin diseases by a priest, because they were highly contagious*).

Mark 1:40-44 - (40) A man with a severe skin disease (*possibly leprosy*) fell on his knees before Jesus and begged him, saying, "If you are willing, you can heal me." (41) Jesus was filled with compassion. He reached out his hand and touched the man, saying, "I am willing. Be healed (*clean*)!" (42) Immediately the skin disease disappeared and he was healed. (43) Jesus sent him away with a strong warning, (44) "Make sure that you don't tell anyone that I healed you, but go and show yourself to the temple priest and offer the sacrifices that the law of Moses commands for your healing (*cleansing*), for this will be a witness to them." (*Leviticus 13-14 provided guidelines for the examination of skin diseases by a priest, because they were highly contagious*).

Luke 5:12-14 - (12) While Jesus was in one of the towns of Galilee, a man walked by who was covered with a severe skin disease (*possibly leprosy*). When he saw Jesus, he fell with his face to the ground and begged him, "Lord, if you are willing, you can heal me and make me clean." (13) Jesus reached out his hand and touched him, saying, "I am willing. Be healed (*cleansed*)!" And the man was immediately healed. (14) Then Jesus ordered him, "Do not tell anyone, but go, show yourself to the temple priest and offer the sacrifices that Moses commanded for your cleansing. This will be a witness to them." (*Leviticus 13-14 provided guidelines for the examination of skin diseases by a priest, because they were highly contagious*).

69 - News About Jesus Continues to Grow
(Mark 1:45, Luke 5:15-16)

Mark 1:45 - But instead the man went out and told everyone, spreading the news about Jesus. As a result, Jesus stayed in rural places because he could no longer go into a town openly. Yet the people still went out to him from everywhere.

Luke 5:15-16 - (15) But the news about Jesus spread even more, so that large crowds of people came to hear him and be healed of their sicknesses. (16) So Jesus would often withdraw from the people to isolated places, so he could be alone and pray.

70 - Jesus Heals a Paralyzed Man
(Matthew 9:1-8, Mark 2:1-12, Luke 5:17-25)

Matthew 9:1-8 - (1) Then Jesus and his disciples got into their boat and went back across Lake Galilee to their home town of Capernaum (*probably staying at Peter's house*). (2) Some men brought to Jesus a paralyzed man, lying on a stretcher. When Jesus saw the faith of those who brought him, he said to the paralyzed man, "My son, take heart; your sins are forgiven." (3) And when some teachers of the law of Moses heard this, they said to one another, "Jesus is blaspheming! He is making himself equal with God!" (4) Jesus knew their thoughts and said, "Why do you allow evil thoughts to enter your hearts? (5) Which is easier for me to say, 'Your sins are forgiven,' or to say, 'Get up and walk'? (6) But I want you to know that the Son of Man (*see Daniel 7:13-14*) has God's authority on earth to forgive sins." So Jesus said to the paralyzed man, "Get up! Take your stretcher and go home." (7) Then the man was healed, and he stood up and went home. (8) When the crowd saw this, they were amazed, and they praised God because he had given such authority to man.

Mark 2:1-12 - (1) A few days later, when Jesus returned to Capernaum, the people heard that he had come home (*probably Peter's house*). (2) So many people came to the house. They gathered in such large numbers that there was no room left, not even outside the door, and he taught them the word of God. (3) Some men came, and four of them carried a paralyzed man to Jesus. (4) Since they could not get him near Jesus because of the crowd, they climbed onto the roof, dug a hole in the roof above Jesus, and lowered the man lying on a stretcher. (5) When Jesus saw their faith, he said to the paralyzed man, "Son, your sins are forgiven!" (6) Now some teachers of the law of Moses were sitting there, thinking to themselves, (7) "How can this man Jesus talk this way? He's blaspheming against God! Who can forgive sins but God alone?" (8) Immediately Jesus knew in his spirit what they were thinking in their hearts, and he said to them, "Why are you thinking this way? (9) What is easier for me to say to the paralyzed man, 'Your sins are forgiven,' or to say, 'Stand up, take your stretcher and walk'? (10) But I want you to know that the Son of Man (*see Daniel 7:13-14*) has authority on earth to forgive sins." So Jesus said to the man, (11) "I tell you, stand up, take your stretcher and go home." (12) The man stood up, took his stretcher, and walked out of the house for all to see."

Luke 5:17-25 - (17) One day Jesus was teaching (*probably in Peter's house in Capernaum*), and Pharisees and teachers of the law of Moses were sitting there from every village of Galilee and Judea and from Jerusalem. And the Lord's power was with Jesus to heal the sick. (18) Some men carried a paralyzed man on a stretcher and tried to take him into the house and lay him before Jesus. (19) But when they couldn't reach him because of the crowd, they went up onto the roof, made a hole, and lowered the man down on his stretcher through the tiles into the middle of the crowd—right in front of Jesus. (20) When Jesus saw their faith, he said, "Friend, your sins are forgiven." (21) The Pharisees and teachers of the law of Moses began thinking to themselves, "Who is this man who speaks blasphemy? Only God can forgive sins." (22) Jesus knew what they were thinking and asked them, "Why are you thinking these things in your hearts? (23) Which is easier for me to say: 'Your sins are forgiven,' or 'Get up and walk'? (24) But I want you to know that the Son of Man (*see Daniel 7:13-14*) has God's authority on earth to forgive sins." So Jesus said to the paralyzed man, "I tell you, stand up, take your stretcher and walk home." (25) Immediately the man stood up in front of them all, took his stretcher, and walked home praising God.

71 - Jesus Teaches the Crowd from Peter's Boat
(Luke 5:2-3)

Luke 5:2-3 - (2) Jesus saw two boats at the water's edge that had been left there by some fishermen, who were washing their nets. (3) He got into Simon Peter's boat, and asked him to push the boat out a short way from the shore. Then he sat down in the boat and taught the people from the boat.

72 - A Miraculous Catch of Fish
(Luke 5:4-10)

Luke 5:4-10 - (4) When Jesus had finished teaching, he told Simon Peter, "Row your boat into deep water, and let down your nets for a catch of fish." (5) Simon Peter said, "Master, we've fished all night and have not caught anything. But because you say so, I will let down my nets." (6) When they did what Jesus had told them, they caught such a large number of fish that their nets began to tear. (7) So they called to their fishing partners in the other boat to come and help them. They came and filled both boats with so many fish that they began to sink. (8) When Simon Peter saw this, he fell at Jesus' feet and declared, "Lord! Go away from me, because I am a sinful man!" (9) For Simon Peter and those with him were amazed at their catch of fish, (10) and so were James and John, Zebedee's sons, who were Simon Peter's fishing partners.

73 - Jesus Calls Peter, Andrew, James, and John
(Matthew 4:18-22, Mark 1:16-20, Luke 5:10-11)

Matthew 4:18-22 - (18) Jesus was walking along the northwestern shore of Lake Galilee near to Capernaum. As he was walking, he saw Simon Peter and his brother Andrew. Peter and Andrew were fishermen, and they were throwing a fishing net into the lake. (19) Jesus said to them, "Come and follow me, and I will send you out to fish for people." (20) At once they left their fishing nets and followed Jesus. (21) Walking a little further, Jesus saw James and John, the sons of Zebedee, in a boat with their father mending their fishing nets. Jesus called them to follow him, (22) and immediately they left the boat and their father and followed Jesus.

Mark 1:16-20 - (16) As Jesus walked along the northwestern shore of Lake Galilee near Capernaum. He saw Simon (*Peter*) and his brother Andrew casting a fishing net into the lake. (17) Jesus called out to them, "Come, follow me! I will send you out to fish for people." (18) And immediately they left their nets and followed him. (19) When Jesus had walked a little farther, he saw James and John the sons of Zebedee in a boat, mending their fishing nets. (20) Jesus immediately called them, and they left their father Zebedee and the hired men in the boat and followed him.

Luke 5:10-11 - (10) Then Jesus said to Simon Peter, "Don't be afraid; from now on you will fish for people." (11) So when they pulled their boats up onto the shore, they left everything and followed Jesus.

74 - The People Praise God
(Matthew 9:8, Mark 6:12, Luke 5:26)

Matthew 9:8 - When the crowd saw this, they were amazed, and they praised God because he had given such authority to man.

Mark 2:12 - Everyone there was amazed and praised God, saying, "We have never seen anything like this before!"

Luke 5:26 - Everyone was filled with amazement and praised God. They were all filled with awe and said, "We have seen miraculous things today.

75 - Jesus Calls Matthew
(Matthew 9:9, Mark 2:13-14, Luke 5:27-28)

Matthew 9:9 - While Jesus walked along the northwestern shore of Lake Galilee near Capernaum he saw a man named Matthew (*also called Levi*) sitting at the tax collector's booth. (*Jewish tax collectors were hated because they were employed as representatives of the Romans*). Jesus said to him, "Follow me!" And Matthew got up and followed him.

Mark 2:13-14 - (13) Once again Jesus walked along the northwestern shore of Lake Galilee and a large crowd of people gathered around him, and he began to teach them. (14) As Jesus continued walking, he saw Levi son of Alphaeus (*also known as Matthew*), sitting at the tax collector's booth. Jesus said to him, "Follow me!" And Levi left the booth and followed him.

Luke 5:27-28 - (27) After these things, Jesus left the house and was walking along the northwestern shore of Lake Galilee. Jesus saw a tax collector by the name of Levi (*Matthew*) sitting at his tax booth. (28) Jesus called out to him, "Follow me!" Levi stood up, left everything, and followed him.

76 - Religious Leaders Object to Jesus Eating With Sinners
(Matthew 9:10-13, Mark 2:15-17, Luke 5:29–32)

Matthew 9:10-13 - (10) While Jesus was eating at Matthew's house, many tax collectors and sinners also came to eat with him and his disciples.(11) When the Pharisees saw this, they asked Jesus' disciples, "Why does your teacher eat with tax collectors and sinners?" (12) Jesus heard them and said, "It is not the healthy who need a doctor, but the sick. (13) You need to go and learn the meaning of Hosea 6:6, 'I desire mercy, not sacrifice.' For I have not come into this world to call the righteous, but sinners."

Mark 2:15-17 - (15) While Jesus and his disciples were eating dinner at Levi's house, many tax collectors and sinners were eating with him and his disciples, because there were many who followed him. (16) When the teachers of the law of Moses who were Pharisees saw Jesus eating with the sinners and tax collectors, they asked his disciples, "Why does Jesus eat with tax collectors and sinners?" (17) Jesus heard them and said, "It is not the healthy who need a doctor, but the sick. I have not come into this world to call the righteous, but sinners."

Luke 5:29-32 - (29) Then Levi held a great banquet for Jesus at his house, and a large crowd of tax collectors and others were eating with them. (30) But the Pharisees and teachers of the law of Moses complained to Jesus' disciples, "Why do you eat and drink with tax collectors and sinners?" (31) Jesus said to them, "It is not the healthy who need a doctor, but the sick. (32) I have not come into the world to call the righteous, but sinners to repent and turn to God."

77 - Jesus is Questioned About Fasting
(Matthew 9:14-15, Mark 2:18-20, Luke 5:33-35)

Matthew 9:14-15 - (14) Then John the Baptizer's disciples came and asked Jesus, "Why do we and the Pharisees fast often, but your disciples do not fast?" (15) Jesus said to them, "How can the wedding guests of the bridegroom mourn while he is with them? But the time will come when the bridegroom will be taken away from them and that is when my disciples will fast."

Mark 2:18-20 - (18) Now John's disciples and the Pharisees were fasting. Some people came and asked Jesus, "Why is it that John's disciples and the disciples of the Pharisees fast, but your disciples do not?" (19) Jesus said to them, "The guests of the bridegroom do not fast as long as the bridegroom is with them. (20) But the time will come when the bridegroom will be taken away from them, and on that day they will fast."

Luke 5:33-35 - (33) The Jewish religious leaders said to Jesus, "John's disciples and the Pharisees' disciples often fast and pray, but your disciples continue to eat and drink." (34) Jesus said to them, "You cannot make the bridegroom's friends fast while he is still with them. (35) But the time will come when the bridegroom will be taken from them; at that time my disciples will fast."

78 - The Parables of Old and New
(Matthew 9:16-17, Mark 2:21-22, Luke 5:36-39)

Matthew 9:16-17 - Jesus said, (16) "No one sews a new cloth patch on an old garment, because the new cloth will shrink when the garment is washed and the old garment will tear even more. (17) Neither do people pour new wine into old wineskins, because the new wine will expand and cause the old wineskins to break open, and the new wine will pour out. The old wineskins will be useless. Instead, they pour new wine into new wineskins, and then both will be preserved."

Mark 2:21-22 - Jesus said, (21) "No one sews a new cloth patch on an old garment, because the new patch will shrink when it is washed and the new patch will tear away from the old, making the tear worse. (22) And neither do people pour new wine into old wineskins, because the new wine will expand and will cause the old wineskins to break open, and the new wine will pour out and the wineskins will be ruined. No, they pour new wine into new wineskins."

Luke 5:36-39 - (36) Jesus told them this parable (*story*): "No one takes a piece of cloth from a new garment and sews it on an old garment. Otherwise, they will have torn the new garment, and the new patch will not match the old garment. (37) And no one pours new wine into old wineskins. Otherwise, the new wine will expand and burst the old wineskins, and the new wine will pour out and the wineskins will be ruined. (38) No, you must put new wine into new wineskins." (39) And no one after drinking old wine wants to drink new wine, for they say, 'The old wine is better.' "

79 - Jesus Attends Passover Feast
(John 5:1)

John 5:1 - Some time later, Jesus walked up to Jerusalem to attend a Jewish feast.

(This was either the Passover Feast or the feast of Tabernacles/Booths, when the people lived in tents to commemorate God's faithfulness to the Israelites during their wanderings in the Sinai Desert).

80 - Jesus Heals a Crippled Man at Pool of Bethesda
(John 5:2-9)

John 5:2-9 - (2) Jesus entered Jerusalem through the Sheep Gate, where he passed a pool of water, which in the Aramaic language is called Bethesda (*which means "house of mercy"*). The pool was surrounded by five roofed colonnades (*a colonnade is a row of columns supporting a roof*). (3) It was here that a large number of disabled people—blind, lame, and paralyzed—lay helplessly on the ground. (4-5) There was a man lying at the pool who had been disabled for 38 years. (6) When Jesus saw him lying on the ground, and learned that he had been in this condition for a long time, he asked him, "Do you want to be healed?" (7) The disabled man said, "Sir, I have no one to put me into the pool when the water stirs. And when I do try to get in, someone else goes down before me." (8) Then Jesus said to him, "Stand up! Pick up your mat and walk." (9) Immediately, the man was healed, and he picked up his mat and walked.

81 - Religious Leaders Question Healed Man
(John 5:9-13)

John 5:9-13 - (9) Now this healing took place on the Sabbath day, (10) and so some religious Jews said to the man who had been healed, "You are breaking the Jewish law by carrying your mat on the Sabbath day." (11) But the man said to them, "The man who healed me told me, 'Pick up your mat and walk.'" (12) So the Jews asked him, "Tell us, who is this man who told you to pick up your mat and walk?" (13) The man who was healed had no idea who it was, because Jesus had slipped away into the crowd of people that was there.

82 - Jesus Talks with the Healed Man
(John 5:14-15)

John 5:14-15 - (14) Later Jesus found the man in the temple and said to him, "See, you are now healed! Stop sinning or something worse can happen to you." (15) The man left and told the Jewish religious leaders that it was Jesus who had healed him.

83 - Jesus is Equal With God
(John 5:16-30)

John 5:16-30 - (16) So the Jewish religious leaders began to persecute Jesus, because he was healing on the Sabbath day. (17) But Jesus said to them in his defense, "My Father is always at his work to this very day, and I too am working." (18) After Jesus said this, the Jews tried even more to kill him, not only because was he breaking the Sabbath law, but because he was also calling God his Father—making himself equal with God. (19) Jesus said to them, "I tell you the truth: The Son can do nothing on his own; he can do only what he sees his Father doing, because whatever the Father does the Son also does. (20) For the Father loves the Son and shows him all he does. Yes, and the Father will show him even greater works than these, so that you will be amazed. (21) For just as the Father raises the dead and gives them life, even so the Son gives life to those he is pleased to give it. (22) Moreover, the Father judges no one, but he has given all judgment to the Son, (23) so that everyone will honor the Son just as they honor the Father. Whoever does not honor the Son does not honor the Father, who sent him into this world. (24) I tell you the truth: Whoever hears my word and believes him who sent me has eternal life and will not be judged but has crossed over from death to life. (25) I tell you the truth: A time is coming and is now here, when the dead will hear the voice of the Son of God, and those who hear will live. (26) For as the Father has life in himself, so he has also granted the Son to have life in himself. (27) And the Father has given the Son authority to execute judgment because he is the Son of Man (*see Daniel 7:13-14*). (28) Do not be surprised at my teaching, because a time is coming when the dead in their graves will hear his voice (29) and be raised to life—those who have done what is good will rise to life, but those who have done what is evil will rise to be condemned. (30) I can do nothing on my own. I judge only what I hear, and my judgment is just, because I do not seek to please myself but the will of the Father who sent me into this world."

84 - Testimonies About Jesus
(John 5:31-47)

John 5:31-47 - Jesus said, (31) "If I testify about myself, then my testimony is not true. (32) But there is another one who testifies about me, and I know that his testimony about me is true. (33) You religious leaders sent men to question John, and he told you the truth. (34) I don't need any human testimony, but I say this so that you will be saved. (35) John was a burning lamp that shined forth light, and you chose for a while to enjoy his light." Jesus said, (36) "But I have a much greater testimony than that of John. For the works that the Father has given me to accomplish—the very works that I am doing—prove that the Father sent me into this world. (37) And the Father who sent me testifies about me. You have never heard his voice nor seen his form, (38) nor does his word live in you, because you do not believe in the one he sent. (39) You study God's word zealously because you think that in it you have eternal life. However, these are the very Scriptures that testify about me, (40) but you still refuse to come to me to receive eternal life." (41) I do not accept glory from human beings, (42) but I know you. I know that you do not have the love of God in your hearts. (43) I came in my Father's name, and you do not believe in me; but if someone else comes in his own name, you will embrace him. (44) How can you believe when you accept praise from one another but make no effort to seek the glory that comes from the only God? (45) But do not think that I will accuse you before the Father. For Moses—the one you put your hope in—is the one who accuses you. (46) For if you believed Moses, you would believe me, because he wrote about me. (47) But since you do not believe in the writings of Moses, how will you believe my teaching?"

_____

_____

_____

_____

_____

85 - Jesus is the Lord of the Sabbath
(Matthew 12:1-8, Mark 2:23-28, Luke 6:1-5)

Matthew 12:1-8 - (1) At that time Jesus and his disciples walked through the grain fields in Galilee on the Sabbath day. His disciples were hungry and so they picked some heads of grain and ate them. (2) But when some Pharisees saw this, they said to Jesus, "Look! Your disciples are doing what is unlawful on the Sabbath day." (3) Jesus said to them, "Haven't you read 1 Samuel 21:1-6 when David and his men were hungry? (4) He went into God's temple, and he and his men ate the holy bread—which was unlawful for them to do, because the holy bread was only for the priests to eat. (5) Or haven't you read in the law of Moses that the priests on Sabbath duty in the temple desecrated the Sabbath but were found innocent? (6) I tell you the truth: Something greater than the temple is here. (7) If you really knew the meaning of Hosea 6:6, 'I desire mercy, not sacrifice,' you would not have accused those who are innocent. (8) For the Son of Man (*see Daniel 7:13-14*) is the Lord of the Sabbath!"

Mark 2:23-28 - (23) Jesus and his disciples were walking through the grain fields in Galilee on the Sabbath day. His disciples picked some grain and ate it. (24) When some Pharisees saw this, they said to Jesus, "Look! Why are your disciples doing what is unlawful on the Sabbath day?" (25) Jesus said to them, "Haven't you read 1 Samuel 21:1-7, when David and his men were in need and were hungry? (26) In the days of Abiathar the high priest, David went into God's temple and ate the holy bread and gave some to his men, which is unlawful because the holy bread is only for the priests to eat." (27) Then he said to them, "The Sabbath day was made for man, and man was not made for the Sabbath. (28) I tell you the truth: The Son of Man (*see Daniel 7:13-14*) is Lord of the Sabbath day!"

Luke 6:1-5 - (1) As Jesus and his disciples were walking through the grain fields in Galilee on the Sabbath day, his disciples picked some heads of grain, rubbed them in their hands and ate the kernels. (2) Some Pharisees asked the disciples, "Why are you doing work which is unlawful on the Sabbath day?" (3) Jesus said to them, "Haven't you read 1 Samuel 21:1-6? David and his men were hungry, (4) and he went into God's temple and took the holy bread to eat and gave some to his men. David ate what was not lawful for him, because the holy bread is only for the priests to eat." (5) Then Jesus said to them, "The Son of Man (*see Daniel 7:13-14*) is Lord of the Sabbath day!"

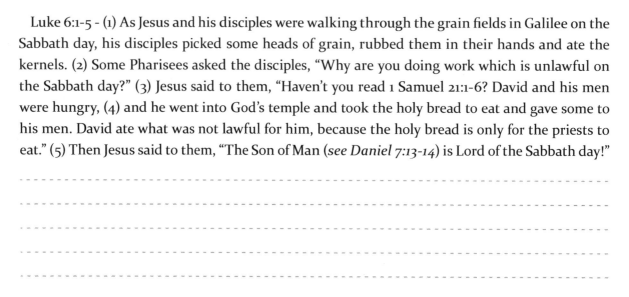

86 - Jesus Heals a Man's Hand in the Synagogue
(Matthew 12:9-13, Mark 3:1-5, Luke 6:6-10)

Matthew 12:9-13 - (9) Then Jesus walked away and went into the synagogue of Capernaum. (10) And a man was in the synagogue who had a shriveled hand. (10) Some Jewish religious leaders were trying to find a way to accuse Jesus of doing something wrong, so they asked him, "Is it lawful to heal on the Sabbath day?" (11) Jesus said to them, "If any of you has a sheep and it falls into a hole on the Sabbath, will you not pull it out of the hole? (12) How much more valuable are people to God than sheep! Therefore it is lawful to do good on the Sabbath day." (13) Then Jesus said to the man, "Hold out your hand." So he held out his hand and it was healed.

Mark 3:1-5 - (1) Another time Jesus entered the Capernaum synagogue, and a man with a withered hand was there. (2) Some Pharisees were looking for a reason to accuse Jesus of doing something wrong, so they watched him closely to see if he would heal the man on the Sabbath day. (3) Jesus said to the man with the withered hand, "Stand up in front of everyone." (4) Then Jesus said them, "Which is lawful on the Sabbath day: To do good or to do evil, to save life or to kill?" But they did not say anything. (5) Jesus looked around at the Pharisees with anger because he was deeply troubled by their stubborn hearts. Jesus said to the man, "Stretch out your hand!" The man stretched it out, and his hand was totally healed.

Luke 6:6-10 - (6) Jesus was teaching in the synagogue on another Sabbath day, and a man was there whose right hand was shriveled. (7) The Pharisees and teachers of the law of Moses were looking for a reason to accuse Jesus, so they watched him closely to see if he would heal on the Sabbath day. (8) But Jesus knew what they were thinking and told the man with the shriveled hand, "Get up and stand in front of everyone." So he got up and stood there. (9) Then Jesus said to the religious leaders, "I ask you, is it lawful to do good or do evil on the Sabbath day, to save life or destroy it?" (10) Jesus looked around at them all, and then said to the man, "Stretch out your hand!" When the man did, it was completely healed.

87 - Religious Leaders Plan to Kill Jesus
(Matthew 12:14, Mark 3:6, Luke 6:11)

Matthew 12:14 - But the Pharisees left the synagogue and began to plan how they could kill Jesus.

Mark 3:6 - Then the Pharisees left the synagogue and began to plot with the Herodians (*a Jewish political party that supported the Herodian rulers*) how they might kill Jesus.

Luke 6:11 - But the Pharisees and teachers of the law of Moses became very angry and began to discuss with one another what they could do against Jesus.

88 - Jesus Heals Many People
(Matthew 12:15-21; Mark 3:7-12)

Matthew 12:15-21 - (15) Knowing that the Jewish religious leaders were planning to kill him, Jesus left the Capernaum synagogue for another place. A large crowd of people followed him, and he healed all who were sick. (16) He ordered them not to tell others about him. (17) This was to fulfill the words written in Isaiah 42:1-4, (18) "Here is my chosen servant, the one I love and in whom I delight (*take pleasure*). I will put my Spirit on him, and he will proclaim justice to the nations. (19) He will not argue or cry out. No one will hear his voice in the streets, (20) because a bruised reed he will not break, and a smoldering wick he will not snuff out. He will lead justice to victory, (21) and the nations will put their hope in his name."

Mark 3:7-12 - (7) Jesus and his disciples withdrew to Lake Galilee, and a large crowd of people from Galilee followed them. (8) When the people heard about all the miracles that Jesus was doing, many people came to him from Judea, Jerusalem, Idumea, the regions east of the Jordan River in Perea, and from around Tyre and Sidon.

(9) Because of the growing crowd Jesus told his disciples to get a small boat ready for him, so that the crowd would not crush him. (10) For Jesus had healed many people, and those with diseases were pushing forward to touch him. (11) Whenever demons saw him, those who were demon-possessed (*demonized*) fell down before him and cried out, "You are the Son of God!" (12) But Jesus commanded the demons not to tell others who he was.

89 - Jesus Prays All Night
(Luke 6:12)

Luke 6:12 - On one of these days Jesus went out and walked up the mountainside (*probably the hills west of Capernaum*) to pray, and he spent the whole night praying to God.

90 - The Twelve Apostles of Jesus
(Mark 3:13-19, Luke 6:13-16)

Mark 3:13-19 - (13) Jesus went up on a mountainside and called to him those he wanted, and they gathered around him. (14) Jesus appointed 12 of his disciples to be with him, that he could send out

46

(*sent ones, apostles*) to preach, (15) and to have God's authority to cast out demons from people. (16) These are the names of the Twelve Apostles that he appointed: Simon (*to whom he gave the name Peter*), (17) James and John the sons of Zebedee (*to them Jesus gave the name Boanerges, which means "sons of thunder"*), (18) Andrew, Philip, Bartholomew, Matthew, Thomas, James son of Alphaeus, Thaddaeus, Simon the Zealot, (19) and Judas Iscariot, who would betray him.

Luke 6:13-16 - (13) In the morning, he called his disciples to him and chose 12 of them, whom he appointed to be his apostles (*sent ones*). (14) The names of the Twelve Apostles were: Simon Peter, his brother Andrew, James, John, Philip, Bartholomew, (15) Matthew, Thomas, James son of Alphaeus, Simon who was called the Zealot, (16) Judas son of James, and Judas Iscariot, who would betray Jesus.

91 - Jesus Heals Many People
(Luke 6:17-19)

Luke 6:17-19 - (17) Jesus walked down the mountainside with his disciples and stood on a plain of land (*possibly a plateau area in the northwestern area of Lake Galilee*). (17) A large crowd of his disciples was there and a great number of people who had come from all over Judea, from Jerusalem, and from the Mediterranean coastal region of Tyre and Sidon (*the non-Jewish region of modern Lebanon*). (18) They came to hear him teach and to be healed of their diseases. Those who were tormented by demons were set free, (19) and the people tried to touch Jesus, because God's power was coming from his body and healing everybody.

92 - The Blessings of the Kingdom of God
(Matthew 5:1-12, Luke 6:20-23)

Matthew 5:1-12 - (1) Now when Jesus saw the crowds, he went up on a mountainside and sat down, and his disciples came to him. (2) He taught them saying: (3) "Blessed are the poor (*humble*) in spirit, because theirs is the kingdom of heaven (*God*). (4) Blessed are those who mourn, because they will be given comfort. (5) Blessed are the meek, because they will inherit the earth. (6) Blessed are those who hunger and thirst for the right ways of God, because they will be filled.

(7) Blessed are the merciful, because they will be shown mercy. (8) Blessed are the pure in heart, because they will see God. (9) Blessed are those who work for peace (*peacemakers*), because they will be called the children of God. (10) Blessed are those who are persecuted for obeying the right ways of God, because theirs is the kingdom of heaven (*God*). (11) Blessed are you when people insult you, persecute you, and say false words about you because of me. (12) Rejoice and be happy, because your reward in heaven will be great, for in the same way they persecuted the (*Old Testament*) prophets who came before you."

Luke 6:20-23 - (20) Jesus looked at his disciples and said, "Blessed are you who are poor, because yours is the kingdom of God. (21) Blessed are you who are hungry now, because you will be filled. Blessed are you who weep now, because you will laugh. (22) Blessed are you when people hate you, exclude and insult you, and call you evil because you are a follower of the Son of Man (*see Daniel 7:13-14*). (23) Rejoice in that day and jump for joy, because great is your reward in heaven. For that is how their ancestors treated the (*Old Testament*) prophets."

93 - Terrible Woes
(Luke 6:24-26)

Luke 6:24-26 - (24) Jesus said, "But how terrible for you who are rich now, because you have already received your comfort. (25) How terrible for you who are well fed now, because you will be hungry. How terrible for you who are laughing (*scoffing*) now, because you will mourn and weep. (26) How terrible for those about whom people say good things, because that is how their ancestors treated the false prophets."

94 - Salt and Light of the World
(Matthew 5:13-16)

Matthew 5:13-16 - Jesus said, (13) "You are the salt of the earth! But if salt loses its taste, it cannot be made to taste like salt again. It is no longer good for anything except to be thrown on the ground and walked on. (14) You are the light of the world! A city built on a hill cannot be hidden. (15) People do not light a lamp and put it under a bowl. Instead they put a lamp on a stand so that it gives light to everyone in the house. (16) In the same way, let your light shine before others, so that they will see your good works and praise your Father in heaven."

95 - Jesus Fulfills the Old Testament
(Matthew 5:17-20)

Matthew 5:17-20 - Jesus said, (17) "Do not think that I came to eliminate the law of Moses and the (*Old Testament*) prophets. I did not come to destroy them but to fulfill them! (18) For I tell you the truth: Until heaven and earth disappear, not the smallest mark of a letter from the law of Moses will be taken away until everything in it is fulfilled. (19) Therefore whoever eliminates one of the least of God's commandments and teaches others to do the same will be called the least in the kingdom of heaven (*God*). But whoever obeys and teaches God's commandments will be called the greatest in the kingdom of heaven (*God*). (20) For I tell you the truth: Unless your righteousness is greater than that of the Pharisees and the teachers of the law of Moses, you will certainly not enter the kingdom of heaven (*God*)."

96 - Hate and Murder
(Matthew 5:21-26)

Matthew 5:21-26 - Jesus said, (21) "You have heard that it was said to the people long ago in Exodus 20:13, 'Do not murder,' and anyone who murders will be subject to judgment. (22) But I say to you that anyone who is angry with another believer will be subject to judgment.

Matthew 5:21-24 - Jesus said, (21) Again, anyone who insults another believer will be brought before the governing council (the Sanhedrin). And anyone who says, 'You are a fool,' to another believer will be in danger of the fire of hell (gehenna). (23) Therefore, if you are offering your gift at God's altar and there remember that your fellow believer has something against you, (24) leave your gift at the altar. First go and heal the relationship (be reconciled) with your fellow believer; then go back and offer your gift to God

Matthew 5:25-26 - Jesus said, (25) "Immediately settle matters with your adversary who is taking you to court. Do it while you are walking together to the courthouse, or he will hand you over to the judge, and the judge will hand you over to a guard, and you will be thrown into prison. (26) I tell you the truth: You will not get out of prison until you have paid the very last penny you owe that person."

97 - Adultery and Causes of Sin
(Matthew 5:27-30)

Matthew 5:27-28 - Jesus said, (27) "You have heard that it was written in Exodus 20:14, 'Do not commit adultery.' (28) But I say to you that anyone who looks at a woman with sexual lust has already committed adultery with her in his heart.

Matthew 5:29-30 - Jesus said, (29) If your right eye causes you to sin, pull it out and throw it away. For it is far better for you to lose one eye than for your whole body to be thrown into hell (*gehenna*). (30) And if your right hand causes you to sin, cut it off and throw it away. For it is far better for you to lose one hand than for your whole body to be thrown into hell (*gehenna*)."

98 - Marriage and Divorce
(Matthew 5:31-32)

Matthew 5:31-32 - Jesus said, (31) "It has been written in Deuteronomy 24:1, 'Whoever divorces his wife must give her a certificate of divorce.' (32) But I say to you that whoever divorces his wife, except for marital unfaithfulness (*sexual immorality*), makes her commit adultery, and whoever marries a divorced woman commits adultery."

99 - Oaths
(Matthew 5:33-37)

Matthew 5:33-37 - (33) Jesus said, "You have heard that it was said to the people long ago in Leviticus 19:12, 'Do not break your oath, but fulfill to the Lord any vows you have made.' (34) But

I say to you: Do not make an oath at all—either by heaven, for it is God's throne; (35) or by the earth, for the earth is God's footstool; or by Jerusalem, for it is the city of the great King. (36) And do not make an oath by your head, for you cannot make even one hair white or black. (37) I tell you to say either 'Yes' or 'No.' To say anything more than this comes from Satan, the evil one."

100 - Non-Violent Resistance
(Matthew 5:38-42, Luke 6:29)

Matthew 5:38-42 - Jesus said, (38) "You have heard that it was said in Exodus 21:24, 'An eye for an eye and a tooth for a tooth.' (39) But I say to you: Do not (*use violence to*) resist an evil person. If anyone slaps you (*with a backhand*) on your right cheek (*in an attempt to humiliate you*), turn your left cheek to them (*in non-violent defiance*). (40) And if anyone sues you in court and takes your inner shirt (*tunic*), give them your outer coat (*cloak*) also (*leaving yourself naked in non-violent defiance*). (41) If anyone forces you to go one mile (*the Roman military often engaged in forced labor, as when Simon of Cyrene was forced to carry Jesus' cross*), insist on going with them for two miles (*in non-violent defiance*). (42) If anyone asks you to give them something, give it to them; do not turn away a person who wants to borrow from you."

Luke 6:29 - Jesus said, "If someone slaps you (*with a backhand*) on your right cheek (*in an attempt to humiliate you*), turn your other cheek to them (*in non-violent resistance*). If someone takes your outer coat (*cloak*), do not stop them from taking your inner shirt (*tunic*) as well (*leaving yourself naked in non-violent defiance*).

101 - Love Your Enemies
(Matthew 5:43-48, Luke 6:27-28, 30-36)

Matthew 5:43-48 - Jesus said, (43) "You have heard that it was written in Leviticus 19:18, 'Love your neighbor,' and also said 'Hate your enemy.' (44) But I say to you: Love your enemies and pray for those who persecute you. (45) If you do this, you will be children of your Father in heaven. For God causes his sun to rise on the evil and the good, and sends rain on the righteous and the unrighteous. (46) If you love only those who love you, why should you get a reward for that? For even tax collectors (*for the Romans*) love those who love them. (47) And if you greet only your friends, you are no better than anyone else, because even the pagans greet their friends. (48) Therefore, you must be holy (*perfect*) like your heavenly Father is holy (*perfect*)."

Luke 6:27-29, 30-36 - Jesus said, (27) "But to you who are willing to listen, I tell you: Love your enemies, do good to those who hate you, (28) bless those who curse you and pray for those who mistreat you. (30) Give to everyone who asks you, and if anyone takes what is yours, do not demand it back. (31) Treat others as you would want them to treat you. (32) Do not expect God's blessing if you love only people who love you, for even sinners love those who love them. (33) Do not expect God's blessing if you do good only to people who do good to you, for even sinners do that. (34) Do not expect God's blessing if you give money to people who will pay you back, for even sinners give money to other sinners who will pay them back in full. (35) But I tell you to love your enemies, do good to them, and give to them without expecting to get your money back. Then your reward in heaven will be great, and you will be the people of the Most High God, because God is merciful to even the ungrateful and wicked. (36) Be merciful, just as your Father is merciful."

102 - How to Give to the Needy
(Matthew 6:1-4)

Matthew 6:1-4 - (1) Jesus said, "Be careful not to practice your righteousness in front of other people, with the desire to be seen by them. If you do, you will not receive a reward from your Father in heaven. (2) Therefore, when you give to people in need, do not draw attention to yourselves by blowing trumpets like the religious hypocrites do in the synagogues and on the streets. They simply want to be praised by people who see them. I tell you the truth: They have received their full reward here on earth. (3) But when you give to people in need, do not let your left hand know what your right hand is doing, (4) so that your giving to others will be done in private (*secret*). Then your Father, who sees everything that is done in private (*secret*), will reward you."

103 - How to Pray
(Matthew 6:5-15)

Matthew 6:5-8 - (5) Jesus said, "When you pray, do not pray like the religious hypocrites. They love to pray standing in the synagogues and on the street corners so that they will be noticed by people. I tell you the truth: They have received their full reward. (6) But when you pray to God, go into a room, close the door and pray to your Father, who is unseen. Then your Father, who sees everything you do in private (*secret*), will reward you. (7) And when you pray, do not repeat the same words over and over again (*babbling*) like the pagans, because they think their gods will hear them because they use many words. (8) Do not pray like them, for your Father knows what you need in life before you even ask him.

Matthew 6:9-15 - (9) "Therefore, this is how you should pray: 'Our Father in heaven, holy be your name, (10) your kingdom come, your will be done, on earth as it is in heaven. (11) Give us today our daily bread (*food*). (12) And forgive us our debts (*what we owe to others*), as we also have forgiven our debtors (*those who owe us*). (13) And lead us not into temptation (*or trial*), but deliver us from Satan, the evil one.' (14) For if you forgive other people when they sin against you, your Father in heaven will also forgive you. (15) But if you do not forgive the sins of others, your Father will not forgive your sins."

---

104 - How to Fast
(Matthew 6:16-18)

Matthew 6:16-18 - (16) Jesus said, "When you fast, do not fast like the religious hypocrites, who put on a sad face (*disfigure their face*) to show other people that they are fasting. I tell you the truth: They have received their full reward on this earth. (17) But when you fast, comb your hair and wash your face, (18) so that other people will not know that you are fasting, but only your Father, who is unseen; and your Father, who sees everything that is done in private (*secret*), will reward you."

---

105 - Treasures in Heaven
(Matthew 6:19-21, Luke 12:33-34)

Matthew 6:19-21 - Jesus said, (19) "Do not store up (*hoard*) treasures for yourselves on earth, where moths and rust destroy and where thieves break in and steal, (20) but store up for yourselves treasures in heaven, where moth and rust do not destroy and where thieves do not break in and steal. (21) For where your treasure is, there your heart will be also.

Luke 12:33-34 - Jesus said, (33) "Sell what you own and give to the poor. Pursue money bags for yourselves that will not wear out, a treasure in heaven that will never fail, where no thieves steal and where moths do not destroy. (34) For where your treasure is, there will your heart be also."

106 - Eyes are the Lamp of the Body
(Matthew 6:22-23)

Matthew 6:22-23 - Jesus said, (22) "The eyes are the lamp of the body. So, if you look at the things that are good, your whole body will be full of light. (23) But if you look at the things that are bad, your whole body will be full of darkness. If then the light in you becomes darkness, your darkness will be great!

107 - You Cannot Serve Both God and Money
(Matthew 6:24)

Matthew 6:24 - Jesus said, "You cannot serve two masters: You will either love one and hate the other, or you will be devoted to one and despise the other. You cannot serve God and money."

108 - Do Not Worry About Your Life
(Matthew 6:25-34, Luke 12:22-32)

Matthew 6:25-34 - (25) Jesus said, "Therefore I tell you the truth: Do not worry about your life, what you will eat or drink, or about the clothes you will wear. Life is much more important than food and clothes. (26) "Watch the birds flying in the sky. They do not work or store crops in barns, and yet your Father in heaven feeds them. People are much more valuable than birds! (27) You cannot add a single hour to your life by worrying. (28) And do not worry about what clothes you will wear. Watch how the flowers grow in the field. They do not work or labor. (29) For I tell you that not even Solomon in all his kingly glory was dressed like one of these flowers. (30) If God clothes the grass, which is here today and tomorrow is thrown into the fire, will he not much more clothe you—you of little faith? (31) So do not worry about your life. Stop saying, 'What will we eat?' or 'What will we drink?' or 'What will we wear?' (32) For pagans live for all these things, and your Father in heaven knows what you need in life. But I tell you to seek first the kingdom of God and his righteousness, and all the things you need in life will be given to you. (34) Therefore do not worry about tomorrow, for tomorrow will have its own worries. Today has enough trouble of its own."

Luke 12:22-32 - (22) Then Jesus said to his disciples, "Therefore I tell you the truth: Do not worry about your life, about what you will eat; or about your body, what clothes you will wear. (23) For life is much more than food, and your body is much more important than what clothes you will wear. (24) Watch how the birds live: They do not plant or harvest. They do not have storerooms or barns for their food, for God feeds them! And you are much more valuable than birds! (25) Who of you by worrying can add a single hour to your life? (26) Since you can't do this, why do you worry about everything else? (27) Watch how the wild flowers grow. They do not labor or work or weave. Yet I tell you the truth: Not even Solomon in all his kingly splendor was dressed like the beauty of the flowers. (28) So if that is how God clothes the grass of the field—which is here today and tomorrow is thrown into the fire—how much more will God clothe you, you of little faith! (29) And do not set your heart on what you will eat or drink. Do not worry about all these things of life! (30) For the people of this world run after all these things, but your Father in heaven knows that you need them. (31) Instead, seek first the kingdom of God and all these things in life will be given to you. (32) Do not be afraid, little flock, because your Father in heaven is pleased to give you the kingdom of God."

---

109 - Do Not Judge Other People
(Matthew 7:1-5, Luke 6:37-42)

Matthew 7:1-5 - Jesus said, (1) "Do not judge others so that you will not be judged. (2) For in the same way you judge others you will be judged, and the measure you use to judge others will be the same measure used against you. (3) Why do you notice the small piece of sawdust in a fellow believer's eye, but ignore the large piece of wood in your own eye? (4) How can you say to a fellow believer, 'Let me remove the small piece of sawdust out of your eye,' when you have a large piece of wood in your own eye? (5) You religious hypocrites! First remove the large piece of wood out of your own eye, and then you can see clearly to remove the small piece of sawdust from the eye of your fellow believer.

Luke 6:37-42 - Jesus said, (37) "Do not judge others, and you will not be judged. Do not condemn others, and you will not be condemned. Forgive others, and you will be forgiven. (38) Give to others, and it will be given to you. You will receive much; it will be poured over into your lap, because the amount you give is the amount that you will receive." (39) Jesus also told the people this parable (story): "Can the blind lead the blind? Won't they both fall into a hole? (40) The student is not above the teacher, but everyone who is fully trained will be like their teacher. (41)

Why do you notice the small piece of sawdust in a fellow believer's eye and ignore the large piece of wood in your own eye? (42) How can you say to a fellow believer, 'Let me take the small piece of sawdust out of your eye,' when you have a large piece of wood in your own eye? You religious hypocrites! First take the large piece of wood out of your own eye, and then you will see clearly to remove the small piece of sawdust from a fellow believer's eye."

110 - Wisdom and Holiness
(Matthew 7:6)

Matthew 7:6 - Jesus said, "Do not give dogs what is holy, or throw pearls before pigs. If you do, they will trample all over them, and then attack you and tear you to pieces."

111 - Keep Asking, Keep Seeking, Keep Knocking
(Matthew 7:7-11)

Matthew 7:7-11 - Jesus said, (7) "Keep asking and it will be given to you. Keep seeking and you will find. Keep knocking and the door will be opened to you. (8) For everyone who asks receives, everyone who seeks finds, and to everyone who knocks, the door will be opened. (9) Which of you parents will give a stone to your child who asks you for bread? (10) Or if he asks for a fish, will give him a snake? Not one of you! (11) Therefore, if you parents—even though you are evil—give good gifts to your children, how much more will your Father in heaven give good gifts to those who ask him!"

112 - How to Treat Other People
(Matthew 7:12)

Matthew 7:12 - Jesus said, "So in all things, do to others what you would have them do to you, because this way of living sums up the teaching of the law of Moses and the prophets (the entire Old Testament)."

- -

- -

- -

- -

- -

113 - The Narrow and Wide Gates
(Matthew 7:13-14)

Matthew 7:13-14 - Jesus said, (13) "Enter through the narrow gate! For the gate is wide and the road is easy that leads to destruction, and many people choose to go this way.

(14) But the gate is narrow and the road is hard that leads to eternal life, and only a few people choose to go this way."

- -

- -

- -

- -

- -

114 - Jesus' Warning About False Prophets
(Matthew 7:15-23, Luke 6:43-45)

Matthew 7:15-23 - Jesus said, (15) "Watch out for false prophets. They come to you wearing sheep's clothing, but on the inside they are ferocious wolves. (16) You can recognize false prophets by their fruit—how they live their lives. People do not pick grapes from thorn bushes, or figs from thistles. (17) Good trees produce good fruit, but bad trees produce bad fruit. (18) Good trees cannot produce bad fruit, and bad trees cannot produce good fruit. (19) Every tree that does not produce good fruit is cut down and thrown into the fire. (20) So, you can recognize false prophets by their fruit—how they live their lives. (21) Not everyone who says to me on the final day, 'Lord, Lord,' will enter the kingdom of heaven (*God*), but only those who do the will of my Father who is in heaven. (22) Many will say to me on the final day, 'Lord, Lord, we prophesied in your name, drove out demons in your name, and performed many miracles in your name.' (23) Then I will tell them directly, 'I never knew you. Away from me! You have lived evil lives!' "

Luke 6:43-45 - Jesus said, (43) "A good tree produces good fruit, and a bad tree produces bad fruit. (44) Each tree is recognized by the kind of fruit it produces. We do not pick figs from thorn bushes, or grapes from thistles. (45) A good man brings good treasure out of the good stored up in his heart, and an evil man brings evil things out of the evil stored up in his heart. For a man speaks out of the abundance that has been stored up in his heart."

115 - The Wise and the Fools
(Matthew 7:24-27, Luke 6:46-49)

Matthew 7:24-27 - Jesus said, (24) "Therefore whoever hears my teaching and puts it into practice is like a wise man who built his house on a rock foundation. (25) The rains came, the rivers rose, and the winds blew and beat against that house, yet it did not fall, because its foundation was on the solid rock. (26) But whoever hears my teaching and does not put it into practice is like a foolish man who built his house on sand. (27) The rains came, the rivers rose, and the winds blew and beat against that house, and it fell with a great crash."

Luke 6:46-49 - Jesus said, (46) "Why do you call me, 'Lord, Lord,' and not do what I teach? (47) Whoever comes to me, hears my teaching, and puts it into practice (48) is like a man building a house who dug down deep and laid the foundation on rock. When a flood came, the waters hit that house but could not shake it, because it was well built.(49) But whoever hears my teaching and does not put it into practice is like a man who built a house on the ground without a rock foundation. As soon as the floodwater hit that house, it fell and was completely destroyed."

116 - Jesus Teaches With God's Authority
(Matthew 7:28-29)

Matthew 7:28-29 - (28) After Jesus finished his teaching, the crowds were amazed at what he said, (29) because he taught as one who had God's authority, and not like the teachers of the law of Moses.

117 - Jesus Heals the Servant of a Roman Military Officer
(Matthew 8:5-13, Luke 7:1-10)

Matthew 8:5-13 - (5) When Jesus entered Capernaum, a Roman military leader (*a centurion*) came and asked him for help, (6) "Lord, my servant lies at home paralyzed, and he is in great suffering." (7) Jesus said to him, "Should I come and heal him?" (8) The military leader said, "Lord, I am not worthy for you to come into my house. Instead, just give a command, and my servant will be healed. (9) For I work under the authority of military leaders, and my soldiers work under me. And I tell a soldier under me to 'Go,' and he goes. I tell a soldier to 'Come,' and he comes. I tell my servant, 'Do this,' and he does it." (10) When Jesus heard this, he was amazed and said to those following him, "I tell you the truth: I have not found anyone in Israel with such great faith. (11) I tell you that many people will come from the east and the west to take their places at the final banquet with Abraham, Isaac, and Jacob in the kingdom of heaven (*God*). (12) But many people in Israel—the subjects of the kingdom—will be thrown out into the darkness, where people will be weeping and grinding their teeth." (13) Then Jesus said to the military leader, "Go! Let your servant be healed as you believed he would." And his servant was healed that very moment.

Luke 7:1-10 - (1) Jesus went into Capernaum after he had finished his teaching. (2) There the beloved servant of a high-ranking Roman military officer (*a centurion*) was very sick and about to die. (3) The military officer heard about Jesus and sent some Jewish elders to ask him to come and heal his servant. (4) When they came to Jesus, they pleaded with him, saying, "This Roman deserves to have you heal his servant (5) because he loves our nation, and he is the one who built our synagogue." (6) So Jesus went with them. As they were coming close to his house, the military officer sent friends to say to Jesus, "Lord, don't trouble yourself, because I am not worthy to have you enter my house. (7) I did not even consider myself worthy enough to come to you. But my servant will be healed if you just say the word. (8) For I am a military officer under authority, with soldiers under my command. I tell one soldier, 'Go,' and he goes, and another soldier, 'Come,' and he comes. I tell my servant, 'Do this,' and he does it." (9) When Jesus heard this, he was amazed at the man, and turning to the crowd of people following him, he said, "I tell you the truth: I have not found such great faith in Israel." (10) Then the Roman officer's friends who had been sent returned to the house and found the servant healed.

118 - Jesus Raises a Dead Man at Nain
(Luke 7:11-15)

Luke 7:11-15 - (11) Soon afterward, Jesus walked to a town called Nain (*located about 6 miles/10 km southeast of Nazareth*), and his disciples and a large crowd followed him. (12) As he approached the town gate, he saw a dead man being carried out of the town. The man was the only son of his mother, who was a widow. And a large crowd from the town was walking with her. (13) When the Lord saw the woman, his heart was filled with compassion for her and he said, "Don't cry." (14) Then Jesus went up and touched the wooden board on which they were carrying her son. Those carrying him stopped. And Jesus said, "Young man, I tell you to get up!" (15) The dead man sat up and began to talk, and Jesus gave him back to his mother.

119 - News About Jesus Spreads Throughout Country
(Luke 7:16-17)

Luke 7:16-17 - (16) The people who saw this were filled with awe and praised God. They declared, "A great prophet has walked among us today; God has come to help his people." (17) This news about Jesus spread everywhere in Judea (*the land of the Jews*) and the surrounding country.

120 - John's Disciples Question Jesus
(Matthew 11:1-6, Luke 7:18-23)

Matthew 11:1-6 - (1) After Jesus had finished teaching his Twelve Apostles, he went on from there to proclaim and teach the gospel (*good news*) throughout the towns of Galilee.(2) When John the Baptizer heard in prison (*he had probably been in prison for about one year, at the fortress Machaerus in the region of Perea, in modern Jordan*) what the Messiah (*Christ*) was doing, he sent his disciples (3) to ask him, "Are you the one to come, or should we look for someone else?" (4) Jesus said to them, "Go back and tell John what you hear and see: (5) The blind receive their sight, the lame walk, lepers are healed, the deaf hear, the dead are raised to life, and the gospel (*good news*) of God is proclaimed to the poor. (6) Blessed is everyone who does not fall away because of me."

Luke 7:18-23 - (18) John's disciples told John (*who probably had been in prison for about one year*) about all that Jesus was teaching and doing. John called two of his disciples (19) and sent them to ask the Lord, "Are you the one who is to come, or should we expect someone else?" (20) When they came to Jesus, they said, "John the Baptizer sent us to ask you, 'Are you the one who is to come, or should we expect someone else?' (21) At that very time Jesus was healing many people who had diseases, sicknesses, and demons, and healing many people who were blind. (22) Jesus told John's disciples, "Go back and tell John what you have seen and heard: The blind see, the lame walk, those who are lepers are cleansed, the deaf hear, the dead are raised to life, and the gospel (*good news*) is proclaimed to the poor. (23) Blessed is the one who does not stumble on account of me."

- -

- -

- -

- -

- -

121 - Jesus Praises John
(Matthew 11:7-15, Luke 7:24-30)

Matthew 11:7-15 - (7) When John's disciples were leaving, Jesus said to the crowd about John: "What did you go out to see in the wilderness of Judea? A fragile desert reed blowing in the wind? (8) What did you go to see? A man dressed in expensive clothes? No, those who wear expensive clothes live in the palaces of kings. (9) Then what did you go to see? A prophet? Yes, I tell you the truth: He is much more than a prophet. (10) John is the one about whom it is written in Malachi 3:1, 'I will send my messenger ahead of you, who will prepare your way before you.' (11) I tell you the truth: Among all the children born of women there has not been one that is greater than John, the Baptizer. But now, whoever is least important in the kingdom of heaven (*God*) is greater than John. (12) From the days of John until now, the kingdom of heaven v has advanced in power (has been subjected to violence), and people of strong faith (*forceful people*) are seizing it (*taking it by force*). (13) For the law of Moses and the prophets (*the entire Old Testament*) foretold of all these things until the coming of John. (14) And if you are willing to accept it, John is Elijah who was to come. (15) Whoever has ears to hear, let them hear!

Luke 7:24-30 - (24) After John's disciples left, Jesus told the crowd of people about John: "What did you go out into the Judean wilderness to see? A weak desert reed blown by the wind? (25) What did you go out to see? A man dressed in fine clothes? No, those who wear expensive clothes and indulge in luxury live in palaces. (26) What did you go out to see? A prophet? Yes, I tell you the truth, more than a prophet. (27) John is the one written about in Malachi 3:1, 'I will send my messenger ahead of you, who will prepare your way before you.' (28) I tell you the truth: Among those born of women there is no one who is greater than John; yet whoever is least in the kingdom of God is greater than John." (29) When all the people and the tax collectors heard Jesus' teaching, they confessed that God's way was right, because they had been baptized by John. (30) But the Pharisees and teachers of the law of Moses rejected God's plan for them, because they had not been baptized by John.

- -

- -

- -

122 - Jesus Rebukes That Generation of Israel
(Matthew 11:16-19, Luke 7:31-35)

Matthew 11:16-19 - Jesus said, (16) "To what can I compare this generation of Israel? They are like children sitting in the public markets and calling out to their playmates, (17) 'We played the flute for you, but you did not dance; we sang a song for the dead, but you did not mourn.' (18) For John did not come eating bread or drinking wine, and they say, 'He has a demon.' (19) The Son of Man (*see Daniel 7:13-14*) came eating and drinking, and they say, 'Look at him! He is a glutton and a drunkard, a friend of tax collectors and sinners!' But wisdom is proved right (*justified*) by her works."

Luke 7:31-35 - (31) Jesus said, "To what do I compare this generation of Israel? What are they like? (32) They are like children sitting in the public market and calling out to each other: 'We played the flute for you, but you did not dance; we sang a song of the dead (*dirge*) for you, but you did not mourn.' (33) For John did not come eating bread or drinking wine, and you say, 'He has a demon.' (34) The Son of Man (*see Daniel 7:13-14*) came eating and drinking, and you say, 'He is a glutton, a drunkard, and a friend of tax collectors and sinners.' (35) But wisdom is shown to be right (*justified*) by all her children."

123 - A Woman Anoints Jesus' Feet
(Luke 7:36-50)

Luke 7:36-50 - (36) When a certain Pharisee invited Jesus to have dinner with him, he entered into the Pharisee's house and sat at the table. (37) Hearing that Jesus was eating at the Pharisee's house, a woman in that town who lived a life of sin came to the house with an alabaster jar filled with expensive fragrant oil. (38) As she stood behind Jesus at his feet weeping, her tears dripped on his feet. She wiped his feet with her hair, kissed them, and poured oil on them. (39) When the Pharisee saw this, he said to himself, "If Jesus was a true prophet, he would know what kind of woman that is touching him—for she is a sinner." (40) Then Jesus said to the Pharisee, "Simon, I have a parable (*story*) to tell you." Simon said, "Tell me, teacher." (41) Jesus said: "Two men were in debt to a moneylender; one man owed him 500 coins and the other 50 coins. (42) Neither of these men had the money to repay the loan, so the moneylender forgave their debts. Now tell me, which man will have a greater love for the moneylender?" (43) Simon said, "The man who was forgiven the largest debt." Jesus said to him, "You are correct." (44) Then Jesus turned toward the woman and said to Simon, "Look at this woman. I came into your house and you did not give me water to wash my feet, but she washed my feet with her tears and wiped them with her hair. (45) You did not give me a kiss, but she, from the time I entered, has not stop kissing my feet. (46) You did not put oil on my head, but she has poured fragrant oil on my feet. (47) Therefore, I tell you the truth: Because her many sins have been forgiven, she has shown me great love. But whoever has been forgiven little shows little love." (48) Then Jesus said to the woman, "Your sins are forgiven." (49) The other guests said to one another, "Who is this Jesus, who forgives sins?" (50) Jesus said to the woman, "Go in peace, because your faith has saved you."

124 - Jesus' Ministry Tour Through Galilee
(Luke 8:1-3)

Luke 8:1-3 - (1) Soon after this, Jesus traveled through Galilee's villages and towns proclaiming the gospel (*good news*) of the kingdom of God. The Twelve Apostles were with him, (2) and also some women who had been healed of demons and diseases: Mary called Magdalene, who had seven demons cast out of her; (3) Joanna the wife of Cuza, the house manager of Herod Antipas; Susanna; and many others. These women were helping to support them out of their own possessions.

125 - Accusations Made Against Jesus
(Matthew 12:22-30, Mark 3:20-27, Luke 11:14-23)

Matthew 12:22-30 - (22) Then the people brought to Jesus a demon-possessed (*demonized*) man who could not see or talk, and Jesus healed him, so that he could see and speak. (23) All the people were amazed and said, "Could this be the Son of David?" (24) But when the Pharisees heard this, they said, "Jesus casts out demons by Satan (*Beelzebub*), the ruler of demons." (25) Jesus knew their thoughts and said to them, "Every kingdom divided against itself will fall, and every city or family divided against itself cannot stand. (26) If Satan casts out demons, he is divided against himself. How then can his kingdom stand? (27) And if I cast out demons by Satan (*Beelzebub*), by whom do your sons cast demons out of people? Therefore, they will be your judges. (28) But if I cast demons out from people by the Spirit of God, then the kingdom of God has come upon you. (29) Or again, how can anyone break into a strong man's house and steal his possessions unless he first ties up the strong man? Then they can take everything in his house. (30) Whoever is not with me is against me, and whoever does not gather with me scatters.

Mark 3:20-27 - (20) Then Jesus went into the house (*probably Peter's home*) in Capernaum, and once again a large crowd gathered, so that he and his disciples were not even able to eat a meal. (21) When Jesus' family in Nazareth heard what was happening in Capernaum, they went there to stop him, because they said, "He is out of his mind." (22) And some teachers of the law of Moses came down from Jerusalem and said, "He is possessed by Satan (*Beelzebub*)! It is by the ruler of demons that he casts demons out of people." (23) So Jesus called them over to him and began to speak to them in parables: "How can Satan cast out demons? (24) If a kingdom is divided against itself, that kingdom cannot stand. (25) If a family is divided against itself, that home cannot stand. (26) And if Satan fights himself and is divided, he cannot stand and that would be his end. (27) The truth is, no one can enter a strong man's house without first tying him up. Then he can rob the strong man's house.

Luke 11:14-23 - (14) Jesus was casting out a demon that caused a man not to be able to speak. The man was able to speak when the demon went out. The people were amazed, but some of them said, "Jesus casts out demons by Satan (*Beelzebub*), the ruler of demons." (16) Other people tested Jesus by asking him to show them a miraculous sign from heaven. (17) But Jesus knew what they were thinking and said to them, "Every kingdom divided against itself will fall in ruin, and a house divided against itself will fall. (18) If Satan's kingdom is divided against himself, how can his kingdom stand? I tell you this because you say that I cast demons out of people by the power of Satan (*Beelzebub*). (19) Now if I cast out demons by Satan (*Beelzebub*), by whom do your followers cast them out? So then, they will be your judges. (20) But if I cast out demons by God's power (*the finger of God*), then the kingdom of God has already come upon you. (21) When a strong man with weapons is guarding his house, all he owns is safe. (22) But when someone stronger attacks and overpowers him, he takes away the armor in which the man put his trust, and divides up all that he stole. (23) Whoever is not with me is against me, and whoever does not gather with me scatters."

126 - Blasphemy Against the Holy Spirit
(Matthew 12:31-32, Mark 3:28-30)

Matthew 12:31-32 - Jesus said, (31) "And I tell you the truth: Every kind of sin and blasphemy can be forgiven, but blasphemy against the Holy Spirit will not be forgiven. (32) Whoever speaks a word against the Son of Man (*see Daniel 7:13-14*) will be forgiven, but whoever speaks against the Holy Spirit will not be forgiven, either in this age or in the age to come."

Mark 3:28-30 - Jesus said, (28) "I tell you the truth: People will be forgiven all their sins and every slanWderous word they say, (29) but whoever blasphemes (*speaks against*) the Holy

Spirit will never be forgiven, because they will be guilty of an eternal sin." (30) Jesus said this because the Jewish religious leaders were saying that he was possessed by Satan.

127 - The Fruit of the Heart
(Matthew 12:33-37)

Matthew 12:33-37 - Jesus said, (33) "Make a tree good and its fruit will be good, or make a tree bad and its fruit will be bad, because a tree is known by its fruit. (34) You are a group of snakes! How can you who are evil say anything good? For what a person says comes out of what fills his heart. (35) A good person speaks good things out of the good stored up in his heart, and an evil person speaks evil things out of the evil stored up in his heart. (36) But I tell you the truth: On the day of God's judgment, everyone will give an account for every bad word they have said. (37) For by your words you will be either set free (*justified*) or condemned."

128 - The Sign of Jonah
(Matthew 12:38-42, Luke 11:29-32)

Matthew 12:38-42 - (38) Then some of the Pharisees and teachers of the law of Moses said to Jesus, "Teacher, we want to see you do a miraculous sign (*miracle*)." (39) Jesus said to them, "You are an evil and unfaithful (*adulterous*) generation that asks for a miraculous sign. But no miracle will be given to you except the sign of the prophet Jonah. (40) For as Jonah was three days and three nights in the stomach of a large fish, so the Son of Man (*see Daniel 7:13-14*) will be three days and three nights in the heart of the earth (*speaking about his burial*). (41) The non-Jews of Nineveh will stand up at God's judgment with this generation of Israel and condemn it, because they repented at the preaching of Jonah, and now something greater than Jonah is here! (*Nineveh was an ancient Assyrian city of upper Mesopotamia, on the eastern bank of the Tigris River. Today it is the city of Mosul, located in northern Kurdish Iraq*). (42) The queen of the South (*the queen of Sheba, modern Yemen; see 1 Kings 10:1-29*) will stand up at God's judgment with this generation of Israel and condemn it; because she came from the ends of the earth to listen to the wise teaching of Solomon, and now something greater than Solomon is here!"

Luke 11:29-32 - (29) - As the crowd of people got bigger Jesus said, "This is a wicked generation in Israel because it seeks a miraculous sign (*miracle*), but the only sign I will give it is the sign of the prophet Jonah. (30) For as Jonah was a sign to the people of Nineveh so also will the Son of Man (*see Daniel 7:13-14*) be a sign to this generation of Israel. (*Nineveh was an ancient Assyrian city of upper Mesopotamia, on the eastern bank of the Tigris River. Today it is the city of Mosul, in northern Kurdish Iraq*). (31) The queen of the South (*the queen of Sheba, in modern Yemen; see 1 Kings 10:1-29*) will stand up at God's judgment with the people of this generation in Israel and condemn them, because she came from the ends of the earth to listen to Solomon's wisdom; and now someone greater than Solomon is here! (32) The people of Nineveh will stand up at God's judgment and condemn this generation of Israel, because they repented at the preaching of Jonah; and now someone greater than Jonah is here!"

129 - The Parable of Demons Returning
(Matthew 12:43-45, Luke 11:24-26)

Matthew 12:43-45 - Jesus told this parable (*story*): (43) "When a demon comes out of a person, it goes through waterless places seeking rest but does not find any. (44) Then it says, 'I will go back inside the person where I used to live.' When the demon returns, it finds the person is empty, swept clean, and put in order. (45) Then the demon goes and brings back seven other demons more evil than itself, and they go live inside the person. And the final condition of that person is worse than he was at first. That is how it will be with this evil generation of Israel."

Luke 11:24-26 - Jesus told this parable (*story*), (24) "When a demon comes out of a person, it goes through dry places seeking rest but finds none. Then it says, 'I will go back to the house I left.' (25) When the demon arrives, it finds the house swept clean and put in order. (26) Then the demon goes and brings back seven demons more wicked than itself, and they go in and live there. And so the final condition of that person is worse than he was at first."

130 - Doing the Word of God
(Luke 11:27-28)

Luke 11:27-28 - (27) As Jesus was saying these things, a woman in the crowd of people yelled out, "Blessed is the mother who gave you birth and nursed you." (28) Jesus said to her, "No, blessed are those who hear God's word and obey it."

131 - The True Family of Jesus
(Matthew 12:46-50, Mark 3:31-35, Luke 8:19-21)

Matthew 12:46-50 - (46) Jesus was teaching a crowd of people in Peter's house in Capernaum. Jesus' mother and brothers came and stood outside the house and asked to talk to him. (47) Someone told Jesus, "Your mother and brothers are outside and want to talk to you." (48) He said to him, "Who are my mother and my brothers?" (49) He pointed to his disciples and said, "These are my mother and my brothers. (50) For whoever does the will of my Father in heaven is my mother, brother, and sister."

Mark 3:31-35 - (31) Then Jesus' mother and brothers arrived in Capernaum from Nazareth. Standing outside Peter's house where Jesus was, they sent someone inside to tell Jesus they were there. (32) A crowd was sitting around Jesus, and they told him, "Your mother and brothers are outside looking for you." (33) Jesus asked, "Who are my mother and brothers?" (34) Then he looked at those sitting in a circle around him and said, "These are my mother and my brothers! (35) Whoever does God's will is my brother, sister, and mother."

Luke 8:19-21 - (19) Now Jesus' mother and brothers came from Nazareth to visit him in Capernaum (*probably in Peter's house*), but they were not able to get near him because of the crowd of people. (20) Someone told Jesus, "Your mother and brothers are standing outside, and they want to see you." (21) Jesus said to them, "My mother and brothers are those who hear God's word and put it into practice."

132 - A Body Full of Light
(Luke 11:33-36)

Luke 11:33-36 - (33) Jesus said, "No one lights a lamp and puts it under a bowl, or in a place where it is hidden. Instead they put a lamp on its stand, so that everyone coming into the house will see the light. (34) Your eye is the lamp of your body. When your eyes are good, your whole body also is full of light. But when your eyes are evil, your body also is full of darkness. (35) Therefore, watch carefully that the light within you is not darkness. (36) Therefore, if your whole body is full of light—having no darkness—it will be just as full of light as when a lamp shines its light on you."

133 - Jesus Condemns the Jewish Religious Leaders
(Luke 11:37-52)

Luke 11:37-52 - (37) When Jesus had finished speaking, a Pharisee invited him to eat with him; so Jesus went into his house and sat at the table. (38) But the Pharisee was surprised when he saw that Jesus did not wash his hands before eating. (39) Then Jesus said to him, "Now you Pharisees clean the outside of the cup and dish, but your hearts are full of greed and wickedness. (40) You are religious fools! Did not the one who made the outside make the inside also? (41) But now as to what is in your heart—be generous to the poor, and everything will be clean for you. Jesus said, (42) "How terrible for you Pharisees! For you give God a tenth (*tithe*) of your mint, rue, and all other kinds of garden herbs, but you neglect justice and the love of God. You should give your offering to God without neglecting the justice and love of God. (43) How terrible for you Pharisees! For you love the most important seats in the synagogues and to be greeted with honor in the public market. (44) How terrible for you Pharisees! You are like unmarked graves, which people do not see and walk over without knowing it." (45) Then one of the experts of the law of Moses said to Jesus, "Teacher, when you say these things, you insult us also." (46) Jesus said to him, "And you experts of the law of Moses, how terrible for you! For you load people down with heavy burdens that they struggle to carry, and you will not lift a finger to help them. (47) How terrible for you! For you build tombs for the prophets, and it was your ancestors who killed them. (48) So you testify that you approve of what your ancestors did; they killed the prophets, and you build their tombs. (49) Because of this, God in his wisdom said, 'I will send them prophets and apostles, some they will persecute and others they will kill.' (50) Therefore this generation of Israel will be held guilty for the blood of all the prophets that has been shed since the beginning of the world, (51) from the blood of Abel to the blood of Zechariah, who was killed between the altar and the sanctuary. Yes, I tell you the truth: This generation of Israel will be guilty for it all. (52) How terrible for you experts in the law of Moses! For you have taken away the key to knowledge. You have not entered, and you hinder others from entering."

134 - Religious Leaders Attack Jesus
(Luke 11:53-54)

Luke 11:53-54 - (53) When Jesus went outside, the Pharisees and teachers of the law of Moses began to viciously oppose him and bombard him with hostile questions, (54) because they wanted to condemn him for something he might say.

135 - Jesus' Warning About Religious Hypocrisy
(Luke 12:1-3)

Luke 12:1-3 - (1) Meanwhile, when a crowd of many thousands of people had gathered so that they were trampling one another, Jesus spoke first to his disciples, "Be on your guard against the religious hypocrisy (*yeast*) of the Pharisees! (2) There is nothing concealed that will not be exposed, or hidden that will not be revealed. (3) What you have said in the darkness of night will be heard in the light of day, and what you have whispered in the ear in the inner rooms will be shouted from the house tops.

136 - Fear God, Not Man
(Luke 12:4-7)

Luke 12:4-7 - Jesus said, (4) "I tell you the truth, my friends: Do not be afraid of those who can kill the body but can do nothing else to you. (5) But I warn you, you should fear God! For after the killing of the body, God has the authority to send you into hell (*gehenna*). Yes, I tell you, fear God! (6) You know that five birds sell for only two pennies. Yet God does not forget one of them. (7) Yes, God knows the exact number of hairs on your head. So don't be afraid, because you are worth much more to God than many birds."

137 - A Public Witness of Jesus
(Luke 12:8-10)

Luke 12:8-10 - Jesus said, (8) "I tell you the truth: Whoever publicly acknowledges me before others, the Son of Man (*see Daniel 7:3-14*) will also acknowledge before God's angels. (9) But whoever denies me before others will be disowned before God's angels. (10) And whoever speaks a word against the Son of Man will be forgiven, but whoever blasphemes against the Holy Spirit will not be forgiven."

138 - The Holy Spirit Will Defend You
(Luke 12:11-12)

Luke 12:11-12 - Jesus said, (11) "When you are brought before synagogues, rulers, and authorities, do not worry about how you will defend yourself, or what you should say, (12) because the Holy Spirit will teach you at that time what you should say."

139 - The Parable About Greed
(Luke 12:13-21)

Luke 12:13-21 - (13) Someone in the crowd said to Jesus, "Teacher, tell my brother to divide the inheritance with me." (14) Jesus said to him, "Man, who appointed me to be a judge between you?" (15) Then he said to them, "Watch out! Be on your guard against all kinds of greed, because true life does not consist of the abundance of one's possessions." (16) And Jesus told the people this parable (*story*): "The land of a rich man produced an abundant harvest. (17) So he thought to himself, 'What should I do? I

have no more space to store all my crops.' (18) Then he said to himself, 'I know what I will do. I will tear down my small barns and build big ones, and then I can store all my extra crops. (19) And I'll say to myself: You now have an abundant amount of food stored up for many years, so I will take life easy. I will eat, drink and be happy.' (20) But God said to the man, 'You rich fool! For this very night your life will be taken from you. Then who will get all the food that you have stored up for yourself?' (21) This is how it will be with whoever stores up things for themselves but is not rich toward God."

140 - The Parable of Faithful Servants
(Luke 12:35-40)

Luke 12:35-40 - Jesus told this parable (*story*): (35) "Be dressed ready to serve and keep your lamps burning. (36) Live like servants waiting for their master to return home from a wedding banquet, so that when he knocks on the door you will immediately open it for him. (37) Blessed are those servants whose master finds them watching when he comes. I tell you the truth: He will dress himself to serve. He will have them take their place at the table and serve them. (38) Blessed are those servants whose master finds them ready, even if he comes in the middle of the night or in the early morning. (39) But understand this: If the owner of a house had known when the thief was coming to break in, he would not have let his house be broken into." (40) Jesus said, "You also must be ready, because the Son of Man (*see Daniel 7:13-14*) will come at a time when you do not expect him."

141 - The Parable of a Faithful and Wise Manager
(Luke 12:41-48)

Luke 12:41-48 - (41) Peter asked Jesus, "Lord, are you telling this parable (*story*) to us, or to the people?" (42) The Lord said to him, "Who then is the faithful and wise manager, whom the master puts in charge of his servants to give them their food to eat at the proper time? (43) Blessed is that servant whom the master finds faithfully doing what he was told to do. (44) I tell you the truth: He will put him in charge over everything he owns.(45) But if the servant says to himself, 'My master is taking a long time in coming,' and so he starts to beat the male and female servants and to eat and drink and get drunk, (46) the master of that servant will come at a time when he does not expect him and at an hour he is not aware of. The master will cut that servant into pieces and send him to the place with the unbelievers. (47) The servant who knows the master's will but does not get ready or does not do what the master wants will receive a severe beating. (48) But the servant who does not know the master's will and does things deserving punishment will receive only a few blows. From everyone who has been given much, much will be demanded of them; and from the one who has been entrusted with much, much more will be required of them."

142 - Separation of Believers and Unbelievers
(Luke 12:49-53)

Luke 12:49-53 - Jesus said, (49) "I came to bring fire (*probably referring to judgment*) on the earth, and how I wish that it was already on fire! (50) But I have a baptism of suffering to experience, and how great is my distress until it is fulfilled. (51) Do you think I came to bring peace on the earth? No, I tell you the truth: I came to bring separation (*between believers and unbelievers*). (52) From now on there will be divisions: Five members of a family will be divided against each other, three against two and two against three. (53) They will be divided—a father will be against his son, and a son will be against his father; a mother will be against her daughter, and a daughter will be against her mother; a mother-in-law will be against her daughter-in-law, and a daughter-in-law will be against her mother-in-law."

143 - Understanding the Times
(Luke 12:54-56)

Luke 12:54-56 - (54) Jesus said to the crowd of people, "When you see a cloud rising in the west, immediately you predict, 'It's going to rain,' and it does rain. (55) And when you feel the wind blowing from the south, you predict, 'It's going to be hot,' and it gets hot. (56) You are hypocrites! You know how to interpret the appearance of the earth and sky, but you don't know how to interpret the present time."

144 - Settle Your Disputes
(Luke 12:57-59)

Luke 12:57-59 - Jesus said, (57) "Why don't you judge for yourselves what is right? (58) As you are going with your adversary to the court, make every effort to settle the dispute (*reconcile*) on the way, or your accuser will drag you before the judge, and the judge will turn you over to the officer, and the officer will put you into prison. (59) I tell you the truth: You will not get out of prison until you have paid the very last penny that you owe.

145 - Repent or Perish
(Luke 13:1-5)

Luke 13:1-5 - (1) Now some people were present who told Jesus about the Galilean Jews who were murdered and whose blood Pontius Pilate had mixed with their sacrifices. (2) Jesus said to them, "Do you think these Galileans were worse sinners than the other Galileans because they suffered in this way? (3) No, they were not! I tell you the truth: Unless you repent and turn to God, you too will perish." (4) Then Jesus said, "What about those 18 people who died when the tower of Siloam (*the pool of Siloam was a water reservoir in the southeastern corner of Jerusalem*) fell on them—do you think they were more guilty than all the others living in Jerusalem? (5) No! I tell you the truth, Unless you repent and turn to God, you too will perish."

146 - The Parable of an Unfruitful Fig Tree
(Luke 13:6-9)

Luke 13:6-9 - Then Jesus told this parable (*story*): (6) "A man had a fig tree growing in his vineyard, and he went out to look for figs on it but did not find any. (7) So he told the gardener of the vineyard, 'For three years now I've been coming for figs on this fig tree and haven't found any. So I want you to cut it down! Why should it use up the soil in the vineyard?' (8) The gardener said to him, 'Sir, let it live for one more year. I'll dig around it and fertilize it. (9) If it produces figs next year that will be great, but if it does not, then you can cut it down.' "

147 - A Crippled Woman Freed from a Demon
(Luke 13:10-17)

Luke 13:10-17 - (10) Jesus was teaching in one of the synagogues on the Sabbath day. (11) And a woman was there who had been crippled by a demon for 18 years. She was bent over and could not stand up straight. (12) When Jesus saw her, he called her to the front of the synagogue and said to her, "Woman, you are set free from your deformity." (13) Then he put his hands on her, and immediately she stood up straight and praised God. (14) The synagogue leader was furious with Jesus because he healed someone on the Sabbath day. He told the people, "Come to be healed on the six days we can work, but do not come to be healed on the Sabbath day." (15) Then Jesus said to the synagogue leader, "You are religious hypocrites! If on the Sabbath day you untie your ox or donkey from the feeding trough and lead it out to drink water, (16) then should not this woman, a daughter of Abraham, whom Satan has kept crippled for 18 years, be set free on the Sabbath day?" (17) When Jesus said these things, all his religious opponents were ashamed, but the people were full of joy because of all the wonderful things he was doing.

---

148 - The Parable of a Sower
(Matthew 13:1-9, Mark 4:1-9, Luke 8:4-8)

Matthew 13:1-9 - (1) That same day Jesus left Peter's house and sat on the northwestern shore of Lake Galilee. (2) Such large crowds gathered around him that he got into a fishing boat and sat down, while all the people stood on the shore. (3) Then Jesus told them many things in parables (*stories*), saying: "A farmer went out and threw seed on his field. (4) Some of the seed fell on the walking path, and the birds ate it. (5) Some seed fell in rocky ground that had little soil, so that it grew very quickly because the soil was shallow. (6) But then the sun burned the plants, and they withered because they had no roots in the soil to keep them alive. (7) Other seed fell among thorns, which grew up and choked the plants. (8) Still other seed fell on good, deep soil that produced a bountiful harvest that was 30, 60, and 100 times what was planted." (9) Jesus declared, "Whoever has ears to hear, let them hear!"

Mark 4:1-9 - (1) Again Jesus taught the people on the northwestern shore of Lake Galilee. The crowd that gathered around him was so large that he sat in a boat out on the lake, while all the people stood along the shore at the water's edge. (2) Jesus taught them many things in parables (*stories*). He told them this parable (*story*): (3) "Listen! A farmer went out to throw seed on his field. (4) As he was throwing the seed, some fell on the walking path, and the birds came and ate it. (5) Some seed fell onto rocky ground where there was very little soil, so that the seed grew very quickly, because the soil was so shallow. (6) But when the sun rose, the plants were burned, and they withered because they had no roots in the soil to keep them alive. (7) Other seed fell among the thorns, which grew up and choked the plants, so that they did not produce grain. (8) Still other seed fell on good, deep soil; it grew and produced an abundant crop, some multiplying 30, some 60, and some 100 times." (9) Then Jesus declared, "Whoever has ears to hear, let them hear!

Luke 8:4-8 - (4) While a large crowd was gathering and people were coming to Jesus from many towns, Jesus told this parable: (5) "A farmer went out and threw seed on his field. As he was throwing the seed, some fell on the walking path; it was trampled on, and the birds came and ate it. (6) Some seed fell on rocky ground, and it grew up, but the plants withered because they had no roots to get water. (7) Other seed fell among thorns, which grew up with the plants and choked them. (8) Other seed fell on good deep soil, where the plants grew up and produced an abundant crop—some multiplying 100 times more than what was planted." (8) After Jesus told them this parable, he called out, "Whoever has ears to hear, let them hear!"

149 - Why Jesus Told Parables
(Matthew 13:10-17, Mark 4:10-13, Luke 8:9-10)

Matthew 13:10-17 - (10) The disciples came to Jesus and asked him, "Why do you teach the people in parables (*stories*)?" (11) Jesus said to them, "Because the knowledge of the secrets (*deep truths*) of the kingdom of heaven (*God*) has been given to you, but it has not been given to them. (12) Whoever has a receptive heart, an abundance will be given to them. But whoever does not have a receptive heart, what they have will be taken from them. (13) This is why I teach the people in parables: Though seeing, they do not see; though hearing, they do not hear or understand. (14) In the people is fulfilled what is written in Isaiah 6:9-10, 'You will be ever hearing but never understanding. You will be ever seeing but never perceiving. (15) The people's hearts have become dull. They are hard of hearing and have closed their eyes. They cannot hear with their ears or see with their eyes. They do not understand with their hearts and turn to me, so that I can heal them.' (16) But blessed are your eyes because they see, and blessed are your ears because they hear. (17) For I tell you the truth: Many prophets and righteous people longed to see what you see but did not see it, and to hear what you hear but did not hear it."

Mark 4:10-13 - (10) When Jesus was alone, the Twelve Apostles and the others around him asked him why he taught the people in parables (*stories*). (11) Jesus told them, "The secrets (*deep truths*) of the kingdom of God have been given to you, but to those on the outside I teach everything by telling parables. (12) This fulfills what is written in Isaiah 6:9-10, so that, 'they may be always looking, but never perceiving, and always hearing, but never understanding; otherwise they might turn to God and be forgiven!' " (13) Then Jesus said to his disciples, "If you don't understand this parable (*story*), how then will you understand any of my parables?"

Luke 8:9-10 - (9) Jesus' disciples asked him the meaning of this parable (*story*). (10) Jesus said, "You have been given the ability to know the secrets (*deep truths*) of the kingdom of God, but to other people I speak in parables, so that what was written in Isaiah 6:9 will be fulfilled: 'Though seeing, they may not see; though hearing, they may not understand.' "

150 - The Meaning of the Parable of the Sower
(Matthew 13:18-23, Mark 4:14-20, Luke 8:11-15)

Matthew 13:18-23 - (18) Jesus said to his disciples: "This is what the parable (*story*) of the sower means. This is the meaning of the seed that was thrown on the walking path. When anyone hears the message of the kingdom of God and does not understand it, Satan comes and quickly steals what was planted in their heart. (20) This is the meaning of the seed that was thrown in rocky ground. This refers to those who hear the message of the kingdom of God and immediately receive it with joy. (21) But since they have no roots, they believe for only a short time. When trouble and persecution come their way because of God's word, they quickly fall away. This is the meaning of the seed that was thrown among the thorns. This refers to those who hear the message of the kingdom of God, but the worries of this life and the deception of wealth choke the word, making it unfruitful. This is the meaning of the seed thrown on good deep soil. It refers to those who hear the message of the kingdom of God and understand it. They produce an abundant crop—some 100 times more than was planted, some 60, or some 30."

Mark 4:18-20 - Jesus said, (18) "Still other people are like the seed thrown into the thorns. They hear God's word, (19) but the worries of this life, the deceitfulness of wealth, and the desire for other earthly things come in and choke the word, making it unfruitful. (14) The seed that the farmer threw into his field was the word of God. (15) Some people are like the seed that fell along the walking path, where the word is sown. As soon as they hear it, Satan comes and steals the word that was sown inside them. (16) Other people are like the seed thrown onto rocky ground. They hear God's word, receive it immediately with joy, (17) but since they do not have deep roots, they last only a short time. When trouble and persecution come because of the word, they quickly fall away. (20) Other people are like the seed thrown into good deep soil. They hear God's word, accept it, and produce an abundant crop—some 30, some 60, some 100 times what was planted."

Luke 8:11-15 - (11) Jesus explained the meaning of the parable (*story*): Jesus said, "The seed is the word of God. (12) The seed falling along the walking path is the people who hear God's word, and then the devil comes and steals the word from their hearts, so that they will not believe and be saved. The seed falling on rocky ground are the people who receive God's word with joy when they hear it, but since they have no roots they only believe for a short time, because they fall away during the time of testing. The seed falling among the thorns are the people who hear God's word, but as they live their lives, they are choked by life's worries, riches, and pleasures, and they do not grow and mature. But the seed falling on good deep soil are the people who have honest and good hearts. They hear God's word, hold fast to it, and by persevering produce an abundant crop."

151 - The Parable of the Weeds
(Matthew 13:24-30)

Matthew 13:24-30 - (24) Jesus told the people another parable (*story*): "The kingdom of heaven (*God*) is like a landowner who threw good seeds of wheat on his field. (25) But while everyone was sleeping, his enemy came and threw seeds of weed (*false wheat*) among the wheat and ran away. (26) When the good seed grew and produced wheat, the weeds also appeared. (27) The landowner's servants came to him and said, 'Sir, didn't you throw good seed on your field? Where then did these weeds come from?' (28) The landowner said to them, 'An enemy did this.' The servants asked him, 'Do you want us to pull up the weeds?' (29) "The landowner said, 'No, because when you pull up the weeds, you will also pull out the wheat. (30) Let both grow together until the harvest. At the harvest time I will tell the harvesters: First gather the weeds and tie them in bundles to be burned; then gather the wheat and store it in my barn.' "

152 - The Parable of the Weeds Explained
(Matthew 13:36-43)

Matthew 13:36-43 - Then Jesus left the crowd by the northwestern shore of Lake Galilee and went into Peter's house in Capernaum. His disciples came to Jesus and said, "Explain to us the parable (*story*) of the weeds in the field." Jesus said to them: "The one who threw the good seed in the field is the Son of Man (*see Daniel 7:13-14*). (38) The field is this world, and the good seed refers to the people of the kingdom of God. The weeds are the people of Satan, (39) and the enemy who sows them is Satan. The harvest is the end of this world (*age*) and the harvesters are angels. (40) As the weeds are pulled up and burned in the fire so it will be at the end of this world (*age*). (41) The Son of Man will send out his angels, and they will remove from his kingdom everyone that causes sin and all who do evil. (42) They will all be thrown into the blazing furnace of fire, where people will be weeping and grinding their teeth. (43) Then the righteous will shine like the sun in the kingdom of their Father." Jesus declared, "Whoever has ears to hear, let them hear!"

153 - The Parable of Light and Understanding
(Mark 4:21-25, Luke 8:16-18)

Mark 4:21-25 - (21) Jesus said to his disciples, "No one lights a lamp and puts it under a bowl or a bed. Instead, they put the lamp on a stand. (22) For whatever is hidden is meant to be revealed, and whatever is concealed is meant to be brought into the open. (23) Whoever has ears to hear, let them hear!" (24) Jesus continued and said, "Consider carefully what you hear, because with the measure you use, it will be measured to you—and even more. (25) Whoever has will be given more; whoever has very little, even what they have will be taken away."

Luke 8:16-18 - Jesus said, (16) "No one lights a lamp and hides it in a clay jar or puts it under a bed. Instead, they put the lamp on a stand, so that those who come into the house can see the light. (17) For there is nothing hidden that will not be revealed, and no secret that will not be known or brought out into the open. (18) Therefore, consider carefully how you listen: For whoever has will be given more, and whoever has little, even what they think they have will be taken away from them."

154 - The Parable About Growing Seed
(Mark 4:26-29)

Mark 4:26-29 - (26) Jesus told this parable (*story*): "The kingdom of God is like a man who throws seed on his field. (27) Day and night, whether he is awake or sleeps, the seed sprouts and grows, although he does not know how it grows. (28) All by itself the earth produces grain—first the stalk, then the head, then the full grain in the head. (29) When the grain is fully grown, then he harvests the grain with a sickle."

155 - The Parable of the Mustard Seed
(Matthew 13:31-32, Mark 4:30-32, Luke 13:18-19)

Matthew 13:31-32 - (31) Jesus told the people another parable (*story*): "The kingdom of heaven (*God*) is like a mustard seed that a man planted in his field. (32) Although the mustard seed is one of the smallest of all seeds, when it has grown it is larger than all the garden plants and becomes a tree, so that the birds come and make nests in its branches."

Mark 4:30-32 - (30) Again Jesus said, "What should we say the kingdom of God is like or what parable should we use to describe it? (31) The kingdom of God is like a mustard seed, which is the smallest of all seeds on earth. (32) But when a mustard seed is planted, it grows and becomes the largest of all garden plants, and the birds can perch in the shade of its large branches."

Luke 13:18-19 - Then Jesus asked: (18) "What is the kingdom of God like? What should I compare it to? (19) It is like a small mustard seed that a man planted in his garden. It grew into a very large bush, and the birds perched in its branches."

156 - The Parable of the Yeast
(Matthew 13:33, Luke 13:20-21)

Matthew 13:33 - Jesus told them another parable: "The kingdom of heaven (*God*) is like yeast that a woman mixed into about 60 pounds of flour until the yeast spreads through all the dough."

Luke 13:20-21 - (20) Again Jesus asked, "What should I compare the kingdom of God to? (21) It is like yeast that a woman took and mixed into about 60 pounds of flour until the yeast spread all through the dough."

157 - The Parable of the Hidden Treasure
(Matthew 13:44)

Matthew 13:44 - Jesus told these parables (*stories*)wwe kingdom of heaven (*God*) is like treasure hidden in a field. When a man discovered the treasure, he buried it again, and then in his joy went and sold all he owned and bought that field."

158 - The Parable of the Expensive Pearl
(Matthew 13:45-46)

Matthew 13:45-46 - Jesus said, (45) "Again, the kingdom of heaven (*God*) is like a merchant searching for valuable pearls. (46) When he found a pearl of great value, he went and sold everything he owned and bought the pearl."

159 - The Parable of a Fishing Dragnet
(Matthew 13:47-51)

Matthew 14:47-51 - Jesus told another parable (*story*): (47) "Once again, the kingdom of heaven (*God*) is like a fishing dragnet that was let down into the lake and caught all kinds of fish. (48) When it was full, the fishermen pulled the dragnet up on the shore. Then they sat down and put the good fish in baskets, but threw the bad fish away. (49) This is how it will be at the end of this world (*age*). God's angels will come and separate the wicked from the righteous (50) and throw them into the blazing furnace of fire, where there will be weeping and grinding of teeth." (51) Jesus asked them, "Do you understand?" His disciples said, "Yes."

160 - The Parable of Old and New Treasures
(Matthew 13:52)

Matthew 13:52 - Jesus said to his disciples, "Therefore every teacher of the law of Moses who has become a disciple in the kingdom of heaven (*God*) is like the owner of a house who brings out of his storeroom both old and new treasures."

161 - Jesus Tells Many Other Parables
(Matthew 13:34-35, Mark 4:33-34)

Matthew 13:34-35 - (34) Jesus spoke all these things to the crowd in parables *(stories)*; he did not teach anything to them without using a parable. (35) So this fulfilled what is written in Psalm 78:2, "I will speak in parables, I will speak about things hidden since the creation of the universe."

Mark 4:33-34 - (33) Jesus told many similar parables, as many as they could understand. (34) He did not teach without a parable. But when he was alone with his disciples, he explained everything to them.

162 - The Cost of Following Jesus
(Matthew 8:18-22, Luke 9:57-62)

Matthew 8:18-22 - (18) When Jesus saw a crowd of people gathering around him, he told his disciples to prepare a boat so that they could go to the eastern side of Lake Galilee. (19) Then a teacher of the law of Moses came to him and said, "Teacher, I will follow you wherever you go." (20) Jesus said to him, "Foxes have holes to live in, and birds have nests, but the Son of Man *(see Daniel 7:13-14)* has no place to lay his head." (21) Another disciple said to Jesus, "Lord, let me first go and bury my father." (22) But Jesus said to him, "Follow me and let the dead bury their own dead."

Luke 9:57-62 - (57) Jesus and his disciples were walking along the road toward Jerusalem. And a man said to Jesus, "I will follow you wherever you go." (58) Jesus said to him, "Foxes have dens and birds have nests, but the Son of Man *(see Daniel 7:13-14)* has no place to lay his head." (59) Jesus said to another man, "Follow me!" But the man said, "Lord, first let me go and bury my father." (60) Jesus said to him, "Let the dead bury their own dead, but you go and proclaim the kingdom of God." (61) And another man said to Jesus, "Lord, I will follow you, but first let me go back and say goodbye to my family." (62) Jesus said to him, "No one who puts his hand to the plow and then looks back is ready to serve in the kingdom of God."

163 - Jesus Calms a Storm on Lake Galilee
(Matthew 8:23-28, Mark 4:35-41, Luke 8:22-25)

Matthew 8:23-28 - (23) Then Jesus got into the boat, and his disciples followed him. (24) As Jesus and his disciples were crossing Lake Galilee, a violent storm suddenly came up and splashing waves began to swamp the boat. But Jesus was sleeping (*in the back of the boat*). (25) So his disciples woke him up, yelling, "Lord! Save us! We are going to die!" (26) But Jesus said to them, "Why are you so afraid? You have such little faith." (27) And the disciples were amazed and asked one another, "What kind of man is this? For even the winds and the waves do what he tells them to do!" (28) Then he got up and commanded the wind and the waves to stop, and the lake became calm.

Mark 4:35-41 - (35) When evening came that day, Jesus said to his disciples, "Let us go to the eastern side of Lake Galilee." (36) Leaving the crowd of people, they took Jesus with them, just as he was, in the boat. There were also other boats with him. (37) Suddenly a violent storm came on the lake, and the waves splashed over the boat, so that it was full of water. (38) Jesus was sleeping in the back of the boat on a pillow. The disciples woke him up and yelled, "Teacher! Don't you care that we are going to die?" (39) Jesus got up, rebuked the wind, and shouted to the waves, "Quiet! Be still!" Then the wind stopped blowing and it became completely calm. (40) Jesus said to his disciples, "Why are you so afraid? Do you still have no faith?" (41) The disciples were terrified and asked one another, "Who is this? For even the wind and the waves obey his commands.

Luke 8:22-25 - (22) One day Jesus said to his disciples, "Let us go over to the eastern side of Lake Galilee." So they got into a boat and set out across the lake. (23) As they sailed, Jesus fell asleep. Suddenly a windstorm came down on the lake, so that high waves began to swamp the boat, and they were in great danger of sinking. (24) The disciples woke Jesus up, yelling, "Lord, Lord, we are going to die!" Jesus got up and rebuked the wind and high waves; immediately the storm stopped and the lake became calm. (25) Jesus asked his disciples, "Where is your faith?" The disciples were filled with fear and amazement, and asked one another, "Who is Jesus? For he even commands the winds and the water, and they obey him."

164 - Jesus Frees Men From Demons
(Matthew 8:28-34, Mark 5:1-20, Luke 8:26-39)

Matthew 8:28-34 - (28) Jesus and his disciples landed on the southeastern shore of Lake Galilee in the non-Jewish region of the Gadarenes. Immediately two demon-possessed (*demonized*) men came running from among the burial tombs to meet him. The two men were so violent that people could not walk by that area. (29) The demons shouted, "Son of God, what do you want with us? Have you come here to torture us before God's appointed time?" (30) A large herd of pigs was feeding in the distance. (31) Then the demons begged Jesus, "If you cast us out of these men, send us into the herd of pigs." (32) Jesus said to them, "Go!" So the demons left the men and went into the pigs, and the herd ran down the steep bank into Lake Galilee and drowned. (33) Those watching the pigs ran into the town, and told the people everything that had happened and about the demon-possessed men. (34) Then the whole town ran out to meet Jesus. And when they saw him, they begged him to leave their region of Galilee.

Mark 5:1-20 - (1) Jesus and the disciples landed their boat on the southeastern shore of Lake Galilee in the non-Jewish region of the Gerasenes. (2) As soon as Jesus stepped out of the boat, a demon-possessed (*demonized*) man came from the burial tombs to meet him. (3) This man lived among the tombs, and no one could tie him up anymore, not even with a chain. (4) For he had chains put around his hands and feet, but he tore the chains apart and broke the irons around his ankles. No one was strong enough to control him. (5) Day and night he wandered among the tombs and in the hills; he would scream out and cut himself with sharp rocks. (6) When the man saw Jesus from a distance (*probably while Jesus was still traveling in the boat*), he ran and fell on his knees in front of him. (7) The demon shouted through the man at the top of his voice, "What do you want with me, Jesus, Son of the Most High God? In God's name don't torture me!" (8) For Jesus was saying to him, "Come out of this man, you evil spirit!" (9) Then Jesus asked the demon, "What is your name?" The demon said, "My name is Legion, because we are many demons." (10) And the demon begged Jesus again and again not to send them out of that region. (11) Now there was a large herd of pigs feeding on a nearby hillside. (12) The demons begged Jesus, "Send us into the pigs; allow us to go into them." (13) Jesus gave them permission, and the demons came out of the man and went into the pigs. The herd—about 2,000 pigs—ran down the steep bank into the lake and drowned. (14) The herders of the pigs ran off into the town and countryside and told everyone what had happened, and the people went to see for themselves. (15) When they came to Jesus, they saw the demon-possessed man sitting there, dressed, and in his right mind; and the people became afraid. (16) Those who had seen everything told the people what had happened to the demon-possessed man and about the pigs. (17) Then the people begged Jesus to leave their region. (18) As Jesus was getting into the boat, the demon-possessed man, who had been set free, begged to go with him. (19) But Jesus did not let him, and said, "Go home to your family and tell them the great things the Lord has done for you, and how he has had mercy on you." (20) So the man went back and began telling everyone in the Decapolis (*the region of ten non-Jewish cities southeast of Lake Galilee*) how much Jesus had done for him. And all the people were amazed.

Luke 8:26-39 - (26) Jesus and his disciples sailed the boat to the non-Jewish region of the Gerasenes. (27) When Jesus stepped onto the shore, he was met by a demon-possessed (*demonized*) man from the town. For a long time this man had been naked and homeless, and he lived among the burial tombs. (29) The demon had seized the man many times, and although he was chained hand and foot and kept under guard, he broke the chains and the demon would drive him into isolated places. (28) When he saw Jesus, he screamed and fell at his feet. The demon shouted through the man at the top of his voice, "What do you want with me, Jesus, Son of the Most High God? I beg you, do not punish me!" (29) For Jesus had already commanded the demon to come out of the man. (30) Jesus asked the demon, "What is your name?" The demon said, "Legion," because many demons lived in the man. (31) And the demons begged Jesus repeatedly not to send them into the world of the dead (*the abyss*). (32) A large herd of pigs was feeding on a hillside nearby. The demons begged Jesus to let them go into the pigs, and he gave them permission. (33) When the demons left the man and went into the pigs, the whole herd ran down the steep bank into Lake Galilee and drowned. (34) When the pig herders saw what had happened, they ran and told everyone in the town and countryside, (35) and the people went out to see what had happened. When they came to Jesus, they found the man sitting at Jesus' feet, dressed and in his right mind; and they became very afraid. (36) Those who had seen everything told the people how the demon-possessed man had been healed. (37) Then the people of the non-Jewish region of the Gerasenes asked Jesus to leave them, because they were filled with fear. So Jesus got into the boat and left. (38) The man who had been set free from the demons begged to go with Jesus, but he sent him away saying, (39) "Go back home and tell everyone what great things God has done for you." So the man went away and told everyone throughout the town all that Jesus had done for him.

(The region of the Gaderenes—or Gerasenes, as used in Mark 5:1 and Luke 28:26—was the southeastern region of Lake Galilee. The exact location of the exorcism was possibly the town of Gerasa on the shore of Lake Galilee, directly across the lake from Tiberius).

165 - Jesus Heals Jairus' Daughter
(Matthew 9:18-19, 23-26, Mark 5:21-24 35-43, Luke 8:40-42, 49-56)

Matthew 9:18-19, 23-26 - (18) While Jesus was saying this, a synagogue leader (*named Jairus*) came and fell on his knees before him and said, "My daughter has just died. But please come and touch her and she will live." (19) Jesus and his disciples got up and went with him. (23) When Jesus entered the synagogue leader's house and saw a noisy crowd and people playing flutes, (24) he told them, "Go away! The girl is not dead, but she is only sleeping." They all laughed at Jesus. (25) After the crowd had gone outside, Jesus went in and took the hand of the girl and raised her from the dead. (26) News of what Jesus did spread through the whole region.

Mark 5:21-24, 35-43 - (21) When Jesus returned to the western shore of Lake Galilee by boat, a large crowd of people gathered around him while he was by the lake. (22) Then Jairus, one of the synagogue leaders, having seen Jesus, ran and fell at his feet. (23) He pleaded earnestly with him, "My little daughter is dying! Please come and put your hands on her so that she will be healed and and live." (24) So Jesus went with him, and a large crowd followed and pressed all around him. (35) While Jesus was still speaking, some men came from the house of Jairus, the synagogue leader, and said, "Your daughter is dead, do not bother the teacher anymore." (36) Overhearing what they told Jairus, Jesus told him, "Do not be afraid; just believe." (37) Jesus did not allow anyone to follow him except Peter, James, and John the brother of James. (38) When they arrived at Jairus' home, Jesus found the house full of noise and disorder, with people crying and wailing very loudly. (39) He entered the house and said to them, "Why are you crying and wailing? The little girl is not dead but is sleeping." (40) And they laughed at him. After Jesus told everyone to leave the house, he took the girl's father and mother and his disciples (*Peter, James, and John*), and went into the child's room. (41) Jesus took her by the hand and said to her, "Talitha koum!" (*which means in Aramaic, "Little girl, I tell you, get up!"*). (42) Immediately the 12-year-old girl stood up and began to walk around the house. (43) When the people saw her, everyone was exceedingly amazed. Jesus gave them strict orders not to let anyone know what had happened, and then he told them to give her something to eat.

Luke 8:40-42, 49-56 - (40) Now when Jesus returned by boat to Capernaum on the northwestern shore of Lake Galilee, a crowd welcomed him, for they had been waiting for him. (41) Then a man named Jairus, a synagogue leader, came and fell at Jesus' feet, pleading with him to go to his house (42) because his only daughter—a girl about 12 years old—was dying. (49) While Jesus was still talking with the woman (*with bleeding*), someone came from the house of Jairus, the synagogue leader. He said, "Your daughter is dead. Don't bother the teacher anymore." (50) But when Jesus heard this, he said to Jairus, "Don't be afraid; just believe, and your daughter will be healed." (51) When Jesus came to Jairus' house, he did not allow anyone to go inside with him except Peter, John, James, and the girl's parents. (52) Meanwhile, all the people there were wailing and mourning for the daughter. But Jesus said to them, "Stop wailing, she is not dead but is sleeping." (53) The people laughed at Jesus because they knew that she was dead. (54) Jesus took the girl's hand and said, "My child, get up!" (55) The girl's spirit came back into her, and immediately she stood up. Then Jesus told them to give her something to eat. (56) Her parents were astonished, but Jesus ordered them not to tell anyone that he had healed their daughter.

166 - Jesus Heals a Sick Woman
(Matthew 9:20-22, Mark 5:25-34, Luke 8:42-48)

Matthew 9:20-22 - (20) Just then a woman who had suffered from bleeding for 12 years (*probably her menstrual period would not stop*). (21) She said to herself, "If I only touch his clothes, I will be healed." See came up behind Jesus and touched the edge of his clothing (*outer cloak*). (22) Jesus turned and said to her, "My daughter, take heart, your faith has healed you." And the woman was healed immediately.

Mark 5:25-34 - (25) And a woman was in the crowd who had suffered from bleeding for 12 years. (26) She had suffered tremendously under the care of many doctors and had spent all of her money, but instead of getting better she became much worse. (27) When she heard about Jesus, she came up behind him in the crowd and touched his clothes (*outer cloak*) (28) because she said to herself, "If I just touch his clothes, I will be healed." (29) Immediately her bleeding stopped and she felt in her body that she had been healed from her suffering. (30) At once Jesus realized that power had gone out from his body. He turned around in the crowd and asked, "Who touched my clothes?" (31) The disciples said to him, "You can see all the people pressing against you, so why do you ask us, 'Who touched me?'" (32) But Jesus kept looking around to see who had touched him. (33) Then the woman knowing what had happened to her, came and fell at Jesus' feet and, shaking with fear, told him the whole truth. (34) Jesus said to her, "Daughter, your faith has healed you, go in peace; you are now free from your suffering."

Luke 8:42-48 - (42) As Jesus was walking to the house (*Jairus' house*), crowds of people were almost crushing him. (43) And there was a woman in the crowd who had suffered for 12 years with continual bleeding, but no one could heal her. (44) She came up behind Jesus and touched the edge of his clothes (*outer cloak*), and immediately her bleeding stopped. Peter said, "Master, the people are crowding and pressing against you from all sides." (45) Jesus asked, "Who touched me?" When all the people denied touching him. (46) But Jesus said, "I know someone touched me, because God's power went out from my body." (47) Then the woman realized that she could not hide, so she came trembling to Jesus and fell at his feet. With many people standing around her, she told Jesus why she had touched him and how she was instantly healed. (48) Then Jesus said to her, "Daughter, go in peace. Your faith has healed you."

167 - Jesus Heals Two Blind Men
(Matthew 9:27-31)

Matthew 9:27-30 - (27) As Jesus left that place, two blind men followed him. They cried out, "Have mercy on us, Son of David!" (28) When Jesus had entered the house the blind men came to him. (28) Jesus asked them, "Do you believe that I am able to make you see?" They said, "Yes, Lord." (29) Then Jesus touched their eyes and said, "You will see because of your faith." (30) Their eyes were healed, and they could see. And Jesus commanded them, "Do not tell anyone that I have healed your eyes." (31) But they went out and spread the news about Jesus all over that region.

168 - Jesus Frees a Man From a Demon
(Matthew 9:32-34)

Matthew 9:32-34 - (32) While Jesus and his disciples were leaving the house a man who was possessed with a demon that did not let him talk was brought to Jesus. (33) And after Jesus cast the demon out, the man could speak. The crowd was amazed and said, "Nothing like this has ever been seen in Israel." (34) But the Pharisees said, "Jesus drives demons out of people by the power of Satan, the ruler of demons."

169 - Jesus Rejected in Nazareth Again
(Matthew 13:53-57, Mark 6:1-6)

Matthew 13:53-57 - (53) When Jesus had finished teaching these parables (*stories*), he left (54) and walked to Nazareth. In Nazareth he taught the people in their synagogue, and they were amazed. They said, "Where did Jesus get this wisdom and these miraculous powers? (55) Isn't this the carpenter's son? Isn't his mother's name Mary, and are not his brothers James, Joseph, Simon, and Judas? (56) Aren't all his sisters here with us? Where then did Jesus get all these things?" (57) And the people were offended and went against Jesus. But he said to them, "A prophet is honored everywhere except in his home town and in his own family."

Mark 6:1-6 - (1) Jesus and his disciples left there and walked to his hometown of Nazareth. (2) On the Sabbath day, Jesus taught in the synagogue and many who heard his teaching were amazed. They asked, "Where did Jesus get these things? What is this wisdom that has been given to him? What are these amazing miracles he is doing? (3) Isn't Jesus the carpenter? Isn't this Mary's son and the brother of James, Joseph, Judas, and Simon? Aren't his sisters here with us?" And the people of Nazareth took offense and went against Jesus. (4) Jesus said to them, "A prophet is honored except in his hometown and among his relatives and in his own family." (5)

He could not do any miracles in Nazareth, except he did touch some sick people and they were healed. (6) Jesus was amazed at the people's lack of faith.

----

170 - Jesus' Ministry Tour Through Galilee
(Matthew 9:35-38, Mark 6:6)

Matthew 9:35-38 - (35) Jesus walked through the villages and towns of Galilee teaching in their synagogues, proclaiming the gospel (*good news*) of the kingdom of God, and healing every disease and sickness. (36) When he saw the crowds, he had deep compassion for them because they were harassed and helpless, like sheep without a shepherd. (37) Then he said to his disciples, "The harvest is great, but the workers are few. (38) Therefore, ask the Lord of the harvest to send out workers into his harvest field."

Mark 6:6 - Then Jesus left Nazareth and walked through the villages of Galilee teaching the people.

----

171 - The Mission of Jesus' Twelve Apostles
(Matthew 10:1-15, Mark 6:7-11, Luke 9:1-5)

Matthew 10: 1-15 - (1) Jesus called his 12 disciples to him (*probably in the hills west of Capernaum*) and gave them God's authority to cast demons out of people and to heal every disease and sickness. (2) These are the names of Jesus' Twelve Apostles: Simon Peter and his brother Andrew; James and John, the sons of Zebedee; (3) Philip, Bartholomew, and Thomas; Matthew the tax collector, James son of Alphaeus, and Thaddaeus; (4) Simon the Zealot, and Judas Iscariot, who betrayed Jesus. (5) Then Jesus sent out these Twelve Apostles on a mission journey and gave them the following instructions, "Do not go among the non-Jews or enter any town of the Samaritans. (6) Go instead to the lost sheep of the house of Israel. (7) As you go, proclaim this message to them, 'The kingdom of heaven (*God*) has come near (is at hand).' (8) Heal the sick, raise the dead, cleanse the lepers, and cast out demons. Freely you have received, so freely give to others. (9) Do not take any money (*gold, silver, or copper*) with you in your belts. (10) Do not take a bag, extra clothes, sandals, or a walking staff, because the worker deserves his food. (11) And whatever Jewish town or village you enter, search there for a worthy person and stay at their home until you leave. (12) As you enter their house, give a greeting. (13) Give a blessing of peace to the homes that deserve it, but do not give a blessing of peace to the homes that do not deserve it. (14) If anyone will not welcome you or listen to your teaching, leave that home or town and shake the dirt off your feet. (15) For I tell you the truth: It will be much better for Sodom and Gomorrah on the day of God's judgment than for that Jewish town."

Mark 6:7-11 - (7) Calling the Twelve Apostles to him, and gave them God's authority over demons. Jesus began to send them out two by two. (8) Jesus told them, "Take nothing for your mission journey except a staff—no bread, no bag, and no money in your belts. (9) Wear your sandals, but do not take an extra inner shirt (*tunic*). (10) Whenever you enter a house, remain there until you leave that town. (11) And if any Jewish town refuses to welcome you or listen to you, leave that place and shake the dirt off your feet as a witness against them."

Luke 9:1-5 - (1) Jesus called the Twelve Apostles together, and he gave them God's power and authority to cast out all demons and to heal diseases. (2) He sent them out to proclaim the kingdom of God and to heal the sick. (3) Jesus told them, "Do not take anything on your mission journey—no staff, no bag, no bread, no money, not even an extra shirt (*inner tunic*). (4) Whatever house you enter, stay there until you leave that Jewish town. (5) If people do not welcome you, leave their town and shake the dirt off your feet as a witness against them."

172 - The Persecution of Jesus' Twelve Apostles
(Matthew 10:16-25)

Matthew 10:16-25 - Jesus said, (16) "I send you out like sheep among wolves, so be as wise as snakes and as harmless as doves. (17) Be on your guard, because you will handed over to local Jewish courts and be flogged in their synagogues. (18) And for my sake you will be dragged before Roman governors and kings as witnesses to them and to the non-Jews. (19) But when they arrest you, do not worry about what to say or how to say it. At that time you will be given what to say, (20) because it will not be you speaking, but the Spirit of your Father will speak through you. (21) Brother will betray brother to death, a father will give his child to be put to death, and children will go against their parents and have them put to death. (22) People will hate you because you are my disciples, but whoever stands strong (*endures*) to the end will be saved. (23) When you are persecuted in one place, flee to another. For I tell you the truth: You will not finish going through all the towns of Israel before the Son of Man comes (*see Daniel 7:13-14*). (24) A student is not above his teacher, and a servant is not above his master. (25) It is enough for students to be like their teachers, and servants to be like their masters. If the master of the house has been called Satan (*Beelzebub*), how much more will they persecute the members of his household.

173 - Do Not Be Afraid
(Matthew 10:26-33)

Matthew 10:26-33 - Jesus said, (26) "So do not be afraid of those who persecute you, because there is nothing concealed that will not be made public, or hidden that will not be revealed. (27) What I tell you in the dark of night, shout in the light of day; whatever is whispered in your ear in private, proclaim it from the housetops. (28) Do not be afraid of those who can kill your body but cannot kill your soul! Instead, you should fear God who can destroy both your body and soul in hell (*gehenna*). (29) Two birds are sold for a penny, but no bird dies without your Father's care. (30) And each hair on your head is numbered. (31) So don't be afraid, because you are much more valuable than birds! (32) Whoever tells others about me, I will tell my Father in heaven about them. (33) But whoever denies me before others, I will deny them before my Father in heaven."

174 - Separation of Believers and Unbelievers
(Matthew 10:34-39)

Matthew 10:34-39 - (34) Jesus said, "Do not think that I came to bring peace to the earth! I did not come to bring peace, but a sword of separation. (35) For I came to turn a man against his father, a daughter against her mother, and a daughter-in-law against her mother-in-law—(36) and a person's enemies will be the members of his own family. (37) Anyone who loves their father, mother, son, or daughter more than me is not worthy of me. (38) Whoever does not take up their cross and follow me is not worthy of me. (39) Whoever finds their life will lose it, and whoever loses their life for my sake will find it."

175 - Kingdom Rewards
(Matthew 10:40-42)

Matthew 19:40-42 - Jesus said, (40) "Whoever welcomes you welcomes me, and whoever welcomes me welcomes my Father who sent me. (41) Whoever welcomes a prophet as a prophet will receive a prophet's reward, and whoever welcomes a righteous person as a righteous person will receive a righteous person's reward. (42) For I tell you the truth: If anyone gives a single cup of cold water to one of these little ones who is my disciple, that person will not lose their reward."

176 - Twelve Apostles' Ministry Tour Through Galilee
(Mark 6:12-13; Luke 9:6)

Mark 6:12-13 - (12) The Twelve Apostles went out and preached that people should repent and turn to God. (13) They cast many demons out of people and anointed many sick people with oil and healed them.

Luke 9:6 - So the Twelve Apostles went out and walked through the villages, proclaiming the gospel (*good news*) of the kingdom of God and healing people everywhere.

177 - Jesus' Ministry Tour Through Galilee
(Matthew 11:1)

Matthew 11:1 - After Jesus had finished teaching his Twelve Apostles, he went on from there to proclaim and teach the gospel (*good news*) throughout the towns of Galilee.

178 - Herod Antipas Beheads John
(Matthew 14:6-12, Mark 6:21-29)

Matthew 14:6-12 - (6) On Herod's birthday, the daughter of Herodias danced for the guests and pleased Herod so much (7) that he promised with an oath to give her whatever she asked for. (8) Advised by her mother Herodias, the daughter said to Herod, "Give me the head of John the Baptizer on a plate." (9) King Herod was very troubled, but because of his oaths and guests he ordered that John's head be cut off. (10) John was beheaded in the prison, (11) and his head was brought in on a plate and given to the girl, who showed it to her mother. (12) John's disciples came and took his body and buried it. Then they went and told Jesus that John was dead.

Mark 6:21-29 - (21) However, an opportune time came for Herodias. On Herod's birthday, he gave a banquet for his high officials and military leaders and the leading men of Galilee. (22) When Herodias' daughter came in and danced for them, she pleased Herod and his dinner quests. So Herod said to the girl, "Ask me for anything you want, and I'll give it to you." (23) And Herod promised her with an oath, "Whatever you ask of me I will give you, up to half of my kingdom." (24) She went out and told her mother what Herod had promised, and asked her, "What should I ask for?" Herodias said, "Ask for the head of John the Baptizer!" (25) Immediately the girl hurried in to Herod and said, "I want you to give me the head of John the Baptizer on a plate." (26) King Herod became greatly troubled, but because of his oaths and his dinner guests, he did not want to deny her request. (27) So Herod immediately sent an executioner with orders to bring John's head. The executioner went into the prison, cut off John's head, (28) and brought it back on a plate. He presented it to the girl, and she gave it to her mother. (29) On hearing of this, John's disciples came and took his body and laid it in a tomb.

(Herod Antipas was a son of Herod the Great, and the Roman governor of the regions of Galilee and Perea. His capital city of Tiberias was located on the western shore of Lake Galilee, around 10 miles/16 km south from Capernaum).

179 - Herod Antipas Hears About Jesus
(Matthew 14:1-2, Mark 6:14-16, Luke 9:7-9

Matthew 12:1-2 - (1) At that time Herod Antipas the tetrarch heard the amazing news about Jesus. (2) He said to his servants, "This must be John the Baptizer; he has risen from the dead! That is why miraculous powers *(miracles)* are working in him."

Mark 6:14-16 - (14) King Herod Antipas heard about this, for Jesus' name had become very well known. Some were saying, "John the Baptizer has been raised from the dead, and that is why these miracles of power are at work in him." (15) Others said, "He is Elijah." And still others said, "He is a prophet, like one of the other (*Old Testament*) prophets." (16) But when Herod heard this, he said, "I cut off the head of John, and he has been raised from the dead!"

Luke 9:7-9 - (7) Now Herod Antipas the tetrarch heard about all that Jesus was doing. And he became very troubled because some people were saying that John the Baptizer had been raised from the dead. (8) Others said that Elijah had appeared, and still others said that one of the (*Old Testament*) prophets of long ago had come back to life. (9) But Herod Antipas said, "I cut off John's head. So who is this person I hear so much about?" Luke 9:9 - And so he looked for an opportunity to see Jesus.

180 - Twelve Apostles Return from Their Mission Journey
(Mark 6:30, Luke 9:10)

Mark 6:30 - The Twelve Apostles returned from their mission journey and gathered around Jesus and told him all they had done and taught.

Luke 9:10 - When the Twelve Apostles returned to Jesus, they told him everything that they had done during their mission journey.

181 - Jesus and Disciples Go to Bethsaida
(Matthew 14:13, Mark 6:31-32, Luke 9:10, John 6:1)

Matthew 14:13 - When Jesus heard that John was dead, he withdrew by boat privately to a place where he could be alone.

Mark 6:31-32 - (31) Then, because so many people were coming and going that they did not have time to eat, Jesus said to them, "Come with me and let's go to an isolated place and get some rest" (32) So they left by themselves in a boat to an isolated area.

Luke 9:10 - Then Jesus took them with him and they withdrew to a town called Bethsaida where they thought they could be alone.

John 6:1 - (1) Some time after this, Jesus went by boat across to the eastern side of Lake Galilee, which is also called Lake Tiberius…

182 - Jesus Heals the Sick People
(Matthew 14:13-14, Mark 6:33-34, Luke 9:11, John 6:2-4)

Matthew 14:13-14 - (13) Hearing that Jesus had left, crowds of people followed him by foot from the towns. (14) So when Jesus' boat landed and he saw a large crowd of people, he had compassion on them and healed the sick.

Mark 6:33-34 - (33) But many people saw them leaving and ran from all the towns and arrived there before Jesus and his disciples. (34) When they landed the boat on the shore, Jesus saw a large crowd, and he had compassion on them, because they were like sheep without a shepherd. So he began teaching them many things.

Luke 9:11 - But crowds of people found out where Jesus went and followed him. Jesus welcomed them and spoke to them about the kingdom of God, and healed the sick.

John 6:2-4 - …and a large crowd of people followed him because they saw the miraculous signs (*miracles*) he had performed when he healed the sick. (3) Then Jesus went up on a mountainside and sat down with his disciples. (4) Now the time of the Passover feast was near (*March/April*).

183 - Jesus Feeds Five Thousand
(Matthew 14:15-21, Mark 6:35-44, Luke 9:12-17, John 6:5-13)

Matthew 14:15-21 - (15) When it was getting dark, the disciples went to Jesus and said to him, "This is an isolated place, and it is getting late. Send the people away, so that they can go to the villages and buy food to eat." (16) Jesus said to them, "They do not need to go away. You give them something to eat." (17) The disciples said, "We have only five loaves of bread and two small fish (*sardines*)." (18) Jesus said, "Bring them to me." (19) And Jesus told the people to sit down on the grass. He took the five loaves of bread and two small fish, looked up to heaven, gave thanks to God, and then broke the loaves of bread. He gave the pieces to his disciples, who then gave them to the people. (20) They all ate and were full, and the disciples collected 12 basketfuls of broken pieces of bread that had not been eaten. (21) There were about 5,000 men who ate (*not including the women and children*).

Mark 6:35-44 - (35) It was getting late in the day, so his disciples said to Jesus, "This is an isolated place, and it is almost evening; (36) send the people away so that they can go into the surrounding countryside and villages and buy food to eat." (37) But Jesus said to them, "You give them something to eat." The disciples said, "Are we to go and spend that much money on bread and give it to them to eat?" (38) And Jesus said to them, "Go and see how many loaves of bread you have." When they found out, they said to Jesus, "We have five loaves of bread and two small fish (*sardines*)." (39) Then Jesus told them to have all the people sit down in groups on the green grass. (40) So they sat in groups of 50 and 100. (41) Taking the five loaves of bread and the two small fish, Jesus looked up to heaven, gave thanks, and broke the bread into pieces. Then he gave the pieces to his disciples to distribute to the people. He also divided the two fish among them all. (42) Everyone ate and was satisfied, (43) and the disciples picked up 12 basketsful of pieces of bread and fish that were left over. (44) The number of the men who ate that day was about 5,000 (*not counting the women and children*).

Luke 9:12-17 - (12) Late in the afternoon the Twelve Apostles came to Jesus and said, "Send the people away so that they can go to the surrounding villages and countryside to find food and lodging, because we are in a very isolated place." (13) Jesus said to them, "You give them something to eat." They said, "We have only five loaves of bread and two small fish (*sardines*)—unless we go and buy food for all of these people."

(14) There were about 5,000 men (*not counting women or children*). Jesus told his disciples, "Have them sit down in groups of about 50 each." (15) The disciples told everyone to sit down on the ground. (16) Taking the five loaves of bread and two fish, Jesus looked up into heaven, gave thanks, and broke the bread and fish into pieces. Then he gave the pieces to the disciples to distribute to the people. (17) All the people ate and were full, and the disciples collected 12 basketsful of broken pieces that were left over.

John 6:5-13 - (5) When Jesus looked up and saw a large crowd of people rushing toward him, he said to Philip, "Where will we buy bread for all these people to eat?" (6) (*Jesus said this to test Philip's faith, for he already knew what he was going to do.*) (7) Philip said to Jesus, "It would take a lot of money—more than six months' pay (*200 denarii*)—to buy enough bread for everyone to just take a single bite." (8) Another of his disciples, Andrew, Simon Peter's brother, spoke up, (9) "Here is a boy who has five small barley loaves and two small fish (*sardines*), but how much more will we need to feed so many people?" (10) Jesus said to his disciples, "Have the people sit down." They were at a very green grassy place, so they all sat down, about 5,000 men (*not counting the women and children*). (11) Jesus then took the five loaves, gave thanks to God, and distributed the pieces to those who were seated as much as they wanted. He did the same with the small fish. (12) After the people had enough to eat, Jesus told his disciples, "Gather up the pieces of food that are left over. Let nothing be wasted." (13) So the disciples gathered the pieces and filled 12 basketsful with the pieces of bread of the five barley loaves left over by those who had eaten.

(*Although the town of Bethsaida is mentioned, the actual feeding of the 5,000 probably took place somewhere on the Plain of Bethsaida, in the northeastern shore region of Lake Galilee. This was a fertile and spacious green grass area about 5 square miles/8 square km*).

184 - The People Try to Make Jesus King
(John 6:14-15)

John 6:14-15 - (14) After the people saw Jesus' miraculous sign, they began saying to one another, "This must be the Prophet that Moses said would come into the world (*as it is written in Deuteronomy 18:15-18*)." (15) Jesus knew the people were planning to come and make him the king of Israel by force.

185 - Jesus Sends the Apostles Away
(Matthew 14:22, Mark 6:45, John 6:16-17)

Matthew 14:22 - Immediately Jesus told the disciples to get into the boat and go on ahead of him to the western side of Lake Galilee (*probably to Capernaum*), while he dismissed the crowd.

Mark 6:45 - Immediately Jesus told his disciples to get into the boat and go on ahead of him to the town of Bethsaida (*on the northeastern coast of Lake Galilee*), while he dismissed the crowd.

John 6:16-17 - (16) Jesus' disciples went down to Lake Galilee that night. (17) They got into a boat and started across the lake toward Capernaum. It was now dark, and Jesus had not yet joined them.

186 - Jesus Prays Alone
(Matthew 14:23, Mark 6:46, John 6:15)

Matthew 14:23 - After he had dismissed the people, he went up on a mountainside by himself to pray.

Mark 6:46 - After leaving the people, Jesus went up on a mountainside to pray.

John 6:15 - ...so he withdrew again up a mountainside so he could be alone.

---

187 - Jesus Walks on Lake Galilee
(Matthew 14:23-33, Mark 6:47-52, John 6:18-21)

Matthew 14:23-33 - (23) Later that night, Jesus was there alone, (24) and the disciples' boat was already far from shore when waves driven by a strong wind smashed against it. (25) Shortly before dawn (*sometime between 3 a.m. and 6 a.m.*) Jesus walked on the lake toward the disciples' boat. (26) When the disciples saw him walking on the water, they were terrified. They cried out in fear and screamed, "It is a ghost!" (27) But Jesus immediately said to them, "It is me! Take courage. Don't be afraid." (28) Peter said to him, "Lord, if it's you, tell me to come to you on the water." (29) Jesus said, "Come!" Then Peter got out of the boat and walked on the water toward Jesus. (30) But when he saw the wind, he became afraid and began to sink. He cried out, "Lord, save me!" (31) Immediately Jesus reached out his hand and grabbed him. Jesus said, "You have such little faith, why did you doubt?" (32) And when they climbed into the boat, the wind stopped. (33) Then the disciples in the boat worshiped Jesus, saying, "It is true, you are the Son of God!"

Mark 6:47-52 - (47) Later that night, Jesus was alone on land, while the disciples' boat was in the middle of the lake. (48) He saw the disciples straining at the oars as they rowed, because the wind was blowing hard against them. Shortly before dawn Jesus walked on the lake toward the disciples' boat. He was about to walk by them, (49) but when they saw him walking on the lake, they thought he was a ghost. They screamed out, (50) because they all saw him and were terrified. Immediately Jesus said to them, "Take courage! It is me. Don't be afraid." (51) Then he climbed into the boat with them, and the wind became calm. They were completely amazed, (52) because they had not understood about the loaves of bread, for their hearts were hardened.

John 6:18-21 - (18) Suddenly a strong wind blew, making huge waves on the lake. (19) After rowing about three or four miles (*5-6 km*), the disciples saw Jesus walking on the water toward the boat, and they became very afraid. (20) But Jesus shouted to them, "It is me. Don't be afraid!" (21) Then they were happy to have Jesus get into the boat...

_____
_____
_____
_____
_____

188 - Jesus and Apostles Land on Plain of Gennesaret
(Matthew 14:34, Mark 6:53, John 6:21)

Matthew 14:34 - When they had crossed back over to the western shore of Lake Galilee, their boat landed in the region of Gennesaret.

Mark 6:53 - They crossed over the lake and anchored at the plain of Gennesaret.

John 6:21 - ...and immediately it arrived at the shore at Capernaum.

(This was probably the crescent-shaped, fertile Plain of Gennersaret, located on the north-western coast of Lake Galilee around 3 miles/5 km south of Capernaum. The size of this plain was about 5 miles/8 km long and 2 miles/3 km wide).

_____
_____
_____
_____
_____

189 - Jesus Heals Many People
(Matthew 14:34-36, Mark 6:54-56)

Matthew 14:35-36 - (35) And when the people there recognized Jesus, they sent word throughout the surrounding region. People brought all their sick to Jesus (36) and begged him to let the sick just touch the edge of his clothes (*outer cloak*), and everyone who touched him was healed.

Mark 6:54-56 - (54) As soon as they got out of the boat, people recognized Jesus.

(55) They ran throughout the whole region and carried the sick on mats to wherever they heard he was. (56) And wherever Jesus went—into villages, towns, or the countryside—they put the sick in the public marketplaces. They begged him to let the sick touch the edge of his clothes (*outer cloak*), and everyone who touched it was healed.

_____
_____
_____
_____

190 - People Search for Jesus
(John 6:22-24)

John 6:22-24 - (22) The next day a large crowd of people that had stayed on the eastern side of the lake realized that only one boat had been there, and that the disciples had left without Jesus because he had gone to the mountainside to be alone. (23) Then some boats from Tiberias landed near the place where Jesus had fed food to the people. (24) When the people realized that neither Jesus nor his disciples were there, they got into their boats and went to Capernaum in search of Jesus.

191 - Jesus is the Bread of Life
(John 6:25-40)

John 6:25-40 - (25) When the people found Jesus in Capernaum, they said to him, "Teacher (*Rabbi*), when did you get here?" (26) Jesus said to them, "I tell you the truth: You are following me not because you saw the miraculous signs (*miracles*) I did but because your stomachs were filled with bread. (27) Stop working for food that rots, but live for food that endures to eternal life, which the Son of Man *(see Daniel 7:13-14)* will give to you. For God the Father has placed his seal of approval on him." (28) Then the people asked Jesus, "What are the works that God requires of us?" (29) Jesus said, "This is the work of God: To believe in the one God has sent into this world." (30) They said to Jesus, "Show us a miraculous sign, then we will see it and believe in you! (31) Our ancestors ate bread (*manna*) from heaven in the desert, as Psalm 78:24 says, 'God gave them bread from heaven to eat.'" (32) Jesus said to them, "I tell you the truth: It was not Moses who gave you the bread from heaven, but it is my Father who gives you the true bread from heaven. (33) For God's bread is the one who comes down from heaven and gives life to this world." (34) They said to Jesus, "Sir, give us this bread forever!" (35) Then Jesus declared, "I am the bread of life! Whoever comes to me will never be hungry, and whoever believes in me will never be thirsty. (36) But as I said, you have seen me and still you do not believe in me. (37) Whoever the Father gives me will come to me, and whoever comes to me, I will never turn away. (38) For I came from heaven not to do my will, but to do the will of the one who sent me. (39) And this is the will of the one who sent me into this world: That I would not lose anyone he has given me, but raise them up at the last day. (40) For this is my Father's will: That whoever comes to the Son and believes in him will receive eternal life, and I will raise them from the dead on the last day."

192 - Eternal Life in Jesus Christ
(John 6:41-51)

John 6:41-51 - (41) After Jesus said these things, the Jewish religious leaders were upset because he said, "I am the bread that came down from heaven." (42) They said, "How can he say that he came down from heaven? Isn't this Jesus, the son of Joseph? We know his father and mother." (43) Jesus said to them, "Stop complaining! (44) No one can come to me unless the Father who sent me brings them to me, and I will raise them from the dead on the last day. (45) For it is written in Isaiah 54:13, 'They will all be taught by God.' Whoever hears and learns from the Father comes to me. (46) No human has ever seen the Father, but only the one who is from God; only he has seen the Father. (47) I tell you the truth: Whoever believes in me has eternal life. (48) I am the bread of life! (49) Your ancestors ate the bread (*manna*) in the wilderness, yet they died. (50) But this is the bread that comes down from heaven, which anyone can eat and not die. (51) I am the living bread that came down from heaven! Whoever eats this bread will live forever. This bread is my body, which I will give for the life of this world.

193 - The Body and Blood of Jesus
(John 6:52-59)

John 6:52-59 - (52) Then the Jews began to argue with each other, saying, "How can Jesus give us his body to eat?" (53) Jesus said to them, "I tell you the truth: Unless you eat the body of the Son of Man (*see Daniel 7:13-14*) and drink his blood, you have no life in you. (54) Whoever eats my body and drinks my blood has eternal life, and I will raise him from the dead on the last day. (55) For my body is true food, and my blood is true drink. (56) Whoever eats my body and drinks my blood lives in me, and I live in them. (57) Just as the living Father sent me into this world, and I live because of the Father, so whoever eats my body will also live because of me. (58) This is the bread that came down from heaven. Your ancestors ate bread (*manna*) and died, but whoever eats this bread will live forever." (59) Jesus taught this message in the synagogue of Capernaum.

194 - Many Disciples Leave Jesus
(John 6:60-66)

John 6:60-66 - (60) When many of his disciples heard Jesus' teaching in the Capernaum synagogue, they said to one another, "This is a very difficult teaching to believe. Who can accept it?" (61) Jesus knew that his disciples were complaining about his teaching and said to them, "Does my teaching offend you? (62) Then what if you see the Son of Man (*see Daniel 7:13-14*) ascend to heaven where he came from! (63) It is the Holy Spirit who gives life; the flesh means nothing. The words of my teaching are full of the Holy Spirit and life. (64) But some of you still refuse to believe in me." For Jesus knew from the beginning which of them would not believe and who would leave him. (65) And Jesus said, "This is why I told you that no one can come to me unless the Father enables them." (66) Because of Jesus' teaching, many of his disciples left and no longer followed him.

195 - Jesus Questions His Twelve Apostles
(John 6:67-71)

John 6:67-71 - (67) Jesus looked at his Twelve Apostles and said, "Are you going to leave me too?" (68) Simon Peter said, "Lord, who are we going to follow? You are the only one who has the words of eternal life. (69) We believe in you! We know that you are the Holy One of God!" (70) Then Jesus said, "Although I have chosen you as my Twelve Apostles, one of you is a demon." (71) Jesus was talking about Judas, the son of Simon Iscariot, who, even though he was one of the Twelve Apostles, would later betray him.

196 - God's Truth, Human Traditions
(Matthew 15:1-9, Mark 7:1-13)

Matthew 15:1-9 - (1) Then some Pharisees and teachers of the law of Moses came to Jesus from Jerusalem and asked him, (2) "Why do your disciples disobey the tradition of the elders? For they eat bread without washing their hands." (3) Jesus said to them, "And why do you disobey God's commandments for the sake of your tradition? (4) For God said in Exodus 20:12, 'Honor your father and mother,' and in Exodus 21:17, 'Anyone who curses his father or mother must be put to death.' (5) But you tell people that any money that could have been used to help their father and mother can now be given to God. (6) And so they don't have to honor their parents with it. Therefore, you have nullified the word of God for the sake of your tradition. (7) You are religious hypocrites! What is written in Isaiah 29:13 is true, (8) 'These people honor me with their lips, but their hearts are far from me. (9) They worship me in vain; their teachings are simply human rules.' "

Mark 7:1-13 - (1) Some Pharisees and teachers of the law of Moses who had come from Jerusalem gathered around Jesus. (2) They saw some of his disciples eating food with unwashed hands, and so they considered them to be religiously unclean. (3) (The Pharisees and all the Jews do not eat unless their hands are ritually washed, according to the tradition of the Jewish elders. (4) When they come from the public marketplace they do not eat unless they wash. And they also observe many other religious traditions, such as the washing of cups, pitchers, and copper kettles.) (5) So the Pharisees and teachers of the law of Moses asked Jesus, "Why don't your disciples live according to the tradition of the Jewish elders, instead of eating their food with unclean hands?"

(6) Jesus said to them, "The prophet Isaiah was right when he prophesied about you religious hypocrites in Isaiah 29:13, 'These people honor me with their lips, but their hearts are far from me. (7) They worship me in vain; their teachings are simply rules taught by men.' (8) You have rejected God's commandments and are obeying human traditions." (9) And Jesus continued, "You are experts at ignoring God's commands so you can observe your own traditions and rules! (10) For Moses wrote in Exodus 20:12, 'Honor your father and mother,' and in Exodus 21:17, 'Anyone who curses his father or mother must be put to death.' (11) But you teach that if anyone declares that what might have been used to help their father and mother is Corban (*that is, devoted to God*)—(12) then you don't let them help their father or mother. (13) So you nullify God's word by your religious tradition that you have handed down. And you do many things like this."

197 - The Clean and the Unclean
(Matthew 15:10-20; Mark 7:14-23)

Matthew 15:10-20 - (10) Jesus called the people to him and said to them, "Listen and understand: (11) It is not what you eat that makes you unclean, but it is what you say that makes you unclean." (12) Then the disciples came and asked Jesus, "Did you know that the Pharisees were offended by what you said?" (13) Jesus said to them, "Every plant that my Father in heaven has not planted will be pulled up by the roots. (14) Leave them alone; they are blind leaders. And if the blind lead the blind, they will both fall into a hole." (15) Then Peter said, "Explain this parable to us." (16) Jesus asked them, "Are you still so dull that you do not understand? (17) What you eat goes into your stomach and then it goes out of your body. (18) But what makes people unclean are the words they say that come from their hearts. (19) For out of the heart come evil thoughts—murder, adultery, sexual perversion, theft, false testimony, and slander. (20) These are what make a person unclean; but eating with unwashed hands does not make anyone unclean."

Mark 7:14-23 - (14) Once again Jesus gathered the crowd of people together and said to them, "Everyone listen to me, and understand what I am telling you. (15-16) There is nothing outside a person that can make them unclean. Rather, a person is made unclean by what comes out from inside him." (17) After Jesus had left the crowd and went into the house (*probably Peter's house in Capernaum*), his disciples asked him the meaning of the parable (*story*). (18) Jesus said to them, "Are you so dumb? Don't you understand that it is not what a person eats that makes him unclean? (19) For what people eat does not go into their heart but into their stomach, and then goes out of their body." By this teaching, Jesus made all foods clean to eat. (20) Jesus then said, "It is what comes out of a person's heart that makes them unclean. (21) For it is out of a person's heart that come evil thoughts, sexual perversion, theft, murder, adultery, (22) greed, hate, deceit, envy, slander, pride, and foolishness. (23) All these evil things come from a person's heart and make them unclean."

198 - Jesus Walks through Galilee Alone
(John 7:1)

John 7:1 - After this, Jesus left Capernaum and walked through Galilee (*in northern Israel*). He would not travel in Judea (*in southern Israel*) because he knew the Jewish religious leaders were looking for a way to kill him.

199 - The Unbelief of Jesus' Brothers
(John 7:2-8)

John 7:2-8 - (2) But when the time for the Jewish feast of Tabernacles was near (*also known as the feast of Booths*), (3) Jesus' brothers said to him, "Leave Galilee and go to Judea, so that your disciples can see the miraculous works (*miracles*) you are doing. (4) For no one who wants to become a public figure hides what he does. Since you are doing these miracles, show yourself to the world!" (5) For even Jesus' brothers refused to believe in him. (6) Therefore Jesus said to his brothers, "It is not God's time for me, but any time is right for you. (7) This world does not hate you, but it hates me because I testify that the ways of this world are evil. (8) You go to the feast. I'm not going to the festival, because my time has not yet fully come."

200 - Jesus Privately Travels to Jerusalem
(John 7:9-10)

John 7:9-10 - (9) After Jesus said this, he stayed in Galilee. (10) However, after Jesus' brothers had left for the festival, Jesus also walked to Jerusalem, not in public but in secret.

201 - Religious Leaders Look for Jesus
(John 7:11-13)

John 7:11-13 - (11) Now the Jewish religious leaders were looking for Jesus at the feast. They asked people, "Where is Jesus?" (12) The crowds of people were whispering many things about Jesus. Some said, "He is a good man." Others said, "No, he deceives the people." (13) But no one would talk about Jesus in public, because they were afraid of the Jewish religious leaders.

202 - Jesus Teaches in the Jerusalem Temple
(John 7:14-24)

John 7:14-24 - (14) Not until the feast of Tabernacles was about half over did Jesus enter the temple courts and begin to teach. (15) The Jews who heard him were amazed and asked, "How does this man have such learning, because he has never been formally taught?" (16) Jesus said, "My teaching is not my own, but it comes from the one who sent me into this world. (17) Whoever chooses to do the will of God discovers whether my teaching is from God or whether I speak on my own authority. (18) Whoever speaks on his own authority seeks his own personal glory, but whoever seeks the glory of the one who sent him is a man of truth, for there is no falsehood in him. (19) Moses gave you the law, but none of you obey it. So why are you trying to kill me?" (20) The crowd of people said, "You are demon-possessed (*demonized*)! Who is trying to kill you?" (21) Jesus said to them, "You were amazed at one miracle that I did. (22) Yet, because Moses gave you circumcision (*although it was not actually given by Moses, but by the patriarchs*), you circumcise a boy on the Sabbath day. (23) Now if you circumcise a boy on the Sabbath day so that the law will not be broken, why are you angry with me for healing a man's whole body on the Sabbath? (24) Stop judging by outward appearances, but judge according to what is right."

203 - Is Jesus the Messiah?
(John 7:25-31)

John 7:25-31 - (25) At this time some of the people in Jerusalem began to ask, "Isn't this the man whom the religious leaders are trying to kill? (26) Look! He is here, teaching publicly, and they are not trying to stop him. Do the authorities now believe that he is the Messiah (*Christ*)? (27) But we know he comes from Galilee, and no one knows where the Messiah (*Christ*) will come from." (28) Then while Jesus was still teaching in the temple courts, he shouted out, "Yes, you know me, and you know I am from Galilee! I am not here on my own authority, but he who sent me is true. You do not know him, (29) but I know him because I came from him, and he sent me into this world." (30) At this the Jewish religious leaders wanted to arrest Jesus, but they did not touch him because God's time had not yet come. (31) And many in the crowd of people believed in Jesus. They said, "When the Messiah (*Christ*) comes, will he do more miraculous signs (*miracles*) than this man?"

204 - Religious Leaders Attempt to Arrest Jesus
(John 7:32-36)

John 7:32-36 - (32) The Pharisees heard the people whispering these things about Jesus, so the chief priests and Pharisees sent temple guards to arrest him. (33) Jesus said, "I am with you for only a short time more, and then I am going back to the one who sent me into this world. (34) You will look for me, but you will not find me. Where I am going, you cannot come." (35) The Jews said to one another, "Where is Jesus planning to go that we cannot find him? Does he plan to go where our people live scattered among the non-Jews (*in the Jewish diaspora*)? Is he going to teach the non-Jews? (36) What did he mean when he said, 'You will look for me, but you will not find me,' and 'Where I am going, you cannot come'?"

- - -

205 - The Holy Spirit as Living Water
(John 7:37-39)

John 7:37-39 - (37) On the last and greatest day of the feast of Tabernacles, Jesus stood up in the temple courts and shouted with a loud voice, "Whoever is thirsty come to me and drink! (38) Whosoever believes in me, as it is written in Isaiah 58:11, 'Out of their hearts will flow rivers of living water.' " (39) By this Jesus was talking about the Holy Spirit that people who believed in him would later receive. Up to that time the Holy Spirit had not been given, because Jesus had not yet been glorified.

- - -

206 - Confusion About Jesus
(John 7:40-44)

John 7:40-44 - (40) When some of the people heard Jesus, they said, "This man is truly the Prophet (*referring to Deuteronomy 18:15-18*)." (41) Others said, "He is the Messiah (*Christ*)!" Still others said, "How can the Messiah (*Christ*) come from Galilee? (42) Doesn't the Bible tell us that the Messiah (*Christ*) will be a descendant of David and come from Bethlehem, the town where David lived?" (43) Therefore the people were divided about Jesus. (44) Some people wanted to arrest him, but no one laid a hand on him.

- - -

207 - Religious Leaders Fail to Arrest Jesus
(John 7:45-49)

John 7:45-49 - (45) Finally the temple guards returned to the Jewish chief priests and Pharisees without Jesus. The religious leaders asked them, "Why didn't you bring Jesus to us?" (46) The guards said, "We have not heard anyone speak the way he does." (47) The Pharisees snapped back, saying, "You mean you have been fooled too? (48) Have any of the Jewish rulers and Pharisees believed in hm? (49) No! But this mob of people that knows nothing about the law of Moses is under a curse."

208 - Nicodemus Defends Jesus
(John 7:50-53)

John 7:50-53 - (50) Nicodemus, who had previously talked with Jesus (*see John 3:1-15*) and who was a member of the governing Jewish council (*the Sanhedrin*), said, (51) "Our law does not condemn a man until we first hear from him and learn what he is doing." (52) The other religious leaders said, "Nicodemus, are you from Galilee, too? Search through the Bible (*the Old Testament*)! You'll find that no prophet comes from Galilee." (53) Then the Jewish religious leaders left for their homes.

209 - Jesus Spends the Night in Bethany
(John 8:1)

John 8:1 - Jesus left and spent the night on the Mount of Olives (*probably in Bethany*).

210 - Jesus Teaches in the Jerusalem Temple
(John 8:2)

John 8:2 - Early the next morning he once again entered the temple courts, sat down, and began teaching a crowd of people that had gathered around him.

211 - Jesus Forgives a Woman Caught in Adultery
(John 8:3-11)

John 8:3-11 - (3) The teachers of the law of Moses and the Pharisees brought in a woman who had been caught in the act of adultery. (4) They made her stand in front of him before the people and said to Jesus, "Teacher, this woman was caught in the act of adultery. (5) As you know, the law of Moses commands us to kill her with rocks. Do you agree with Moses?" (6) They were using this question to trap Jesus, so that they could have evidence to bring charges against him. But Jesus bent down and began to write on the ground with his finger. (7) When the religious leaders continued questioning him, Jesus stood up and said to them, "Whoever among you is without sin should throw the first rock at her." (8) Then Jesus bent down again and went on writing on the ground. (9) In response, those who heard Jesus' words began to leave one by one—the older ones left first, until Jesus was left alone with the woman standing there. (10) Jesus stood up and asked her, "Woman, where are the people? Did any of them condemn you?" (11) She said, "Sir, no one." Jesus said, "Then neither do I condemn you. Go now and leave your life of sin."

212 - Jesus is the Light of the World
(John 8:12-20)

John 8:12-20 - (12) Jesus spoke again to the people, saying, "I am the light of this world! Whoever follows me will never live in darkness, but will have the light that gives life." (13) But some of the Pharisees confronted Jesus, saying to him, "You are giving witness about yourself, so your testimony is false." (14) Jesus said, "Even if I testify about myself, my testimony is true, because I know where I came from and where I am going. But you do not know where I came from or where I am going. (15) You judge me by human standards, but I do not judge anyone. (16) Yet, if I do judge, my judgments are true, because I am not alone. I judge with the Father, who sent me into this world.

(17) As Moses wrote in Deuteronomy 17:6, 'The testimony of two witnesses is true.' (18) I am one who testifies about myself, and my other witness is the Father, who sent me into this world." (19) Then the religious leaders asked Jesus, "Where is your father?" Jesus said, "You don't know me or my Father. If you knew me, you would also know my Father." (20) Jesus taught these things in the area of the temple courts where the offerings were given. Yet no one tried to arrest him, because God's time had not yet come.

213 - Jesus Confronts the Religious Leaders
(John 8:21-30)

John 8:21-30 - (21) Jesus began to teach once again, saying, "I am going away, and you will search for me, but you will die in your sin. Where I am going, you cannot come." (22) The Jews asked one another, "Is he going to kill himself? Is that why he says, 'Where I am going, you cannot come'?" (23) But Jesus said, "You are from this world below, but I am from heaven above. You are of this world, but I am not of this world. (24) I tell you the truth: You will die in your sins if you refuse to believe that I am the Messiah (*Christ*). Yes, you will die in your sins." (25) They said, "Who are you?" Jesus said, "From the beginning, I have told you many times. (26) I have much more to say in judgment of you, but the one who sent me into this world is true, and what I have heard from him I have told this world." (27) They did not understand that Jesus was speaking to them about his Father. (28) So Jesus said, "When you have lifted up the Son of Man (*see Daniel 7:13-14*), then you will know that I am he and that I do nothing on my own authority. For I speak only what I have learned from the Father. (29) The one who sent me into this world is with me; he has never left me alone, for I always do what pleases him." (30) Even while Jesus was speaking, many people believed in him.

214 - Religious Leaders Are Not Abraham's Children
(John 8:31-47)

John 8:31-47 - (31) Jesus said to the Jews who had believed in him, "If you continue to follow my teaching, then you are truly my disciples. (32) Then you will know the truth, and the truth will set you free." (33) But they said, "We are Abraham's descendants, and we have never been slaves of anyone. How can you say that we can be set free?" (34) Jesus said, "I tell you the truth: Whoever sins is a slave to sin. (35) A slave has no permanent status in the family, but a son always belongs to the family. (36) So if the Son sets you free, you will be truly free. (37) I know that you are Abraham's descendants, but you are looking for a way to kill me, because my teaching finds no place in your hearts. (38) I tell you what I have seen in the Father's presence, but you are doing what you have heard from your father." (39) They said to Jesus, "Our father is Abraham." Jesus said, "If you were Abraham's children then you would live the life that Abraham did. (40) But instead, you are looking for a way to kill me, even though I tell you the truth that I heard from God. Abraham did not do these things. (41) You are doing the works of your real father." They said, "We aren't illegitimate children, because God alone is our father." (42) Jesus said to them, "If God were your Father, you would love me, because I came into this world from God. He sent me into this world, I did not come on my own authority. (43) You are not able to understand what I am saying because you are not able to hear my teaching. (44) I tell you the truth: You belong to your true father, the devil, and your desire is to do your father's will. He was a murderer from the beginning, never holding to the truth, for there is no truth in him. When he lies, he speaks his own language, because he is a liar and the father of lies. (45) Yet, even though I tell you the truth, you still refuse to believe me! (46) Which one of you can prove that I am guilty of sin? If I am telling you the truth, why don't you believe me? (47) Whoever belongs to God hears what God says. The reason you do not hear God is because you do not belong to God."

---

215 - Jesus Was Before Abraham
(John 8:48-59)

John 8:48-59 - (48) The Jews said to Jesus, "Aren't we right to say that you are a Samaritan and demon-possessed (*demonized*)?" (49) Jesus said, "I'm not possessed by a demon, but I honor my Father and you dishonor me. (50) I do not seek my own glory, but there is one who seeks it, and he is the true judge. (51) I tell you the truth: Whoever obeys my teaching will never die." (52) The Jews declared, "Now we know that you are demon-possessed (*demonized*)! Abraham died and so did the prophets, but you say that whoever obeys your teaching will never die. (53) Who do you think you are? Are you greater than our father Abraham and the prophets who died?" (54) Jesus said, "If I glorify myself, it is worth nothing. But my Father—whom you claim is your God—is the one who glorifies me. (55) I know God, but you do not. I would be a liar like you if I said I did not know him. For I do know him and obey his word. (56) Your father Abraham rejoiced at the thought of seeing my day. And indeed he did see it and was glad." (57) The Jews said, "You are not yet 50 years of age, and you have seen Abraham?" (58) Jesus said, "I tell you the truth: Before Abraham was born, I am, (*for as Moses wrote in Exodus 3:14, 'I AM WHO I AM).'*" (59) When the Jews heard this, they picked up rocks to kill Jesus, but he hid himself and left the temple courts.

216 - Jesus Heals a Blind Man's Eyes
(John 9:1-12)

John 9:1-12 - (1) While Jesus was walking away from the temple, he saw a man who was blind from birth. (2) His disciples asked Jesus, "Teacher (*Rabbi*), why was this man born blind? Was it because of his sins or the sins of his parents?" (3) Jesus said, "Neither this man nor his parents sinned, but he was born blind so that the acts of God would be seen in what happens to him. (4) While it is still day, we must do the work of him who sent me into this world. The darkness of night is coming, when no one can do works. (5) As long as I am in this world, I am the light of the world!" (6) After saying this, Jesus spit on the ground, made mud with his saliva, and smeared it on the blind man's eyes. (7) Jesus said to him, "Go, wash the mud from your eyes in the Pool of Siloam," which means "Sent." (*The Pool of Siloam was located southeast of the temple complex*). So the man went and washed the mud off his eyes, and he went to his home seeing. (8) His neighbors and those who knew him as a blind man said, "Look! Isn't this the blind beggar?" (9) Some said he was. Others said, "No, he only looks like him." But the healed blind man kept insisting, "I am the man!" (10) They asked him, "How can you now see?" (11) He said to them, "The man called Jesus made some mud and put it on my eyes. He told me to go wash my eyes in the Pool of Siloam. So I went and after I washed my eyes, then I could see." (12) They asked, "Where is this Jesus?" The man said, "I don't know."

217 - Religious Leaders Question the Healed Man
(John 9:13-17)

John 9:13-17 - (13) They took the man who was once blind to the Pharisees (*probably at a Jerusalem synagogue*). (14) Now it was on the Sabbath day that Jesus had the man make mud and healed his eyes. (15) Therefore the Pharisees asked the man how he had received his sight. The man said, "Jesus put mud on my eyes, and after I washed my eyes, then I could see." (16) Some of the Pharisees said, "This Jesus is not from God, because he violated the Sabbath day." But others said, "How can a sinner do these miracles?" (17) Then they turned again to the man and asked, "Since it was your eyes that were healed, what do you think about this man Jesus?" The man said, "He is a prophet!"

218 - Religious Leaders Question the Healed Man's Parents
(John 9:18-23)

John 9:18-23 - (18) They still would not believe that the man was born blind and that his eyes were healed, so they sent for his parents. (19) They asked his parents, "Is this your son? Was he born blind? How can he now see?" (20) His parents said, "Yes, this is our son, and he was born blind. (21) But we don't know how he can now see, nor who it was that healed him. Ask him; he is an adult, he can speak for himself." (22) His parents said this because they were afraid of the Jewish religious leaders, who had already said that anyone who believed that Jesus was the Messiah *(Christ)* would be put out of the synagogue. (23) That is why his parents told the religious leaders to ask their son.

219 - Religious Leaders Question Healed Man Again
(John 9:24-34)

John 9:24-34 - (24) Now a second time, the religious leaders called for the man born blind and they told him, "Give all the glory to God by telling the truth, because we know that this Jesus is a sinner." (25) The man said, "I don't know whether he is a sinner or not, but one thing I do know: I was once blind, and now I see!" (26) Then the religious leaders asked him again, "What did this man Jesus do to you? How did he heal your eyes?" (27) The man said, "I have told you already, but you refuse to listen. Why do you want me to tell you over and over again? Do you want to become his disciples too?" (28) Then the religious leaders heaped insults on him, saying, "You are this man's disciple! But we are disciples of Moses! (29) We know that God spoke to Moses, but as for this man, we don't even know where he comes from." (30) The man said, "Now I am amazed! He healed my eyes, and you say you don't know where he comes from? (31) We all know that God does not listen to sinners. He only listens to those who worship him and do his will. (32) Nobody has ever heard of someone who heals the eyes of a man born blind. (33) If this Jesus did not come from God, he could not do anything." (34) The religious leaders said, "You were completely steeped in sin at birth! How dare you lecture us?" And they threw the man out of the synagogue.

220 - Healed Blind Man Believes in Jesus
(John 9:35-41)

John 9:35-41 - (35) Jesus heard that the Jewish religious leaders had thrown the healed blind man out of the synagogue. When he found him, he said, "Do you believe in the Son of Man (*see Daniel 7:13-14*)?" (36) The man said, "Sir, who is he? Tell me so that I can believe in him." (37) Jesus said, "You are now looking at him; he is the one speaking with you." (38) Then the man said, "Lord, I believe in you," and he worshiped Jesus. (39) Jesus said to him, "I came into this world to bring judgment, so that the blind will see, and those who see will become blind." (40) Some Pharisees who were with him heard Jesus say this and asked him, "What? Are you saying that we are blind?" (41) Jesus said, "If you were blind, you would not be guilty of sin; but since you claim you can see, you remain guilty in your sins."

221 - The Faith of a Non-Jewish Woman in Tyre and Sidon
(Matthew 15:21-28, Mark 7:24-30)

Matthew 15:21-28 - (21) Leaving that place, Jesus traveled northwest of Galilee to the region of Tyre and Sidon. (22) There a pagan Canaanite woman from that region came to Jesus, crying out, "Lord, Son of David, have mercy on me! My daughter is demon-possessed (*demonized*) and suffers terribly." (23) Jesus did not answer her. So his disciples came to him and told him, "Send her away, for she keeps crying out after us." (24) Jesus said, "I was sent only to the lost sheep of the house of Israel." (25) The woman came and fell on her knees before Jesus and said, "Lord, help me!" (26) Jesus said to her, "It is not right to take the children's bread and throw it to the dogs." (27) She said, "This is true, Lord, but even the dogs eat the crumbs of food that fall from their master's table." (28) Then Jesus said to her, "Woman, you have great faith! I will do what you ask me." And her daughter was healed immediately.

Mark 7:24-30 - (24) Jesus left Capernaum and traveled into the region of Tyre and Sidon. He entered a house and did not want anyone to know that he was there, but he could not keep it a secret. (25) In fact, as soon as a woman heard that Jesus was there, she went and fell at his feet because her little daughter was demon-possessed (*demonized*). (26) The woman was a non-Jew, born in Syrian Phoenicia (*the Mediterranean coastal part of the Roman province of Syria*). She begged Jesus to cast the demon out of her daughter. (27) Jesus told her, "First let the children eat all they want, because it is not right to take their bread and toss it to the dogs." (28) The woman said to him, "Lord, even the dogs under the table eat the children's crumbs." (29) Then Jesus said, "Because this is a good answer, go, because the demon has left your daughter." (30) She went home and found her daughter lying on the bed, and the demon was gone.

(The non-Jewish region of Tyre and Sidon bordered Galilee to the west along the Mediterranean Sea coast. Tyre was the main seaport of the Roman province of Syria and Phoenicia. Both are today located in modern Lebanon, with Tyre around 20 miles/32 km south of Sidon and only 12 miles/19 km north of the Israel-Lebanon border).

222 - Jesus Walks to the Decapolis
(Mark 7:31)

Mark 7:31 - Then Jesus left the region of Tyre and walked north about 25 miles (*40 km*) through Sidon, down to Lake Galilee and into the region of the Decapolis (*the region of the ten non-Jewish cities on the southeastern coast of Lake Galilee*).

223 - Jesus Heals a Deaf Man
(Mark 7:32-35)

Mark 7:32-35 - (32) There some people brought Jesus a man who was deaf and could hardly talk, and they begged him to place his hand on him. (33) After Jesus took the man away from the crowd, he put his fingers into the man's ears. Then he spit and touched the man's tongue. (34) Jesus looked up to God in heaven, took a deep sigh, and said to the man, "Be opened (*"Ephphatha" in Aramaic*)!" (35) Immediately the man could hear, and his tongue was released and he could talk clearly.

224 - News About Jesus Spreads
(Mark 7:36-37)

Mark 7:36-37 - (36) Jesus commanded them not to tell anyone about the healing, but the more Jesus told them this, the more they kept talking about it publicly. (37) People were overcome with amazement and said, "Everything Jesus does is good; he even makes deaf people hear and mute people speak."

225 - A Large Crowd Gathers in Decapolis
(Mark 8:1)

Mark 8:1 - During those days another large crowd gathered (*probably in the non-Jewish region of the Decapolis, ten cities, on the southeastern side of Lake Galilee*).

226 - Jesus Heals Many People
(Matthew 15:29-31)

Matthew 15:29-31 - (29) Jesus left there and walked along the shore of Lake Galilee. Then he went up on a mountainside and sat down. (30) Large crowds of people came to him, bringing the lame, the blind, the crippled, those who could not speak, and many others, and laid them at Jesus' feet; and he healed them. (31) The people were amazed when they saw the mute speak, the crippled made whole, the lame walking, and the blind seeing. And they all praised the God of Israel.

227 - Jesus Feeds Four Thousand
(Matthew 15:32-38, Mark 8:1-9)

Matthew 15:32-38 - (32) Jesus called his disciples to him and said, "I have compassion for these people; they have been with me for three days and have had nothing to eat. I do not want to send them away hungry, or they will faint walking back to their homes." (33) His disciples said to Jesus, "Where in this isolated place could we get enough bread for so many people?" (34) Jesus asked them, "How many loaves of bread do you have?" They said, "Seven, and a few small fish (*sardines*)." (35) Jesus told the people to sit down on the ground. (36) Then he took the seven loaves and the fish, and after he had given thanks to God, he broke them into pieces and gave them to his disciples, and they gave them to the people. (37) They all ate and were full. Afterward the disciples picked up seven basketful of broken bread that were not eaten. Matthew (38) There were 4,000 men who ate, not including the women and children.

Mark 8:1-9 - (1) Since they had nothing to eat, Jesus called his disciples to him and said, (2) "I have compassion for these people, because they have been with me three days and have not had anything to eat. (3) If I send them home hungry, they will faint along the road, because some of them have walked a long distance to be with me." (4) His disciples said to him, "But where in this isolated place can anyone get enough bread to feed them?" (5) Jesus asked, "How many loaves of bread do you have?" They said, "We have seven loaves of bread." (6) Jesus told the people to sit down on the ground. He took the seven loaves of bread and gave thanks to God, then he broke the bread into pieces and gave them to his disciples to distribute to the people, which they did. (7) They also had a few small fish (*sardines*); Jesus gave thanks for them also and told the disciples to distribute them to the people. (8) The people ate until they were full. Afterward the disciples picked up seven basketfuls of broken pieces that were left over. (9) There were about 4,000 men who ate (*not counting women and children*).

228 - Jesus and Apostles Land in Magadan/Dalmanutha
(Matthew 15:39, Mark 8:9-10)

Mathew 15:39 - After Jesus had sent the people away, he and the disciples got into the boat and went to the region of Magadan.

Mark 8:9-10 - (9) After Jesus had sent the people to their homes, (10) he and his disciples got into the boat and went to the region of Dalmanutha.

(*Magadan, also later identified as Magdala, was located on the western coast of Lake Galilee, around 6 miles/10 km south of Capernaum. Although uncertain, it is possible that Magadan/ Magdala was the home town of Mary Magdalene. Mark 8:9 refers to Dalmanutha instead of Magadan, which was possibly the port of Magadan*).

229 - Religious Leaders Ask Jesus for a Sign From Heaven
(Matthew 16:1-4, Mark 8:11-12)

Matthew 16:1-4 - (1) Then some Pharisees and Sadducees came to test Jesus, asking him to show them a miraculous sign (*miracle*) from heaven. (2) Jesus said to them, "When it is evening you say, 'It will be good weather, for the sky is red.' (3) And in the morning you say, 'It will be stormy weather today, for the sky is red and overcast.' You know how to interpret the sky's appearance, but you cannot interpret the signs of the times. (4) This wicked and unfaithful (*adulterous*) generation of Israel demands a miraculous sign (*miracle*), but no sign will be given it except the sign of the prophet Jonah." Then Jesus left them and went away.

Mark 8:11-12 - (11) Some Pharisees came and began to question Jesus. To test him, they asked him to show them a miraculous sign (*miracle*) from heaven. (12) Jesus took a deep breath and said, "Why does this generation of Israel seek a miraculous sign? I tell you the truth: I will not show this generation of Israel a sign."

230 - Jesus and Apostles Go to Bethsaida
(Matthew 16:5, Mark 8:13)

Matthew 16:5 - When Jesus and the disciples went to the eastern side of Lake Galilee... (*Bethsaida on the northeastern coast of Lake Galilee; see Mark 8:22*)...

Mark 8:13 - Then Jesus left them, got back into the boat and crossed over to Bethsaida on the northeastern side of Lake Galilee (*see Mark 8:22*).

231 - Jesus' Warning About the Religious Leaders
(Matthew 16:5-12, Mark 8:14-21)

Matthew 16:5-12 - (5)...the disciples had forgotten to bring bread. (6) Jesus said to them, "Be careful! Be on your guard against the yeast of the Pharisees and Sadducees." (7) The disciples discussed this among themselves and said, "Jesus knows that we did not bring bread." (8) Jesus knew what they were talking about and said, "You have so little faith! Why are you talking with each other about not bringing bread? (9) Do you not understand? Don't you remember that we fed 5,000 men with five loaves of bread, and that there were basketsful of bread left over? (10) Or when we fed 4,000 men with seven loaves of bread, and how many basketsful of bread you gathered? (11) How can it be that you don't understand that I was not talking about bread? I am telling you to be on your guard against the yeast of the Pharisees and Sadducees." (12) Then they finally understood that Jesus was not telling them to beware of the yeast used to make bread, but to be on guard against the false teaching of the Pharisees and Sadducees.

Mark 8:14-21 - (14) The disciples had forgotten to bring bread, except for the one loaf they had with them in the boat. (15) Jesus warned his disciples, "Be on your guard. Watch out for the yeast of the Pharisees and that of Herod." (16) The disciples discussed Jesus' statement with one another and said, "He said this because he knows that we did not bring any bread." (17) Jesus knew what they were talking about and asked them, "Why are you talking about having no bread? Do you still not see or understand? Are your hearts so hard? (18) Are your eyes not able to see? Are your ears not able to hear? And don't you remember (19) when I broke the five loaves of bread to feed 5,000 men; how many basketsful of pieces did you collect?" They said, "We collected 12 baskets." (20) Jesus asked, "And do you remember when I broke the seven loaves of bread to feed 4,000 men; how many basketsful of pieces did you collect?" They said, "We collected seven baskets." (21) Jesus said to them, "Do you still not understand?"

232 - Jesus Heals a Blind Man in Bethsaida
(Mark 8:22-26)

Mark 8:22-26 - (22) Jesus and his disciples came to Bethsaida (*on the northeastern coast of Lake Galilee*) and some people brought a blind man and begged Jesus to touch him. (23) He took the hand of the man and led him outside of the village. After Jesus had spit on the man's eyes and put his hands on them, he asked the man, "Do you see anything?" (24) He looked around and said, "I see people, but they look like trees walking around." (25) Once again Jesus put his hands on the man's eyes. Then his eyes were healed, and he could see everything clearly. (26) Jesus sent the man home, saying, "Do not even enter the village."

233 - Jesus and Apostles Walk to Northern Galilee
(Matthew 16:13, Mark 8:27, Luke 9:18)

Matthew 16:13 - Jesus and his disciples left Bethsaida and traveled north to the region of the city of Caesarea Philippi.

Mark 8:27 - Jesus and his disciples left Bethsaida and walked north to the villages around the city of Caesarea Philippi.

Luke 9:18 - Jesus was praying alone with his disciples.

(The region of Caesarea Philippi was primarily non-Jewish and located abou`vt 25 miles/40 km north of the Sea of Galilee, near Mount Hermon. The region was governed by Herod Philip, a son of Herod the Great).

234 - Jesus is the Messiah
(Matthew 16:13-20, Mark 8:27-30, Luke 9:18-21)

Matthew 16:13-20 - (13) He asked his disciples, "Who do people say the Son of Man is (*see Daniel 7:13-14*)?" (14) The disciples said to him, "Some say John the Baptizer, others say Elijah, and still others say Jeremiah, or one of the other (*Old Testament*) prophets." (15) Jesus asked them, "Who do you say I am?" (16) Peter said to Jesus, "You are the Messiah (*Christ*), the Son of the living God!" (17) Jesus said to him, "Blessed are you, Peter, son of Jonah, because this was not revealed to you by flesh and blood, but by my Father in heaven. (18) I tell you the truth: You are Peter (*meaning little pebble*), and on this rock (*meaning large boulder*) I will build my church, and the defense gates of death (*hades*) will not be strong enough to stop it. (19) I will give you disciples the knowledge (*keys*) of the kingdom of heaven (*God*): whatever you bind on earth will have already been bound in heaven, and whatever you loose on earth will have already been released in heaven." (20) Then Jesus ordered his disciples not to tell anyone that he was the Messiah (*Christ*).

Mark 8:27-30 - (27) As they were walking, Jesus asked his disciples, "Who do people say that I am?" (28) They said, "Some say you are John the Baptizer; others say you are Elijah; and still others say you are one of the (*Old Testament*) prophets." (29) Jesus asked, "But who do you say that I am?" Peter said to him, "You are the Messiah (*Christ*)!" (30) Jesus warned them not to tell anyone who he was.

Luke 19:18-21 - (18) He asked them, "Who do the crowds of people say I am?" (19) They said, "Some people say John the Baptizer, others say Elijah, and others say that you are one of the (*Old*

Testament) prophets of long ago who has come back to life." (20) Then Jesus asked his disciples, "Who do you say that I am?" Peter said, "You are the Messiah (*Christ*) of God!" (21) Jesus ordered them not to tell anyone who he was.

235 - Jesus Speaks About His Death and Resurrection
(Matthew 16:21-23, Mark 8:31-33, Luke 19:22)

Matthew 16:21-23 - (21) From that time on Jesus began to explain to his disciples that he must travel to Jerusalem and suffer many things at the hands of the Jewish elders, chief priests, and teachers of the law of Moses, and that he must be killed and on the third day be raised to life. (22) Peter took Jesus aside and rebuked him, saying, "Never, Lord! This will never happen to you!" (23) Jesus turned and said to Peter, "Get behind me, Satan! You are a stumbling block to me; you are not thinking about God's purposes, but only human concerns!"

Mark 8:31-33 - (31) Then Jesus began to teach his disciples that the Son of Man (*see Daniel 7:13-14*) must suffer many things and be rejected by the Jewish elders, chief priests, and teachers of the law of Moses. He told them that he would be killed, and after three days rise again. (32) Jesus spoke to them very clearly about this. Peter pulled Jesus away from the others and began to rebuke him. (33) But when Jesus turned and looked at his disciples, he rebuked Peter and said, "Satan, get behind me! You are not thinking about God's purposes, but only human concerns."

Luke 19:22 - Then he said, "The Son of Man (*see Daniel 7:13-14*) must suffer many things and be rejected by the Jewish chief priests, elders, and teachers of the law of Moses. He will be killed, but he will be raised from the dead on the third day."

236 - The Cost of Following Jesus
(Matthew 16:24-28, Mark 8:34-38, 9:1, Luke 9:23-27)

Matthew 16:24-28 - (24) Then Jesus said to his disciples, "Whoever wants to be my disciple must deny themselves and pick up their cross and follow me. (25) For whoever wants to save their life will lose it, but whoever loses their life for me will find it. (26) What good will it be for someone to gain the whole world, yet lose their soul? What can anyone give in exchange for their soul? (27) For the Son of Man (*see Daniel 7:13-14*) will come again in his Father's glory with his angels, and then he will reward each person according to how they have lived on earth. (28) I tell you the truth: There are some standing here who will not die before they see the Son of Man coming in his kingdom."

Mark 8:34-38, 9:1 - (34) Then Jesus called the crowd to him along with his disciples. He said, "Whoever wants to be my disciple must deny themselves and take up their cross and follow me. (35) For whoever wants to save their life will lose it, but whoever gives up their life for my sake and for the gospel (*good news*) will save it. (36) What good is it for someone to gain the whole world, yet lose their soul? (37) Or what can a person give in exchange for their soul? (38) If anyone is ashamed of me and my words in this unfaithful and sinful generation of Israel, the Son of Man (*see Daniel 7:13-14*) will be ashamed of them when he comes in his Father's glory, with the holy angels." (*Mark 9:1*) And Jesus said to them, "I tell you the truth: There are some standing here who will not die until they see the kingdom of God has come with power."

Luke 9:23-27 - (23) Then Jesus said to them all, "Whoever wants to be my disciple must deny (*surrender*) themselves and pick up their cross daily and follow me. (24) For whoever wants to save their life will lose it, but whoever loses their life for me will save it. (25) Tell me, what good is it if someone gains the whole world, but then loses his life? (26) Whoever is ashamed of me and my words in this world, the Son of Man (*see Daniel 7:13-14*) will be ashamed of him when he comes again in his glory, and in the glory of the Father and of the holy angels. (27) I tell you the truth: There are some people standing here who will not die before they see the kingdom of God."

237 - Jesus Take Apostles on a High Mountainside
(Matthew 17:1, Mark 9:2, Luke 9:28)

Matthew 17:1 - After six days Jesus led Peter, James, and John up on a high mountainside by themselves.

Mark 9:2 - Six days later Jesus led Peter, James, and John up a tall Galilean mountainside.

Luke 9:28 - About eight days after his teaching, Jesus took Peter, John, and James with him and walked up a mountainside to pray.

(*Probably on Mount Hermon in northern Galilee*).

238 - Jesus' Appearance Changes
(Matthew 17:2-13, Mark 9:2-13, Luke 9:29-36)

Matthew 17:2-13 - (2) There Jesus' appearance was transformed (*transfigured*) before their eyes. His face shone as bright as the sun, and his clothes became as white as light. (3) Suddenly Moses and Elijah appeared before them, talking with Jesus. (4) Peter said to Jesus, "Lord, it is good for us to be here. If you want, I can put up three tents—one for you, one for Moses, and one for Elijah." (5) While he was still speaking, suddenly a bright cloud covered them (*possibly the presence of God*), and a voice from the cloud said, "This is my Son, whom I love; with him I am very pleased. Be sure to listen to him!" (6) When the disciples heard this, they fell facedown to the ground because they were terrified. (7) But Jesus came and touched them, saying, "Get up, do not be afraid!" (8) When they looked up, they saw no one except Jesus. (9) As they were walking down the mountainside, Jesus told his disciples, "Do not tell anyone what you have seen, until the Son of Man (*see Daniel 7:13-14*) has been raised from the dead." (10) The disciples asked Jesus, "Why do the teachers of the law of Moses say that Elijah must come first?" (11) Jesus said, "Yes, Elijah will come and will restore all things. (12) But I tell you the truth: Elijah has already come, and the religious leaders did not recognize him, but they mistreated him. In the same way, the Son of Man is going to suffer at their hands." (13) Then the disciples understood that Jesus was talking to them about John the Baptizer.

Mark 9:2-13 - (2) While they were there alone, Jesus' appearance was changed (*transfigured*) in front of them. (3) His clothes became blazing white, whiter than any tailor in the world could bleach them. (4) And suddenly Moses and Elijah appeared to them, talking to Jesus. (5) Peter said to Jesus, "Teacher (*Rabbi*), it is good for us to be here together. I can put up three tents—one for you, one for Moses, and one for Elijah." (6) Peter did not know what to say, because the disciples were so terrified. (7) Then a cloud appeared and covered them (*possibly the presence of God*), and a voice from the cloud said, "This is my Son, whom I love. Listen to him!" (8) Suddenly, when they looked around, they saw no one with them except Jesus. (9) As they were walking down the mountainside, Jesus told them not to tell anyone what they had seen until the Son of Man (*see Daniel 7:13-14*) had risen from the dead. (10) The disciples did not tell anyone, but asked each other, "What does 'rising from the dead' mean?" (11) And the disciples asked Jesus, "Why do the teachers of the law of Moses say that Elijah must come first?" (12) Jesus said to them, "It is true, Elijah does come first, and restores all things. Why then is it written that the Son of Man must suffer and be rejected? (13) But I tell you the truth: Elijah has come, and they treated him very badly, just as it was written about him."

Luke 9:29-36 - (29) As Jesus was praying, the appearance of his face changed, and his clothes became bright and shining white. (30) Suddenly two men—Moses and Elijah—appeared in glorious light and began talking with Jesus. (31) They spoke to him about his coming departure (*ascension*) from the earth, which he was about to bring to fulfillment in Jerusalem. (32) Peter, James, and John were very tired, but when they woke up, they saw Jesus' glory and Moses and Elijah standing with him. (33) As Moses and Elijah were leaving Jesus, Peter said, "Master, it is good for us to be here. Let me make three tents—one for you, one for Moses, and one for Elijah." Peter was confused and did not know what he was saying. (34) While Peter was talking, a cloud (*probably the presence of God*) appeared and covered them. As the cloud surrounded them, they were terrified. (35) A voice came from the cloud and said, "This is my Son; listen to him." (36) After the voice had spoken, the disciples were alone with Jesus. And the disciples did not tell anyone what they had seen.

---

239 - Jesus Frees a Boy From a Demon
(Matthew 17:14-21, Mark 9:14-29, Luke 9:37-43)

Matthew 17:14-21 - (14) When Jesus and his disciples came down from the mountainside, they met a crowd of people, and a man came and fell on his knees before Jesus and said, (15) "Lord, have mercy on my son. He has seizures and experiences tremendous suffering. He often falls into the fire or into the water. (16) I brought him to your disciples, but they could not heal him. (17) You unbelieving and perverse generation of Israel, how long will I stay with you? How long will I put up with you? Bring your son to me." (18) Jesus rebuked the demon, and it came out of the boy, and he was healed immediately. (19) Then the disciples came to Jesus in private and asked, "Why couldn't we cast the demon out of the boy?" (20-21) Jesus said to them, "Because you have so little faith. I tell you the truth: If you have faith as small as a mustard seed, you can say to this mountain, 'Move from this place to another place,' and it will move. Nothing will be impossible for you."

Mark 9:14-29 - (14) When Jesus and the disciples came down from the mountainside, they met the other disciples and saw a large crowd of people around them and the teachers of the law of Moses arguing with them. (15) As soon as the people saw Jesus, they were overcome with wonder and ran to greet him. (16) Jesus asked them, "What are you arguing with them about?" (17) A man in the crowd answered, "Teacher, I brought you my son who is demon-possessed (*demonized*) and so he cannot speak. (18) The demon attacks him and throws him to the ground. He foams at the mouth, grinds his teeth, and his body becomes stiff. I asked your disciples to cast out the demon, but they couldn't do it." (19) Jesus said to him, "Oh! You unbelieving generation of Israel, how long must I stay with you? How long will I tolerate you? Bring your son to me." (20) So they brought the boy to Jesus. And when the demon saw him, it immediately threw the boy into a severe convulsion. He fell to the ground and rolled around, foaming at the mouth. (21) Jesus asked the boy's father, "How long has your son been acting like this?" The father answered, "Since he was a child. (22) The demon tries to kill him by throwing him into fire or water. But if you can do anything, please have mercy on us and help us." (23) Jesus said, "Why do you ask me if I can help you? Everything is possible for a person who believes." (24) Immediately the boy's father yelled out, "I do believe! Help me overcome my unbelief!" (25) When Jesus saw that a crowd of people was running toward them, he rebuked the demon, saying, "You deaf and mute evil spirit, I command you to come out of him and never enter him again!" (26) The demon cried out and shook the boy violently and came out of him. When the demon left, the boy looked like a corpse, so that many people said, "He's dead." (27) But Jesus took the hand of the boy and lifted him to his feet, and he stood up. (28) After Jesus had entered the house, his disciples asked him privately, "Why couldn't we cast out that demon from the boy?" (29) Jesus said, "Because this kind of demon can be cast out only by prayer (*and fasting*)."

Luke 9:37-43 - (37) On the next day, when Jesus and the disciples walked down the mountainside, a large crowd met him. (38) A man in the crowd called out, "Teacher, I beg you to help my son, for he is my only child. (39) A demon seizes him and he suddenly screams; it causes him to have convulsive seizures so that he foams at the mouth. The demon seldom leaves him, and it is destroying his life. (40) I begged your disciples to cast the demon out of my son, but they could not do it." (41) Jesus said, "You faithless and perverted generation of Israel; how long can I stay with you and put up with you? Bring your son to me." (42) As the boy was going to Jesus, the demon threw him to the ground in a convulsion. But Jesus rebuked the demon, healed the boy and gave him back to his father. (43) And all the people were amazed at the majesty of God.

----

240 - Jesus Speaks About His Death and Resurrection
(Matthew 17:22-23, Mark 9:30-31, Luke 9:43-45)

Matthew 17:22-23 - (22) When Jesus and his disciples gathered together in Galilee, he said to them, "The Son of Man (*see Daniel 7:13-14*) will soon be delivered over to the custody of men. (23) They will kill him, but on the third day he will be raised to life." And the disciples became very troubled.

Mark 9:30-31 - (30) Jesus and his disciples left that place and walked through Galilee.

Jesus did not want anyone to know where they were, (31) because he was teaching his disciples. He said to them, "The Son of Man (*see Daniel 7:13-14*) is going to be delivered over to the custody of men. They will kill him, and after three days he will rise from the dead." But the disciples did not understand what he was telling them and were afraid to ask him about it.

Luke 9:43-45 - (43) While everyone was still in awe at all that Jesus had done, he said to his disciples, (44) "Listen carefully to me! I tell you the truth: The Son of Man (*see Daniel 7:13-14*) is going to be delivered into the custody of men." (45) But the disciples did not understand what Jesus was telling them because its meaning was hidden from them, and they were afraid to ask him what he meant.

241 - Jesus Teaches About the Temple Tax in Capernaum
(Matthew 17:24-27)

Matthew 17:24-27 - (24) When Jesus and his disciples entered Capernaum, the collectors of the annual temple tax of two drachma (worth about two days' wages) came to Peter and asked him, "Doesn't your teacher pay the temple tax?" (25) Peter said, "Yes, he does." When Peter went into his house, Jesus asked him, "What do you think, Simon (*Peter*)? From whom do the kings of the earth collect duty and taxes—from their own children or from others?" (26) Peter said, "From others." So Jesus said, "Then their children do not pay taxes. (27) But so that we will not offend anyone, go to the lake and throw out your fishing line. Open the mouth of the first fish you catch, and you will find a four-drachma coin in its mouth. Take it and give it to them for my tax and yours."

242 - The Greatest in the Kingdom of God
(Matthew 18:1, Mark 9:33-34, Luke 9:46)

Matthew 18:1 - At that time the disciples came to Jesus and asked him, "Who is the greatest in the kingdom of heaven (*God*)?"

Mark 9:33-34 - (33) When they went into the house (*probably Peter's house*) in Capernaum, Jesus asked his disciples, "What were you arguing about when we were walking on the road?" (34) But his disciples did not say anything, because they had been talking about who was the greatest among them.

Luke 9:46 - The disciples started arguing among themselves about which one of them would be the greatest.

243 - Disciples Must Become Like Little Children
(Matthew 18:2-4, Mark 9:35, Luke 9:47-48)

Matthew 18:2-4 - (2) Jesus called a little child to him and had him stand among them. (3) And he said, "I tell you the truth: Unless you change and become like little children, you will not enter the kingdom of heaven (*God*). (4) Therefore, whoever humbles himself like this child will be the greatest in the kingdom of heaven (*God*).

Mark 9:35 - Sitting down, Jesus called the Twelve Apostles together and said to them, "Whoever wants to be first must be the last, and the servant of all."

Luke 9:47-48 - (47) Knowing what they were arguing about, Jesus took a little child and had him stand beside him. (48) For it is the one who is least among you all who is the greatest."

244 - Jesus Speaks About Little Children
(Matthew 18:5-6,10-14, Mark 9:36-37,42, Luke 9:48)

Matthew 18:5-6 - Jesus said, (6) "And whoever receives such a child in my name receives me." (6) If anyone causes one of these little children—who believe in me—to sin, it would be much better for them to have a large millstone hung around their neck and be thrown into the deep sea to drown."

Matthew 18:10-14 - Jesus said, (10-11) "Make sure that you do not mistreat one of these little children. For I tell you the truth: Their angels in heaven always see the face of my Father in heaven. (12) Tell me what you think: If a man owns 100 sheep, and one of them wanders away and gets lost, will he not leave the 99 sheep on the hill grazing and go to search for the one that is lost? (13) I tell you the truth: When he finds the lost sheep, he is happier for that one sheep than for the 99 that were not lost. (14) In the same way, your Father in heaven does not want one of these little children to be lost (to perish)."

Mark 9:36-37, 42 - (36) And then he had a little child come and stand among them. Taking the child in his arms, he said to them, (37) "Whoever receives one of these little children in my name receives me; and whoever receives me does not receive me but the one who sent me into this world." (42) Jesus said, "If anyone causes one of these little children—those who believe in me—to sin, it would be much better for them if a large millstone were hung around their neck and they were thrown into the sea."

Luke 9:48 - Then Jesus said to his disciples, "Whoever welcomes a little child in my name welcomes me; and whoever welcomes me welcomes the one who sent me into this world.

---

245 - Jesus' Warning About Sin
(Matthew 18:7-9, Mark 9:43-50)

Matthew 18:7-9 - (7) Jesus said, "How terrible (*woe*) for the world because of the temptations that cause people to sin! It is necessary that temptations will come, but how terrible for the person through whom these temptations come! (8) If your hand or your foot causes you to sin, cut it off and throw it away. For it is much better for you to enter eternal life with one hand or one foot than to be thrown into eternal fire. (9) And if your eye causes you to sin, pluck it out and throw it away. For it is much better for you to enter eternal life with one eye than be thrown into the fire of hell (*gehenna*)."

Mark 9:43-50 - Jesus said, (43) "If your hand causes you to sin, you should cut it off. It is much better for you to enter eternal life with one hand than to be thrown into hell (*gehenna*) with two hands, because in hell (*gehenna*) the fire never goes out. (44-45) And if your foot causes you to sin, you should cut it off. It is much better for you to enter eternal life with one foot than to be thrown into hell (*gehenna*) with two feet. (46-47) And if your eye causes you to sin, you should pluck it out. It is much better for you to enter the kingdom of God with one eye than to be thrown into hell (*gehenna*) with two eyes, (48) because in hell (*gehenna*) the worms that eat them do not die, and the fire does not go out. (49) Everyone will be salted with fire. (50) Salt is good, but if it does not taste like salt anymore, it can never be made to taste like salt again. You should have salt among yourselves, and be at peace with one another."

---

246 - For or Against Jesus
(Mark 9:38-41, Luke 9:49-50)

Mark 9:38-41 - (38) John said to Jesus, "Teacher, we saw someone casting out demons in your name and we told him to stop, for he was not one of us." (39) But Jesus said, "Do not tell him to stop. For no one who does a miracle in my name can then say bad things about me, (40) because whoever is not against us is for us. (41) I tell you the truth: Whoever gives you a cup of water in my name because you belong to the Messiah (*Christ*) will certainly not lose their reward."

Luke 9:49-50 - (49) John said, "Master, we saw a man casting demons out of people in your name, and we tried to stop him because he is not one of us." (50) Jesus said, "Do not stop him, because whoever is not against you is for you."

-----

247 - When People Sin Against You
(Matthew 18:15-17)

Matthew 18:15-17 - Jesus said, (15) "If your brother or sister sins (*does something wrong*) against you, go in private and tell them their sin against you, just between the two of you. If they listen to you, you have restored your relationship with them. (16) But if they refuse to listen to you, take one or two other believers along with you, for as it is written in Deuteronomy 19:15, 'Let every matter be settled by the testimony of two or three witnesses.' (17) If they still refuse to listen, tell it to the church; and if they refuse to listen to the church, treat them as you would a pagan or a tax collector.

-----

248 - When Believers Agree
(Matthew 18:18-20)

Matthew 18:18-20 - Jesus said, (18) "I tell you the truth: Whatever you bind on earth will have already been bound in heaven, and whatever you set free on earth will have already been set free in heaven. (19) Again, I tell you the truth: When two believers on earth agree about anything they ask for, it will be done for them by my Father in heaven. (20) For where two or three believers gather in my name, there I am with them (*in their midst*)!"

-----

249 - Forgiveness
(Matthew 18:21-22, Luke 17:3-4)

Matthew 18:21-22 - (21) Then Peter came and asked Jesus, "Lord, how many times must I forgive a fellow believer who sins against me? Do I have to forgive him up to seven times?" (22) Jesus said to him, "I tell you the truth: You must not just forgive a fellow believer seven times but 77 times."

Luke 17:3-4 - (3) "If another believer sins against you, talk with them; and if they repent, forgive them. (4) Even if they sin against you seven times in a day and seven times come back to you saying, 'I repent,' you must forgive them."

250 - The Parable of an Unforgiving Servant
(Matthew 18:23-35)

Matthew 18:23-35 - Jesus told this parable (*story*): (23) "Therefore, the kingdom of heaven (*God*) is like a king who told his servants to pay back all the money they owed him. (24) As he began to settle his accounts, a servant who owed the king 10,000 talents (*about 20 years' wages*) was brought to him. (25) Because the servant was not able to pay, the king ordered that he and his family and all that he owned be sold to repay his debt. (26) After hearing this, the servant fell on his knees before him, begging, 'Please be patient with me, and I will pay you back everything I owe you.' (27) The king showed mercy toward the servant and forgave him his entire debt and let him go. (28) "But when that servant left, he found one of his fellow servants who owed him 100 denarii (*about a day's wages*). He grabbed him and began to choke him, demanding, 'Pay me back all that you owe me!' (29) His fellow servant fell to his knees and begged him, 'Please be patient with me, and I will pay you back everything I owe you.' (30) But he refused to forgive him his debt. Instead, he had the man thrown into prison until he could pay his entire debt. (31) When the other servants saw what had happened, they were very angry and went and told their king everything that had happened. (32) Then the king called the servant in and said, 'You are a wicked servant! I forgave you of all your debt because you begged me. (33) You should have had mercy on your fellow servant just as I had mercy on you.' (34) In his anger the king handed him over to the jailers to be punished, until he paid back all he owed. (35) Jesus said, "This is how my Father in heaven will treat each of you unless you forgive your fellow believers from your heart."

251 - The Shepherd and the Sheep
(John 10:1-5)

John 10:1-5 - (1) Jesus said, "You Pharisees, I tell you the truth: Whoever does not enter the sheep pen by the gate, but climbs in by any other way, that one is a thief and a robber. (2) The one who enters by the gate is the shepherd of the sheep. (3) The gatekeeper opens the gate for him, and the sheep listen to his voice. He calls his sheep by name and leads them out. (4) When the shepherd brings out all his sheep, he walks ahead of them, and his sheep follow him because they know his voice. (5) But his sheep will never follow a stranger; in fact, they will run away from him because they do not recognize a stranger's voice."

252 - Jesus is the Good Shepherd
(John 10:6-18)

John 10:6-18 - (6) Jesus had spoken to the Pharisees using a parable but they did not understand what he was telling them. (7) Therefore Jesus explained the parable to them: "I tell you the truth: I am the gate of the sheep! (8) All who have come before me are thieves and robbers, but the sheep would not listen to them. (9) I am the gate! Whoever enters through me will be saved. They will come in and go out, and find pasture. (10) The thief comes only to steal and kill and destroy, but I have come into this world that they will have life abundantly (*life to its fullest*). (11) I am the good shepherd! The good shepherd lays down his life for his sheep. (12) A hired worker is not the shepherd and does not own the sheep. So when he sees a wolf coming, he runs away and leaves the sheep. Then the wolf attacks and kills the sheep and scatters them. (13) The hired worker runs away because he is simply an employee and does not care about the life of the sheep. (14) I am the good shepherd! I know my sheep, and my sheep know me—(15) just as the Father knows me and I know the Father—and I lay down my life for my sheep. (16) I have other sheep that are not from this sheep pen. I must bring them also. They too will listen to my voice, so that there will be one flock under one shepherd. (17) The reason my Father loves me is because I lay down my life—and I will take it up again. (18) No one takes my life from me, but I lay it down by my own choice. I have authority to lay my life down, and I have the authority to take it up again. This command I received from my Father."

253 - Jews Disagree About Jesus
(John 10:19-21)

John 10:19-21 - (19) Once again the Jews were divided over what Jesus was saying. (20) Many of them said, "He is demon-possessed (*demonized*)! He is insane! Why even listen to him?" (21) But others said, "These are not the sayings of someone who is possessed by a demon. A demon cannot heal a man who was born blind."

254 - Jesus Leaves Galilee for Perea
(Matthew 19:1-2, Mark 10:1, Luke 9:51)

Matthew 19:1-2 - (1) When Jesus finished his teaching, he left Galilee and traveled into the region of Judea to the region of Perea on the eastern side of the Jordan River. (2) Large crowds of people followed him there, and he healed them.

Mark 10:1 - Then Jesus left Capernaum and went into the region of Judea and east of the Jordan River. Again large crowds of people came to Jesus, and he taught them as was his practice.

Luke 9:51 - The time for Jesus to be taken up into heaven was getting close, so he immediately left Galilee and began to walk toward Jerusalem.

(*The primarily Jewish region east of the Jordan River was called Perea, today in modern Jordan. Perea occupied the eastern side of the Jordan River valley, from about one third the way down from Lake Galilee to about one third the way down the eastern shore of the Dead Sea. Herod Antipas, a son of Herod the Great, was the governor of both Galilee and Perea*).

255 - A Samaritan Town
(Luke 9:52-56)

Luke 9:52-56 - (52) And Jesus sent messengers ahead of him, and they went into a Samaritan village to get things ready for him to come. (53) But the Samaritans would not welcome Jesus, because he was traveling to Jerusalem. (54) When the disciples James and John saw this, they asked

Jesus, "Lord, do you want us to call fire (*judgment*) down from heaven to destroy them?" (55) But Jesus turned and rebuked them. Then Jesus and his disciples walked on to another village.

(The Samaritans were the offspring of Israelites left behind from the Assyrian exile of the northern kings and non-Jews. Because of this, there was hostility between the Jews and Samaritans).

256 - Jesus Heals Ten Men With a Skin Disease
(Luke 17:11-19)

Luke 17:11-19 - (11) Jesus was walking toward Jerusalem and was along the border between Samaria and Galilee. (12) As he was going into a village, 10 men with a skin disease (*possibly leprosy*) met him. They stood at a distance (13) and yelled out, "Jesus, Master, have mercy on us!" (14) When Jesus saw them, he said, "Go, show yourselves to the temple priests." As they were going to the temple priests, they were healed (*cleansed*). (15) When one of them saw that he was healed, he went back to Jesus, praising God in a loud voice. (16) He was a Samaritan and threw himself at Jesus' feet and thanked him. (17) Jesus asked him, "I healed 10 of you. Where are the other nine? (18) No one has come back to praise God except this foreign Samaritan?" (19) Then Jesus told the Samaritan, "Stand up and go; your faith has healed you."

257 - Jesus Sends Seventy-Two Disciples on a Mission
(Luke 10:1-12)

Luke 10:1-12 - (1) After this the Lord chose 72 disciples and sent them two by two ahead of him to every town and place he would pass through on his way to Jerusalem. (2) Jesus told them, "Yes, there is an abundant harvest, but there are only a few workers to gather it in. Therefore, ask the Lord of the harvest to send out workers into his harvest field. (3) Go now! I send you out like lambs among wolves. (4) Do not take a money bag or pouch or sandals; and do not stop to greet anyone along the road. (5) When you enter a home, say, 'God's peace be on this home.' (6) If a person of peace lives there, your blessing of peace will rest on them; if not, it will return to you. (7) Stay only in that home and do not move around from house to house; eat and drink whatever is given you, because a worker deserves to be paid. (8) "When you enter a town and are welcomed, eat whatever they give you. (9) Heal the sick who are there and tell them, 'The kingdom of God has come near to you.' (10) But when you enter a town and are not welcomed, stand in its streets and declare, (11) 'We wipe the dirt of your town from our feet as a warning to you. You can be sure of this: The kingdom of God has come near.' (12) I tell you the truth: It will be much better on the day of judgment for Sodom than for that town."

258 - Jesus Condemns Jewish Cities
(Matthew 11:20-24, Luke 10:13-16)

Matthew 11:20-24 - (20) Then Jesus began to denounce the Jewish towns (*around Lake Galilee*) in which he did most of his miracles, but they refused to repent and turn to God. (21) Jesus said, "How terrible it will be for the Jewish towns of Corazin (*located around 2 miles/3 km from Capernaum on the top northwestern shore of Lake Galilee*) and Bethsaida (*located around 6 miles/10 km from Capernaum on the northeastern shore of the Sea of Galilee*)! For if the miracles that I did in you were done in Tyre and Sidon, they would have repented long ago, wearing coarse cloths and covered with ashes. (22) But I tell you the truth: It will be much better for the non-Jewish towns of Tyre and Sidon on the day of God's judgment than for you. (23) And you, Capernaum (*located on the northwestern shore of Lake Galilee*), will you be lifted to the heavens? Absolutely not! You will go down to the realm of the dead (*hades*)! For if the miracles that were done in you had been done in Sodom, it would still exist today. (24) I tell you the truth: It will be much better for Sodom on the day of God's judgment than for you."

Luke 10:13-16 - Jesus declared, (13) "How terrible for the Jewish towns of Chorazin! (*located around 2 miles/3 km from Capernaum on the top northwestern shore of Lake Galilee*) and Bethsaida (*located around 6 miles/10 km from Capernaum on the northeastern shore of the Sea of Galilee*). For if the miracles that I did in you had been done in the non-Jewish cities of Tyre and Sidon, they would have repented in sackcloth and ashes a long time ago. (14) But it will be much better for Tyre and Sidon at God's judgment than for you. (15) And will the Jewish town of Capernaum (*located on the northwestern shore of Lake Galilee*) be lifted up to the heavens? Absolutely not! You will descend into the realm of the dead (*hades*). (16) Whoever listens to you listens to me; whoever rejects you rejects me; but whoever rejects me rejects him who sent me into this world."

259 - Jesus' Seventy-Two Disciples Return
(Luke 10:17-20)

Luke 10:17-20 - (17) The 72 disciples returned from their mission journey full of joy, and said to Jesus, "Lord, even the demons obey what we say in your name." (18) Jesus said to them, "I saw Satan fall like a lightning bolt from heaven. (19) I gave you God's authority to walk over snakes and scorpions and to overcome all the power of Satan our enemy. Nothing can hurt you! (20) However, do not rejoice that demons obey your commands, but rejoice that your names are written in heaven."

260 - The Prayer of Jesus
(Matthew 11:25-27, Luke 10:21-24)

Matthew 11:25-27 - (25) At that time Jesus prayed, "I praise you, Father, Lord of heaven and earth, because your ways are hidden from the wise and educated, but are revealed to little children. (26) Yes, Father, for this was your gracious will. (27) And all things have been given to me by my Father. Only the Father knows the Son, and only the Son knows the Father, and those to whom the Son chooses to reveal him."

Luke 10:21-24 - (21) At that time Jesus was full of joy through the Holy Spirit and prayed: "I praise you, Father—Lord of heaven and earth—because you have hidden these things from the wise and educated, and have revealed them to little children. Yes, Father, for this was your good pleasure. (22) All things have been delivered to me by my Father. No one knows who the Son is except the Father, and no one knows who the Father is except the Son and those to whom the Son chooses to reveal him." (23) Then Jesus turned to his disciples and said in private, "Blessed are your eyes because you see what you see. (24) For I tell you the truth: Many prophets and kings wanted to see what you see but did not see it, and to hear what you hear but did not hear it."

261 - Rest for the Heavy-Burdened in Life
(Matthew 11:28-30)

Matthew 11:28-30 - (28) Then Jesus declared, "Come to me, all who are tired of carrying the heavy burdens of life, and I will give you rest. (29) Live the way I live (*take my yoke upon you*) and learn from me, because I am gentle and humble in heart, and you will find rest for your souls. (30) For my way of life (*yoke*) is easy and my burden is light."

262 - The Parable of a Good Samaritan
(Luke 10:29-37)

Luke 10:29-37 - (29) But the expert in the law of Moses wanted to prove that he was a righteous person, so he asked Jesus, "Who is my neighbor?" (30) So Jesus answered him in this parable (*story*): "A man was walking down the road that leads from Jerusalem to Jericho, and he was attacked by robbers. They took his clothes, beat him, and left him lying there nearly dead. (*The winding road from Jericho to Jerusalem was around 18 miles/29 km long through the dry desert. There were many robbers along this road*). (31) A Jewish priest walked down the same road, but when he saw the dying man, he passed by him on the other side of the road. (32) Also, a Jewish Levite walked down that road and saw the dying man, but he passed by him on the other side of the road. (33) But when a Samaritan walked down that road and saw the dying man, he had compassion on him. (34) He poured oil and wine on his wounds and bandaged them. Then, putting him on his donkey, he took the man to a hotel (*inn*) and took care of him. (35) The next day the Samaritan paid the hotel manager two coins (*denarii*), and told him, 'Take care of him, and when I return from my journey, I will pay you for any extra costs you may have when I return.'" (36) Jesus asked the Jewish teacher, "Which of these three men do you think was a neighbor to the man who was attacked by robbers?" (37) The expert in the law of Moses said, "The one who had compassion for him and showed him mercy." Jesus said to him, "You go and do the same for others."

263 - Jesus Visits Mary and Martha in Bethany
(Luke 10:38-42)

Luke 10:38-42 - (38) As Jesus and his disciples were walking toward Jerusalem, they entered a village (*Bethany, on the Mount of Olives*) where a woman named Martha opened her home to Jesus. (39) She had a sister named Mary, who sat at the Lord's feet listening to his teaching. (40) But Martha was distracted by all the preparations that had to be done. So she asked Jesus, "Lord, Mary has left me to serve all alone; don't you care? Tell her to help me!" Jesus said to her, (41) "Martha, Martha, why are you anxious and worried about so many things? (42) For there is only one thing that is truly important. And Mary has chosen what is truly good, and I will not take it away from her."

264 - Jesus Teaches How to Pray
(Luke 11:1-4)

Luke 11:1-4 - (1) One day Jesus was praying in a certain place. When he finished, one of his disciples said to him, "Lord, teach us to pray, just as John the Baptizer taught his disciples to pray." (2) Jesus said to them, "When you pray, say, 'Father, holy be your name, your kingdom come. (3) Give us our daily bread. (4) Forgive us our sins, as we forgive everyone who sins against us. And lead us not into temptation.' "

265 - Keep Asking, Keep Seeking, Keep Knocking
(Luke 11:5-13)

Luke 11:5-13 - (5) Then Jesus told them this parable (*story*): "Suppose you go to your friend at midnight and tell him, 'My dear friend, lend me three loaves of bread, (6) because a guest has come to visit my home, and I have nothing to feed him.' (7) And suppose your friend says, 'Don't bother me! My door is already locked, and my family is all sleeping. I can't get up out of bed and give you any bread.' (8) I tell you the truth: Even though your friend will not at first get out of bed to give you bread, yet if you are persistent and keep asking, he will finally get up and give you as much as you need. (9) I tell you the truth: Keep asking and it will be given to you; keep seeking and you will find; keep knocking and the door will be opened to you. (10) For everyone who asks receives; everyone who seeks finds; and to the one who knocks, the door will be opened. (11) Tell me, which of you fathers, if your son asks for a fish, will give him a snake instead? (12) Or if he asks you for an egg, will give him a scorpion? (13) So then if earthly fathers—who have evil in their hearts—give good gifts to their children, how much more will the Father in heaven give the Holy Spirit to those who ask him!"

266 - Jesus Attends Hanukkah Feast in Jerusalem
(John 10:22)

John 10:22 - It was winter (*December*) and the time to celebrate the feast of Dedication in Jerusalem (*Hanukkah or the Festival of Lights, which celebrates the rededication of the temple in December 164 BC*).

267 - Jesus and the Father Are One
(John 10:23-30)

John 10:23-30 - (23) Jesus was walking in Solomon's Colonnade along the eastern side of the temple complex. (24) The Jews who were there gathered around Jesus, and said, "How long will you keep us wondering? If you you are the Messiah (Christ), tell us in plain language." (25) Jesus said to them, "I have already told you, but you refuse to believe. The works of power (*miracles*) that I do in my Father's name tell you who I am, (26) but you don't believe because you are not my sheep. (27) I know my sheep. My sheep listen to my voice and follow me. (28) And I give them eternal life, and they will never perish; for no one has the power to seize them out of my hand. (29) My Father, who has given them to me, is greater than all things; no one has the power to seize my sheep out of my Father's grasp. (30) The Father and I are one!"

268 - Religious Leaders Try to Kill Jesus
(John 10:31-39)

John 10:31-39 - (31) Because Jesus said that he was one with the Father, his Jewish opponents picked up rocks to throw at him. (32) But Jesus said to them, "I have shown you many good works of power from the Father. For which one of these good works do you want to stone me to death?" (33) The Jews said, "We do not want to stone you because you do good works, but because you blaspheme—you are a mere man, but claim to be God." (34) Jesus said to them, "It is written in

Psalm 82:6, 'I have said you are "gods." ' (35) And if he called them 'gods,' to whom the word of God came—and we know that God's word cannot be broken—(36) what about the one whom the Father set apart as his very own and sent into this world? Why then do you accuse me of blasphemy because I said to you, 'I am the Son of God'? (37) Don't believe me unless I do the miraculous works of my Father. (38) But if I do them—even if you do not believe in me—believe in the miraculous works that I do. Then you will know and understand that the Father is in me, and I am in the Father." (39) Once again, the Jewish religious leaders tried to arrest Jesus, but he escaped.

269 - Jesus Travels to the Region of Perea
(John 10:40-42)

John 10:40-42 - (40) Then Jesus traveled east across the Jordan River to the place where John had been baptizing people in the early days. (*This region east of the Jordan River was known as Perea, in modern Jordan*). (41) There Jesus stayed, and many people came to him. They said, "Although John never did a miraculous sign (*miracle*), everything he said about Jesus was true." (42) And in the region of Perea many people believed in Jesus.

270 - Enter Through the Narrow Door
(Luke 13:22-30)

Luke 13:22-30 - (22) As Jesus journeyed toward Jerusalem, he taught in the towns and villages through which he traveled. (23) Someone asked him, "Lord, are only a few people going to be saved?" Jesus said, (24) "Make every effort to enter through the narrow door, because I tell you the truth, many will try to enter and will not be able to. (25) Once the owner of the house gets up and closes the door, you will stand outside knocking and begging, 'Sir, open the door for us.' But the owner will declare, 'I don't know you or where you come from!' (26) Then you will tell him, 'We ate and drank with you, and you taught in our streets.' (27) But the owner will declare, 'I don't know you or where you come from! Go away from me, all you workers of evil!' (28) There will be weeping and grinding of teeth there, when you see Abraham, Isaac, Jacob, and all the (*Old Testament*) prophets in the kingdom of God, but you have been thrown out. (29) People will come from east and west and north and south, and will take their places at the banquet feast in the kingdom of God. (30) For there are those who are last who will be first, and those who are first who will be last."

271 - Jesus is Warned About Herod Antipas
(Luke 13:31)

Luke 13:31 - At that time some Pharisees came to Jesus and said to him, "Hurry, leave this place because Herod Antipas (*a son of Herod the Great and the ruler of Galilee and Perea*) wants to kill you."

272 - Jesus Speaks About His Death and Resurrection
(Luke 13:32-33)

Luke 13:32-33 - (32) Jesus said to them, "Go tell that fox, 'Today and tomorrow I will continue to cast out demons and heal the sick, and on the third day I will reach my goal.' (33) Believe me, I will keep walking today and tomorrow and the next day, because surely no prophet can die outside of Jerusalem!"

273 - Jesus Heals a Sick Man on the Sabbath
(Luke 14:1-6)

Luke 14:1-6 - (1) Jesus went to eat in the house of a prominent Pharisee on the Sabbath day, and he was being carefully watched to see what he would do. (2) There was a man there who was suffering from a swollen body (*possibly dropsy*). (3) Jesus asked the Pharisees and the experts in the law of Moses, "Is it lawful to heal on the Sabbath day?" (4) But they did not say anything. So Jesus took hold of the man, healed him, and sent him away. (5) Then Jesus said to the religious leaders, "If one of you had a child or an ox that fell into a well on the Sabbath day, you would immediately pull it out." (6) Again, they did not say anything.

274 - Live a Life of Humility
(Luke 14:7-11)

Luke 14:7-11 - (7) When Jesus saw how the guests chose the places of honor at the table (*sitting on each side of the host*), he told them this parable (*story*): (8) "When someone invites you to a wedding feast, do not take the place of honor, because a more important person than you may have been invited. (9) And then the wedding host who had invited both of you will tell you, 'Give this person your seat of honor.' Then you will be put to shame, and you will have to sit in a less honorable seat. (10) Instead, when you are invited, take the least important place, so that when your host comes, he will tell you, 'Friend, move to a more honored place at the table.' Then you will be honored in the presence of all the other guests. (11) For whoever exalts himself will be humbled, and whoever humbles himself will be exalted."

275 - Compassion for the Poor
(Luke 14:12-15)

Luke 14:12-15 - (12) Then Jesus said to his host, "When you give a luncheon or dinner, do not invite your friends, family, relatives, or your rich neighbors; if you do, they might invite you back to repay you. (13) Instead, when you give a banquet, invite the poor, crippled, lame, and blind. (14) If you do, you will be blessed. Although they cannot repay you, you will be repaid at the resurrection of the righteous." (15) When someone at the table heard this, he said to Jesus, "Blessed is the one who will eat at the feast in the kingdom of God."

276 - The Parable of a Wedding Banquet
(Luke 14:16-24)

Luke 14:16-24 - (16) Jesus told this parable (*story*): "A man was preparing a great banquet and invited many guests. (17) At the time of the banquet he sent his servant to tell everyone who had been invited, 'Come, for everything is now ready!' (18) But they all made excuses. The first person said, 'I have just bought land and I must go see it. Please excuse me.' (19) Another person said, 'I have just bought five teams of oxen and I'm on my way to try them out. Please excuse me.' (20) Still another person said, 'I have just got married, so I can't come.' (21) The servant returned and told his master about all the excuses that those who were invited had made. Then the owner of the house became angry and ordered his servant, 'Go out quickly into the streets and alleys of the town and bring in the poor, crippled, blind, and lame.' (22) The servant said, 'Sir, what you asked us to do, we have already done, but there is still room in the banquet room.' (23) Then the master told his servant, 'Go out to the roads and country paths and persuade people to come in, so that my house will be full. (24) For I tell you the truth: Not one of these people who were invited will eat at my banquet.'"

277 - The Cost of Following Jesus
(Matthew 10:37-38, Luke 14:25-33)

Matthew 10:37-39 - (37) "Anyone who loves their father, mother, son, or daughter more than me is not worthy of me. (38) Whoever does not take up their cross and follow me is not worthy of me. (39) Whoever finds their life will lose it, and whoever loses their life for my sake will find it."

Luke 14:25-32 - (25) Large crowds were walking with Jesus, and he turned to them and said, (26) "Whoever comes to me and does not hate father and mother, wife and children, brothers and sisters—yes, and even their own life—such a person cannot be my disciple. (27) And whoever does not carry their cross and follow me cannot be my disciple. (28) For if any of you wants to build a tower, won't he first sit down and find out what it will cost to make sure he has enough money to finish it? (29) For if you lay the foundation and are unable to finish it, (30) everyone who sees it will ridicule you, saying, 'He started to build, but was not able to finish it.' (31) Or suppose a king is about to go to war against an enemy king. Won't he sit down and determine whether his 10,000 soldiers can defeat his enemy's 20,000 soldiers? (32) If the king concludes that he is not able to win, he will send a delegation to his far-off enemy and will ask to make peace. (33) Jesus said, "In the same way, those of you who do not give up everything you have cannot be my disciple."

278 - Good Salt and Bad Salt
(Luke 14:34-35)

Luke 14:34-35 - Jesus said, (34) "Salt is good, but if it loses its saltiness, it cannot become salty again. (35) It is not useful either for the soil or for the manure pile. It is worthless and is thrown away. Whoever has ears to hear, let them hear!"

279 - Tax Collectors and Sinners Follow Jesus
Luke 15:1-2

Luke 15:1-2 - (1) Now many tax collectors and sinners were crowding around to hear Jesus. (2) But the Pharisees and teachers of the law of Moses complained, "Jesus welcomes sinners and eats with them."

280 - The Parable of the Lost Sheep
(Luke 15:3-7)

Luke 15:3-6 - (3) Then Jesus told this parable (*story*): (4) "Suppose someone has 100 sheep and loses one of them. Wouldn't he leave the 99 sheep in the field and search for the one lost sheep until he finds it? (5) And when he finds the lost sheep, he puts it on his shoulders rejoicing (6) and goes home. Then he calls together his friends and neighbors and says, 'Rejoice with me, because I have found my lost sheep!'" (7) Jesus said, "In the same way, I tell you the truth: There is more rejoicing in heaven over one sinner who repents and turns to God than over 99 righteous people who do not need to repent."

281 - The Parable of a Lost Coin
(Luke 15:8-10)

Luke 15:8-10 - Jesus told this parable (*story*): (8) "Suppose a woman has 10 silver coins and loses one of them. Wouldn't she light a lamp, sweep the house, and look everywhere until she finds it? (9) And when she finds the lost coin, she calls together her friends and neighbors and says, 'Rejoice with me, because I have found my lost coin!'" (10) Jesus said, "In the same way, I tell you the truth: There is rejoicing in the presence of God's angels over one sinner who repents and turns to God."

282 - The Parable of a Lost Son
(Luke 15:11-32)

Luke 15:11-32 - Jesus told this parable (*story*): (11) "There was a man who had two sons. (12) The younger son said to his father, 'Father, give me my share of the estate.' So the father divided his property between his two sons. (13) Not long after that, the younger son took all that he owned, and went on a journey to a faraway country where he wasted his wealth in sinful living. (14) After he spent all his money, there was a severe famine in that whole country, and he began to be in desperate need. (15) So he went and was hired by a citizen of that country to feed the pigs in the field. (16) He became so hungry that he even wanted to eat the pigs' food, but no one gave him anything. (17) When the son realized that his life had hit bottom, he said, 'My father's hired servants have plenty of food to eat, but here I am starving to death! (18) I will go back to my father and tell him, "Father, I have sinned against heaven and against you. (19) I am no longer worthy to be called your son, so just make me one of your hired servants."' (20) So the son left and was on his way back to his father. But while the son was still a long way off, his father saw him and was filled with compassion for him; he ran to meet his son, threw his arms around him and kissed him. (21) The son said to him, 'Father, I have sinned against heaven (*God*) and against you. I am no longer worthy to be called your son.' (22) But the father told his servants, 'Go! Bring the best robe and put it on him. Put a ring on his finger and sandals on his feet. (23) Bring the well-fed calf and kill it. Let's have a feast and celebrate. (24) For my son was dead, but now he lives again; he was lost, but now he is found.' So they began to celebrate. (25) Meanwhile, the older son was working in the field. When he came near to the house, he heard music and dancing. (26) So he called one of the servants and asked him why everyone was celebrating. (27) He said to him, 'Your younger brother has come home, and your father has killed the well-fed calf because his son is back home safe and sound.' (28) The older brother became very angry and refused to go into the house and join the celebration. So his father went outside and pleaded with him. (29) But the older son told his father, 'Look! I've worked slaving for you many years, and I have done everything you have told me to do. But you never gave me even a young goat so that I could celebrate with my friends. (30) But when this son of yours who after wasting all your property with prostitutes comes home, you kill a well-fed calf for him!' (31) The father said to him, 'My son, you are always with me and everything I own is yours. (32) But we had to celebrate and rejoice, because your brother was dead and is now alive again. He was lost, but now he is found.'"

283 - The Parable of a Wise Manager
(Luke 16:1-12)

Luke 16:1-12 - (1) Jesus told his disciples this parable (*story*): "There was a rich man whose manager was accused of wasting his possessions. (2) So the rich man called his manager in and asked him, 'What are these bad reports that I am hearing about you? You need to give me an account of your management of my money, because you cannot be my manager any longer.' (3) The manager said to himself, 'What should I do now? My master is taking away my job. And I'm not strong enough to dig, and I'm ashamed to beg. (4) I know what I'll do so that, when I lose my job, people will welcome me into their homes.' (5) So the manager called in each person who owed money to his master. He asked the first person, 'How much do you owe my master?' (6) The man said, 'Around 900 gallons (3,000 *liters*) of olive oil.' The manager told him, 'Take your bill, sit down quickly, and write 450 gallons (1,500 *liters*)' (7) Then he asked the second person, 'How much do you owe my master?' He said, 'A thousand bushels of wheat.' The manager told him, 'Take your bill and write 800 bushels.' (8) The rich man praised the dishonest manager because he acted with good judgment (*shrewdness*). For the people of this world (*age*) are more shrewd when dealing with their own kind than are the people of the light. (9) I tell you, use the wealth of this world to make friends, so that when your earthly wealth is gone, you will be welcomed into eternal homes. (10) Whoever can be trusted with very little can also be trusted with much, and whoever is dishonest with very little will also be dishonest with much. (11) So if you have not been faithful in handling worldly wealth, who will trust you with true riches? (12) And if you have not been faithful with someone else's property, who will give you property of your own?"

284 - You Cannot Serve Both God and Money
(Luke 16:13)

Luke 16:13 - Jesus said, "No servant can serve two masters. Either he will hate the one and love the other, or he will be devoted to the one and despise the other. You cannot serve both God and money."

285 - Religious Leaders Mock Jesus
(Luke 16:14-15)

Luke 16:14-15 - (14) When the Pharisees heard this, they made fun of Jesus because they were lovers of money. (15) Jesus said to them, "You are those who justify yourselves in the eyes of others, but God knows your hearts. What people value highly in this world is detestable in God's sight."

286 - The Good News of the Kingdom of God
(Luke 16:16-17)

Luke 16:16-17 - Jesus said, (16) "The law of Moses and the (*Old Testament*) prophets was proclaimed until the coming of the prophet John. Since the coming of John, the gospel (*good news*) of the kingdom of God is being preached, and whoever has strong faith is entering it (*forcing their way into it*). (17) It is easier for heaven and earth to disappear than for the smallest stroke of a pen to be left out of the law of Moses."

287 - Divorce
(Luke 16:18)

Luke 16:18 - Jesus said, "Whoever divorces his wife and marries another woman commits adultery, and the man who marries a divorced woman commits adultery."

288 - The Parable of a Rich Man and Lazarus
(Luke 16:19-31)

Luke 16:19-31 - Jesus told this parable (*story*): (19) "There was a rich man who was dressed in purple and fine linen and lived in luxury every day. (20) A poor beggar named Lazarus—whose body was covered with sores—was laid at the rich man's gate (21), hoping to eat what fell from the rich man's table. Even the dogs came and licked Lazarus' sores. (22) Lazarus died and the angels carried him to Abraham's side. The rich man also died and was buried, (23) and was being tormented in the realm of the dead (*hades*). He looked up and saw Abraham far away and Lazarus at his side. (24) The rich man called out, 'Father Abraham, have compassion on me and send Lazarus to dip his finger in water and cool off my tongue, because I am suffering in this fire.' (25) "But Abraham said to the rich man, 'Son, you received all your luxurious things during your life on earth, while Lazarus only received bad things, but now he is comforted here and you are suffering. (26) And besides, a great canyon has been placed between us, so that no one is able to cross to either side.' (27) The rich man said, 'Then I beg you, Father Abraham, send Lazarus to my family, (28) for I have five brothers. Have Lazarus warn them, so that they will not also come to this place of torment.' (29) Abraham said, 'They can believe Moses and the (*Old Testament*) prophets; let them listen to them.' (30) But the rich man said, 'No, Father Abraham, for if someone from the dead goes to them, they will repent and turn to God.' (31) Abraham said to him, 'If they will not listen to Moses and the (*Old Testament*) prophets during their life on earth, they will not be convinced even if someone rises from the dead.' "

289 - Jesus Explains Coming Kingdom of God to Religious Leaders
(Luke 17:20-21)

Luke 17:20-21 - (20) Some Pharisees asked Jesus when the kingdom of God would come. Jesus said to them, "The kingdom of God is not something you can see with your eyes, (21) nor will people say, 'Here it is,' or 'There it is,' because the kingdom of God is within you (*or in the midst of you*)."

290 - Jesus Explains the Coming Kingdom of God to His Disciples
(Luke 17:22-35)

Luke 17:22-35 - (22) Then Jesus said to his disciples, "The time is coming when you will want to see one of the days of the Son of Man (*see Daniel 7:13-14*), but you will not see it. (23) People will tell you, 'There he is!' or, 'Here he is!' But do not run after them or follow them. (24) For the coming of the Son of Man will be like flashes of lightning; it will light up the sky from one end to the other. (25) But first he must suffer many things and be rejected by this generation in Israel. (26) Just as it was in the time of Noah, so also it will be in the time of the Son of Man. (27) People were eating, drinking, marrying, and being given in marriage up to the day Noah entered the ark. Then the flood came and destroyed them all. (28) It was the same in the time of Lot; people were eating and drinking, buying and selling, and planting and building. (29) But the day Lot left Sodom, fire and sulfur thundered down from heaven and destroyed them all. (30) This is how it will be on the day the Son of Man comes. (31) On that day no one who is on the housetop (*houses had flat roofs*) should go down inside the house to get their possessions. Likewise, those in the field should not go back for anything. (32) Remember Lot's wife! (33) Whoever seeks to save their life will lose it, but whoever loses their life will keep it. (34) I tell you the truth: On that night there will be two people in bed; one will be taken and the other left. (35) There will be two women grinding grain together; one will be taken and the other left."

291 - Disciples Ask Jesus Where the Kingdom Will Come
(Luke 17:36-37)

Luke 17:36-37 - Then the disciples asked, "Lord, where will this take place?" Jesus said, "Where there are dead bodies, there vultures will gather to eat them."

292 - The Parable of Persistent Prayer for Justice
(Luke 18:1-8)

Luke 18:1-8 - (1) Then Jesus told this parable (*story*) to teach his disciples that they should always pray and never give up. (2) He said, "In a certain town there was a judge who did not fear God or care about people. (3) But there was a widow in that town who kept going to the judge, pleading, 'Give me justice against my enemy.' (4) For a long time the judge refused to listen, but finally he said to himself, 'Although I do not fear God or care about people, (5) but because this widow keeps bothering me, I will give her justice, so that she won't one day come back and attack me!' " (6) And the Lord said, "Listen to what this unjust judge said. (7) Will not God give justice to his chosen ones, who cry out to him day and night (*from morning to evening*)? Will he continue to ignore them? (8) I tell you the truth: God will give justice to them, and quickly. However, when the Son of Man (*see Daniel 7:13-14*) comes, will he find faith on the earth?"

293 - The Parable of True Righteousness
(Luke 18:9-14)

Luke 18:9-14 - (9) Jesus told this parable (*story*) to some who trusted in their own righteousness, and looked down with religious pride on everyone else: (10) "Two men went up into the temple to pray—one a Pharisee and the other a tax collector. (11) The Pharisee stood by himself and prayed, 'God, I thank you that I am not like sinners—robbers, evildoers, adulterers—or even like this tax collector. (12) I fast twice a week and give a tenth (*tithe*) of all I get.' (13) But the tax collector stood at a distance. He would not even lift his eyes to heaven (*God*), but beat his chest and prayed, 'God, have mercy on me, a sinner.' (14) I tell you the truth: This tax collector is the only one who went home in right standing (*justified*) before God. For whoever exalts themselves will be humbled, and whoever humbles themselves will be exalted."

294 - The Parable of a Landowner
(Matthew 20:1-16)

Matthew 20:1-16 - Jesus told this parable (*story*): (1) "For the kingdom of heaven (*God*) is like a landowner who went out early in the morning (*before 6 a.m.*) to hire men to work in his vineyard. (2) He agreed to pay them a day's wage (*a denarius*) and sent them into his vineyard. (*A work day was normally from 6 a.m. to 6 p.m.*). (3) The landowner went out again about 9 a.m. and saw men standing in the public market doing nothing. (4) He told them, 'You also can go and work in my vineyard, and I will pay you a day's wage.' (5) So they went out to work. The landowner went out about noon and again at 3 p.m. and hired more workers. (6) The landowner went out again about 5 p.m. and found more men standing around doing nothing. So he asked them, 'Why have you been standing here all day doing nothing?' (7) They answered, 'Because no one has hired us to work for them.' The landowner replied, 'You also can go and work in my vineyard.' (8) When evening came, the landowner told his foreman, 'Call all the workers and pay them their day's wage—beginning with the last ones hired to the first ones hired.' (9) The workers who were hired last came and each received a day's wage. (10) So when those came who were hired first, they expected to receive more money than the others, but they also received only a day's wage. (11) When they received their pay, they began to complain to the landowner. (12) They said, 'Those hired last worked only one hour, and you gave them a wage equal to ours, even though we did most of the work and worked through the heat of the day.' (13) But the landowner said to one of them, 'Friend, I am not being unfair to you. Didn't you agree to work for a day's wage? (14) Take your money and leave. I want to give the same wage to the one who was hired last. (15) Don't I have the right to do what I want with my own money? Or are you envious because I am generous?' (16) Jesus said, "So the last will be first, and the first will be last."

295 - The Death of Lazarus in Bethany
(John 11:1-16)

John 11:1-16 - (1) Now a man named Lazarus was very sick. He lived in Bethany, on the Mount of Olives, the village of Mary and Martha. (2) This Mary, whose brother Lazarus was sick, was the same woman who poured fragrant oil on the Lord and wiped his feet with her hair (*see John 12:1-8*). (3) So Lazarus' sisters, Mary and Martha, sent this message to Jesus, "Lord, Lazarus, the one you love is very sick." (4) When Jesus received the news, he said, "Lazarus' sickness will not lead to his death. No, his sickness is for God's glory, so that the Son of God will be praised through it." (5) Now Jesus loved Mary, Martha, and Lazarus. (6) So after hearing that Lazarus was sick, Jesus stayed east of the Jordan River in the region of Perea for two more days. John (7) Then he said to his disciples, "Let us go back to Judea." (8) His disciples said, "But Teacher (*Rabbi*), a short while ago the Jewish religious leaders in Judea were trying to stone you to death. Why are you going back there?" (9) Jesus said, "There are 12 hours of light in a day. Whoever walks during the day will not stumble, because they see by this world's light. (10) But it's when a person walks in the darkness of night that they stumble, because they have no light to see." (11) Jesus continued and said to them, "Our friend Lazarus has fallen asleep, but I am going there to wake him up." (12) His disciples said, "Lord, if he is asleep, he will wake on his own." (13) Jesus was telling them of Lazarus' death, but his disciples thought he was saying that Lazarus was just sleeping. (14) So then Jesus told them directly, "Lazarus is dead, (15) and I rejoice for you that I was not there when Lazarus died, so that you will believe. But let's go to Lazarus." (16) Then Thomas (*also known as Didymus, the Twin*), said to the other disciples, "Let us also go, so that we will die with him."

296 - Jesus Arrives at Bethany
(John 11:17-20)

John 11:17-20 - (17) When Jesus arrived at Bethany, on the Mount of Olives, Lazarus had already been in the rock tomb for four days. (18) Now Bethany was less than two miles (*3 km*) from Jerusalem, (19) and many Jews had come to comfort Mary and Martha because of their brother's death. (20) When Martha heard that Jesus was coming to Bethany, she went out to meet him, but Mary stayed home.

297 - Jesus Talks with Martha
(John 11:21-27)

John 11:21-27 - (21) Martha said to Jesus, "Lord, if you had been here, my brother Lazarus would not have died. (22) But I know that even now God will do whatever you ask him." (23) Jesus said to her, "Your brother will be raised from the dead." (24) Martha said, "I know he will rise from the dead in the resurrection at the last day." (25) Jesus said to her, "I am the resurrection and the life! Whoever believes in me will live, even though they die. (26) Whoever lives by believing in me will never die. Do you believe what I tell you is true?" (27) Martha said, "Yes, Lord! I believe that you are the Messiah (*Christ*), the Son of God, who has come into this world."

298 - Jesus Talks with Mary
(John 11:28-33)

John 11:28-33 - (28) After saying this, Martha went back to Bethany and called her sister Mary aside, and said, "The Teacher is here, and he is asking to see you." (29) When Mary heard this, she left quickly and went out to meet him. (30) Now Jesus had not yet entered the village of Bethany, but was still at the place where Martha had met him. (31) When the Jews who were with Mary in the house, comforting her, saw how quickly she got up and left, they followed her, because they thought that she was going to Lazarus' tomb to mourn. (32) When Mary came to Jesus, she fell at his feet and said, "Lord, if you had been here, my brother Lazarus would not have died." (33) When Jesus saw Mary weeping, and the Jews who had come with her also weeping, he was deeply moved in his spirit and greatly troubled.

299 - Jesus Raises Lazarus from the Dead
(John 11:34-44)

John 11:34-44 - (34) Jesus asked, "Where did you put Lazarus' body?" They said, "Lord, come and we will show you." (35) Jesus wept. (36) Then the Jews said to one another, "See how much he loved Lazarus." (37) But some of the Jews said, "He healed the man who was born blind (*see John 9:1-12*). Couldn't he have stopped Lazarus from dying?" (38) Jesus arrived at the tomb, and he was deeply moved in his spirit. Now it was a cave tomb, and a large stone had been rolled across the tomb entrance. (39) Jesus said, "Roll away the stone." Martha, Lazarus' sister, said, "But Lord, he has been dead four days and by this time his body will stink." (40) Then Jesus said to her, "Didn't I tell you that if you believe you will see the glory of God?" (41) So they rolled the stone away from the tomb's entrance. Then Jesus looked up to heaven and prayed, "Father, I thank you that you hear me. (42) I know that you always hear me, but I said this so the people standing around me will believe that you sent me into this world." (43) After Jesus had prayed, he shouted, "Lazarus, come out of that tomb!" (44) Lazarus walked out of the tomb, his hands and feet wrapped with linen strips, and his face wrapped with a cloth. Jesus told the people, "Take off his grave clothes and set Lazarus free!"

300 - Religious Leaders Plan to Kill Jesus
(John 11:45-53)

John 11:45-53 - (45) Therefore many of the Jews who had come to visit Mary believed in Jesus after they saw him raise Lazarus from the dead. (46) But some other Jews went and told the Pharisees what Jesus had done. (47) So the chief priests and Pharisees called a meeting of the Jewish governing council (*the Sanhedrin*). They asked, "What are we going to do? For this man Jesus is doing many miraculous signs (*miracles*). (48) If we do not stop him, everyone will believe in him, and then the Romans will come and destroy our temple and our nation." (49) Then one of them, named Caiaphas, who was the high priest that year, said, "You know nothing at all! (50) You don't realize that it is better for you that one man die for the people than that the whole nation be destroyed." (51) Caiaphas did not say this in his own ability, but as high priest that year he prophesied that Jesus would die for the Jewish nation, (52) and not only for the nation, but also to gather together as one the children of God who were scattered abroad (*the Jewish diaspora*). (53) So from that day on the Jewish religious leaders made plans to kill Jesus.

301 - Jesus Leaves Judea to Ephraim
(John 11:54-57)

John 11:54-57 - (54) Therefore Jesus decided not to walk around openly among the people of Judea, because the Jews were planning to kill him. So Jesus and his disciples left Jerusalem and traveled to a region near the wilderness of Judea to stay in the village of Ephraim. (55) When the time of the Jewish Passover was near, many people went up from the country to Jerusalem for their ceremonial purification (*cleansing*) before the Passover began. (56) People were looking for Jesus, and when they were in the temple courts they asked each other, "What do you think? Isn't he coming to celebrate Passover at all?" (57) But the Jewish chief priests and the Pharisees gave orders that whoever found out where Jesus was must report it so that they could arrest him.

302 - Religious Leaders Question Jesus About Divorce
(Matthew 19:3-9, Mark 10:2-9)

Matthew 19:3-9 - (3) Some Pharisees came to test Jesus by asking him, "Is it lawful for a man to divorce his wife for any reason?" (4) Jesus said to them, "Haven't you read Genesis 1:27? From the beginning, God the Creator 'made them male and female,' (5) and it is written in Genesis 2:24, 'For this reason, a man will leave his father and mother and be united to his wife, and the two will become one body.' (6) So in marriage they are no longer two, but one body. Therefore what God has united as one, let no one separate." (7) The religious leaders asked, "Why then did Moses say that a man can give his wife a certificate of divorce and send her away?" (8) Jesus said to them, "Moses allowed you to divorce your wives because your hearts were hard. But it was not this way from the beginning of creation. (9) I tell you the truth: A man who divorces his wife—except for marital unfaithfulness (*sexual immorality*)—and marries another woman commits adultery."

Mark 10:2-9 - (2) And some Pharisees came and tested him by asking, "Is it lawful for a man to divorce his wife?" (3) Jesus said to them, "What did Moses teach you?" (4) They said, "Moses allowed a man to write a certificate of divorce and send his wife away." (5) Jesus said, "Moses wrote you this command because your hearts were hard. (6) But from the beginning of creation, as it is written in Genesis 1:27, God 'created them male and female,' (7) and it is written in Genesis 2:24, 'For this reason, a man will leave his father and mother and be united to his wife, (8) and the two will become one body.' I tell you the truth: They are no longer two in marriage, but one body. (9) Therefore what God joined together as one, let no one separate."

303 - Disciples Question Jesus About Divorce
(Matthew 19:10-12; Mark 10:10-12)

Matthew 18:10-12 - (10) The disciples said to Jesus, "If this is true between a husband and wife, then it is better not to marry." (11) Jesus said, "Not everyone can accept my teaching, but only those to whom it has been given. (12) For there are eunuchs (*some men*) who were born that way (*spiritually gifted not to marry*), and there are eunuchs (*some men*) who have been made eunuchs by others (*having been castrated*)—and there are eunuchs (*some men*) who choose not to marry for the sake of the kingdom of heaven (*God*). Whoever can accept my teaching should receive it."

Mark 10:10-12 - (10) When they were in the house again, his disciples asked Jesus about his teaching on divorce. (11) Jesus said to them, "Whoever divorces his wife and marries again commits adultery against her. (12) And if she divorces her husband and marries again, she commits adultery."

304 - Jesus Welcomes Children
(Matthew 19:13-15, Mark 10:13-16, Luke 18:15-17)

Matthew 19:13-15 - (13) Then people brought little children to Jesus for him to put his hands on them and pray for them. But the disciples told them to stop. (14) Jesus said, "Let the little children come to me, and do not stop them, because the kingdom of heaven (*God*) belongs to them." (15) When Jesus had placed his hands on them, he then left that place.

Mark 10:13-16 - (13) People were bringing little children to Jesus for him to put his hands on them, but the disciples rebuked them. (14) When Jesus saw this he became very angry and said to his disciples, "Let the little children come to me and do not stop them, because the kingdom of God belongs to such as these. (15) I tell you the truth: Whoever does not receive the kingdom of God like a little child will never enter it." (16) And Jesus took the little children in his arms, put his hands on them, and blessed them.

Luke 18:15-17 - (15) People were bringing children to Jesus, so that he could put his hands on them. When his disciples saw this, they tried to stop them. (16) But Jesus called the children around him and told his disciples, "Let the children come to me and, do not stop them, because the kingdom of God belongs to them. (17) I tell you the truth: Whoever will not receive the kingdom of God like a little child will never enter it."

---

305 - A Rich Young Ruler and Eternal Life
(Matthew 19:16-22, Mark 10:17-22, Luke 18:18-23)

Matthew 19:16-22 - (16) Just then a man (*a young civil ruler*) came up to Jesus and asked, "Teacher, what good work must I do to enter eternal life?" (17) Jesus said, "Why do you ask me about what is good? God is the only one who is good. If you want to enter eternal life, keep God's commandments." (18) The man asked, "Which commandments?" Jesus said, "Do not murder, do not commit adultery, do not steal, do not give false testimony, (19) honor your father and mother, and love your neighbor as yourself." (20) The man said, "I have kept all of these commandments. What else must I do?" (21) Jesus said, "If you want to be perfect, go and sell everything you own and give it to the poor, and you will have treasure in heaven. Then come and follow me." (22) When the young man heard this, he went away sad, because he was very rich.

Mark 10:17-22 - (17) As Jesus started out on his journey, a young man (*a young civil ruler*) ran up to him and fell on his knees. He asked Jesus, "Good teacher, what must I do to inherit eternal life?" (18) Jesus said, "Why do you call me good? Only God is good. (19) You know Moses' commandments: Do not murder, do not commit adultery, do not steal, do not give false witness, do not cheat, and honor your father and mother." (20) The man said, "Teacher, I have obeyed all these commandments since I was a boy." (21) Jesus looked at him and loved him. He said, "There is one thing that you lack. Go, sell everything you own and give it to the poor, and you will have treasure in heaven. Then come and follow me." (22) When the man heard this, he went away very sad, because he was very rich.

Luke 18:18-23 - (18) A civil ruler asked Jesus, "Good teacher, what must I do to inherit eternal life?" (19) Jesus said, "Why do you call me good? God is the only one who is good! (20) You know God's commandments: Do not commit adultery, do not murder, do not steal, do not give false testimony, and honor your father and mother." (21) The man said, "I have kept all these commandments since I was a boy." (22) When Jesus heard his answer, he said to him, "You still lack one thing: Sell everything you own and give it to the poor, and you will have treasure in heaven. Then come and follow me." (23) When the ruler heard Jesus' words he became sad, because he was very rich.

306 - It is Hard for the Rich to Enter God's Kingdom
(Matthew 19:23-26, Mark 10:23-27, Luke 18:24-27)

Matthew 19:23-26 - (23) Then Jesus said to his disciples, "I tell you the truth: It is hard for a rich person to enter the kingdom of heaven (*God*). (24) Again I tell you: It is easier for a camel to go through the hole of a sewing needle than for a rich person to enter the kingdom of God." (25) When Jesus' disciples heard this, they were greatly amazed and asked, "Who then can be saved?" (26) Jesus stared at them and said, "For humans this is impossible, but with God all things are possible."

Mark 10:23-27 - (23) Jesus looked around and said to his disciples, "It is hard for a rich person to enter the kingdom of God." (24) The disciples were amazed at his words. But Jesus said again, "My children, it is hard for a rich person to enter the kingdom of God. (25) It is easier for a camel to go through the hole of a sewing needle than for a rich person to enter the kingdom of God." (26) The disciples were even more amazed, and said to one another, "Who then can be saved?" (27) Jesus looked at them and said, "With humans it is impossible, but not with God, because all things are possible with God."

Luke 18:24-27 - (24) Seeing the sadness on the face of the ruler, Jesus said, "It is hard for a rich person to enter the kingdom of God! (25) Yes, it is easier for a camel to go through the hole of a sewing needle than for a rich person to enter the kingdom of God." (26) Those who heard Jesus say this, asked him, "Then who can be saved?" (27) Jesus said to them, "What is impossible with man is possible with God."

307 - Following Jesus, Eternal Rewards
(Matthew 19:27-30, Mark 10:28-31, Luke 18:28-30)

Matthew 19:27-30 - (27) Peter answered Jesus, "We have left everything to follow you! What then will there be for us?" (28) Jesus said to his disciples, "I tell you the truth: At the renewal (*regeneration*) of heaven and earth, when the Son of Man (*see Daniel 7:13-14*) sits on his glorious throne, you who have followed me will also sit on 12 thrones, judging the 12 tribes of Israel. (29) And whoever has left houses or brothers or sisters or father or mother or wife or children or lands for my sake will receive 100 times more and will inherit eternal life. (30) But many people who are first will be last, and many who are last will be first."

Mark 10:28-31 - (28) Then Peter said to Jesus, "We have left everything to follow you!" (29) Jesus said, "I tell you the truth: No one who has left home or brothers or sisters or mother or father or children or land for me and the gospel (30) will fail to receive 100 times more in this present age: homes, brothers, sisters, mothers, children, and lands—along with persecutions—and in the age to come, eternal life. (31) But many people who are first will be last, and the last will be first."

Luke 18:28-30 - (28) Peter said to Jesus, "We have left everything to follow you!" (29) Jesus said to them, "I tell you the truth: Whoever has left home or wife or brothers or sisters or parents or children for the sake of the kingdom of God (30) will receive much more on earth in this age, and eternal life in the age to come."

308 - Jesus Speaks About His Death and Resurrection
(Matthew 20:17-19, Mark 10:32-34, Luke 18:31-33)

Matthew 20:17-19 - (17) Now while Jesus was walking up to Jerusalem, he took his Twelve Apostles away from the people and said to them, (18) "We are going up to Jerusalem, and the Son of Man (*see Daniel 7:13-14*) will be delivered over to the Jewish chief priests and teachers of the law of Moses. They will condemn him to death (19) and will turn him over to the Romans to be mocked and flogged and crucified. But God will raise him to life on the third day!"

Mark 10:32-34 - (32) Jesus was leading his disciples on the way up to Jerusalem, and the disciples were amazed, while those who followed were afraid. Once again Jesus took the Twelve Apostles away from the people and told them what was about to happen to him. (33) He said, "We are going up to Jerusalem, and the Son of Man (*see Daniel 7:13-14*) will be delivered over to the Jewish chief priests and teachers of the law of Moses. They will condemn him to death and will hand him over to the Romans (*non-Jews*), (34) who will mock him, spit on him, flog him, and crucify him. But after three days he will rise from the dead."

Luke 18:31-33 - (31) Jesus took the Twelve Apostles away from the other people and told them, "We are going up to Jerusalem, and everything that is written about the Son of Man (*see Daniel 7:13-14*) in the Bible (*Old Testament*) will be fulfilled. (32) For he will be delivered over to the Romans. They will mock him, slander him, and spit on him. (33) After flogging him, they will crucify him, but on the third day he will rise from the dead."

309 - James and John Makes a Request of Jesus
(Matthew 20:20-23, Mark 10:35-40)

Matthew 20:20-23 - (20) Then the mother of apostles James and John came to Jesus with her sons and, kneeling before him, she asked him a favor. (21) Jesus asked, "What is it that you want?" She said, "Let one of my sons sit at your right and the other sit at your left in your kingdom." (22) Jesus said, "You don't know what you are asking me." Jesus said to James and John, "Can you drink the cup that I am going to drink?" They answered, "Yes, we can." (23) Jesus said to them, "You will drink from my cup, but to sit at my right or left is not for me to grant. These places of honor belong to those for whom they have been prepared by my Father."

Mark 10:35-40 - (35) Then James and John, the sons of Zebedee, came to Jesus and said, "Teacher, we want you to do something for us, whatever we ask." (36) Jesus said to them, "What do you want me to do for you?" (37) They answered, "Let one of us sit at your right side, and the other at your left side in your glory." (38) Jesus said, "You don't know what you are asking me. Can you drink the cup I drink, or be baptized with the baptism I am baptized with?" (39) They answered, "Yes, we can." Jesus said to them, "You will drink the cup of suffering I drink and be baptized with the baptism I am baptized with, (40) but who will sit at my right or left is not for me to grant. These places belong only to those for whom they have been prepared."

310 - Apostles Became Angry at James and John
(Matthew 20:24, Mark 10:41)

Matthew 20:24 - When the other 10 apostles heard about this, they became angry (*jealous*) with James and John.

Mark 10:41 - When the other 10 apostles heard about this they became very angry with James and John.

311 - Become a Servant of All
(Matthew 20:25-28, Mark 10:42-45)

Matthew 20:25-28 - (25) Jesus called his Twelve Apostles together and said to them, "You know that the rulers of the non-Jews lord it over their people, and their high officials exercise authority over them. (26) But this is not true with you. Instead, whoever wants to become great among you must be your servant, (27) and whoever wants to be first among you must serve all others—(28) just as the Son of Man (*see Daniel 7:13-14*) did not come to be served, but to serve, and to give his life as a ransom payment for many people."

Mark 10:42-45 - (42) Jesus called his Twelve Apostles together and said to them, "You know that the non-Jewish rulers lord it over them, and their high officials exercise authority over them. (43) But this is not true among you. Instead, whoever wants to become great among you must be your servant, (44) and whoever wants to be first must be a servant of all. (45) For even the Son of Man (*see Daniel 7:13-14*) did not come to be served, but to serve, and to give his life as a ransom payment for many people."

312 - Jesus Heals Blind Bartimaeus in Jericho
(Mark 10:46-52, Luke 18:35-43)

Mark 10:46-52 - (46) Then Jesus and the disciples came to the city of Jericho. And as they, together with a large crowd, were leaving Jericho, a blind man named Bartimaeus (*which means "son of Timaeus"*), was sitting on the roadside begging. (47) When he heard that Jesus of Nazareth was walking by him, he began shouting, "Jesus, Son of David, have mercy on me!" (48) Many people rebuked him and told him to be quiet, but he shouted even louder, "Son of David, have mercy on me!" (49) Jesus stopped and told his disciples to bring Bartimaeus to him. So the disciples called to the blind man, "Take heart! Stand on your feet! Jesus is calling for you." (50) Throwing his garment (outer cloak) aside, he jumped to his feet and went to Jesus. (51) Jesus asked him, "What do you want me to do for you?" Bartimaeus said, "Teacher (*Rabbi*), I want you to heal my eyes so that I can see." (52) Jesus said, "Go, your faith has healed you." Immediately he could see and followed Jesus as he walked along the road toward Jerusalem.

Luke 18:35-43 - (35) As Jesus was about to enter the city of Jericho, a blind man (*named Bartimaeus; see Mark 10:46-52*) was sitting by the road begging. (36) When he heard a crowd of people walking by, he asked what was happening. (37) They told him, "Jesus of Nazareth is walking by." (38) The blind man yelled out, "Jesus, Son of David, have mercy on me!" (39) The people who were walking in front of Jesus told him to be quiet, but he shouted even more, "Son of David, have mercy on me!" (40) Jesus stopped and told them to bring the blind man to him. When he came, Jesus asked him, (41) "What do you want me to do for you?" The blind man said, "Lord, I want to see." (42) Jesus said to him, "Receive your sight; your faith has healed you." (43) Immediately the blind man could see and followed Jesus, praising God. When all the people saw this, they also praised God.

313 - Jesus and the Tax Collector Zacchaeus in Jericho
(Luke 19:1-10)

Luke 9:1-10 - (1) Jesus was walking through Jericho. (2) There was a man living there named Zacchaeus; he was the chief tax collector (*Jewish tax collectors were hated because they were hired representatives of the Romans*) and was very rich. (3) He wanted to see Jesus, but because he was short he could not see over the crowd of people. (4) So he ran ahead of the crowd and climbed a sycamore tree (*which had large branches near the ground, like an oak tree*) to see Jesus as he walked by. (5) When Jesus walked by, he looked up into the tree and said to him, "Zacchaeus, come down immediately from the tree, for I must stay at your house tonight." (6) Zacchaeus came down at once and welcomed Jesus with joy. (7) All the people saw this and began to complain, "He has gone to be a house guest of a sinner." (8) But Zacchaeus stood up and said to the Lord, "Look, Lord! I will give half of what I own to the poor, and I will pay back the people that I have cheated. I will give them four times the amount of money I cheated from them." (9) Jesus said to him, "Zacchaeus, today salvation has come to your house, because you are also a son of Abraham. (10) For the Son of Man (*see Daniel 7:13-14*) came to seek and to save the lost!"

314 - Jesus Heals Two Blind Men in Jericho
(Matthew 20:29-34)

Matthew 20:29-34 - (29) As Jesus and his disciples were leaving the city of Jericho toward Jerusalem, a large crowd followed them. (30) Two blind men were sitting by the road, and when they heard that Jesus was walking by, they shouted, "Lord, Son of David, have mercy on us!" (31) The people tried to stop the blind men from yelling and told them to shut up, but they shouted even louder, "Lord, Son of David, have mercy on us!" (32) Jesus stopped and called out to them, "What do you want me to do for you?" (33) They answered, "Lord, we want you to heal our eyes." (34) Jesus had compassion on them and touched their eyes, and immediately they could see, and followed him.

(The winding road from Jericho to Jerusalem was around 18 miles/29 km long and ascended about 3,000 feet/914 meters through the dry desert. The journey would have taken around eight hours of uphill walking).

315 - The Parable of Faithful Stewardship
(Luke 19:11-27)

Luke 19:11-27 - (11) While they were listening to Jesus, he told them a parable *(story)* because he was near Jerusalem and the people expected the kingdom of God to appear immediately. (12) He said, "A man of royal birth traveled to a far country to have himself appointed king and then to return. (13) So he called 10 of his servants and gave them 10 valuable coins *(a mina coin was about three months' wages)*, saying, 'Invest this money until I come back.' (14) But his citizens hated him and sent messengers after him to the far country, saying, 'We don't want this man to be our king.' (15) But the man was made king and came back home. Then he sent for the servants to whom he had given his money to invest. He wanted to find out how much money they had earned for him. (16) The first servant came and said, 'Sir, your coin has earned 10 more coins.' (17) The king said, 'Well done, my good servant! Because you have been faithful in little, I will give you charge of 10 cities.' (18) The second servant came and said, 'Sir, your coin has earned five more coins.' (19) The king said, 'You take charge of five cities.' (20) Then another servant came and said, 'Sir, here is your coin; I have kept it safe by wrapping it in a piece of cloth. (21) I was afraid of you, because you are a very hard man. You take out what you did not put in and harvest what you did not plant.' (22) The king said harshly, 'I will judge you by your own words, you wicked servant! You knew that I am a hard man, taking out what I do not put in and harvesting what I did not plant. (23) Why then didn't you put my money in the bank, so that I could have collected some interest when I returned?' (24) Then the king said to those standing by, 'Take his coin away from him and give it to the one who has 10 coins.' (25) They said, 'Sir, he already has 10 coins!' (26) The king said, 'I tell you that to whoever has much, more will be given, but whoever has little, even what he has will be taken away. (27) And bring my enemies who did not want me to be king over them—bring them in front of me and kill them.'

316 - People Go to Jerusalem for Passover
(John 11:55-57)

John 11:55-57 - (55) When the time of the Jewish Passover was near, many people went up from the country to Jerusalem for their ceremonial purification (*cleansing*) before the Passover began. (56) People were looking for Jesus, and when they were in the temple courts they asked each other, "What do you think? Isn't he coming to celebrate Passover at all?" (57) But the Jewish chief priests and the Pharisees gave orders that whoever found out where Jesus was must report it so that they could arrest him.

317 - Jesus Arrives at Bethany
(Matthew 21:1, Mark 11:1, Luke 19:28-29)

Matthew 21:1 - As they approached Jerusalem from Jericho, they came to the town of Bethphage on the Mount of Olives.

Mark 11:1 - As Jesus and his disciples approached Jerusalem, they walked up to the towns of Bethphage and Bethany on the Mount of Olives.

Luke 19:28-29 - (28) After Jesus had said these things, he walked ahead from Jericho up the road to Jerusalem (29) and approached the towns of Bethphage and Bethany, on the hill of Mount of Olives.

(*The road from Jericho to Jerusalem came onto the Mount of Olives and then passed through the villages of Bethphage and Bethany, which are around 2 miles/3 km southeast of Jerusalem. The Mount of Olives was a mountain ridge east of and adjacent to the city of Jerusalem, separated by the Kidron Valley*).

318 - Mary Anoints Jesus' Feet
(John 12:1-8)

John 12:1-8 - (1) Six days before the start of the Passover, Jesus walked from Ephraim to Bethany on the Mount of Olives, where Lazarus, whom Jesus had raised from the dead, lived. (2) So they gave a dinner for him there. Martha served, and Lazarus sat with Jesus at the table. (3) Then Mary took a pound of expensive fragrant oil that had been extracted from a pure nard plant, and poured it on Jesus' feet and wiped them with her hair. And the whole house was filled with the oil's fragrance. (4) But Judas Iscariot, one of Jesus' disciples, who would later betray him, said to Mary, (5) "Why didn't you sell this oil for a day's wage (300 denarii) and give the money to the poor?" (6) Judas did not say this because he cared about the poor; he was a thief. He was the one who carried the money bag and would often steal from it. (7) Jesus told Judas, "Leave Mary alone! For she has kept this oil for my burial. (8) You will always have the the poor with you, but you will not always have me."

---

319 - A Woman Anoints Jesus' Head at Simon's House
(Matthew 26:6-13, Mark 14:3-9)

Matthew 26:6-13 - (6) When Jesus was in Bethany on the Mount of Olives in the home of Simon the Leper, (7) a woman came to Jesus with an alabaster jar of very expensive fragrant oil, and she poured it on his head as he was eating at the table. (8) When the disciples saw this, they became very angry and said to her, "Why are you wasting this expensive oil? (9) This oil could have been sold for lots of money and it given to the poor." (10) But Jesus, aware of this, said to his disciples, "Why are you rebuking this woman? For she has done a beautiful thing to me. (11) You will always have the poor with you, but you will not always have me with you. (12) In pouring this fragrant oil on my body, she has prepared me for my burial. (13) I tell you the truth: Wherever the gospel (good news) is proclaimed around the world, what she did to me will be told in her memory."

Mark 14:3-9 - (3) While Jesus was in Bethany on the Mount of Olives, eating in the home of Simon the Leper, a woman came with an alabaster jar of very expensive fragrant oil, extracted from a genuine nard plant. She broke the jar and poured the fragrant oil on Jesus' head. (4) Some of those present were angry, saying to one another, "Why did she waste this expensive oil? (5) It could have been sold for more than a year's wages (100 denarii) and the money given to the poor." And they rebuked her harshly. (6) Jesus said to them, "Leave her alone. Why are you causing her so much trouble? She has done a beautiful thing to me. (7) The poor you will always have with you, and you can help them any time you want. But you will not always have me with you. (8) She did what she could do. She poured the fragrant oil on my body to prepare it for my burial. (9) I tell you the truth: Wherever the gospel (good news) is proclaimed throughout the world, what she has done to me will also be told, in her memory."

320 - The Plan to Kill Lazarus
(John 12:9-11)

John 12:9-11 - (9) Now when a large crowd of Jews heard that Jesus was in Bethany, they went to visit him. They went not only because of Jesus, but also to see Lazarus whom Jesus had raised from the dead. (10) So the Jewish chief priests made plans to kill Lazarus too, (11) because on account of him many Jews were leaving them and believing in Jesus.

321 - Jesus Sends for Colt
(Matthew 21:1–6, Mark 11:1–6, Luke 19:29–34)

Matthew 21:1-6 - (1) Jesus said to two of his disciples (*Peter and John*), (2) "Go to the village ahead of us, and you will find a donkey tied there, with her colt beside her. Untie them and bring them to me. (3) If anyone says anything to you, tell them that the Lord needs them, and he will let you go." (4) This happened to fulfill what is written in Zechariah 9:9, (5) "Say to the Daughter Zion: See, your king comes to you, gentle and riding on a donkey, and on a colt, the foal of a donkey." (6) The disciples did what Jesus had told them to do.

Mark 11:1-6 - (1) Jesus sent two of his disciples (*Peter and John*), (2) saying to them, "Go to the village ahead of us. When you enter it, you will find a colt tied there, which no one has ever ridden. Untie it and bring it to me. (3) If anyone asks you, 'Why are you taking this colt?' tell them, 'The Lord needs it and will send it back here soon.'" (4) They went and found the colt outside in the street, tied at a doorway. As they untied it (5) some people standing there asked them, "Why are you taking this colt?" (6) The disciples answered as Jesus had told them to, and the people let them go.

Luke 19:29-34 - (29) Jesus told two of his disciples (*Peter and John*), (30) "Go to the village ahead of us. When you enter, you will find a colt tied there, which no one has ever sat on. Untie it and bring it here. (31) If anyone asks you, 'Why are you untying the colt?' tell them, 'The Lord needs it.'" (32) The two disciples found the colt as Jesus had said. (33) As they were untying the colt, its owners asked them, "Why are you taking the colt?" (34) The disciples said, "The Lord needs it."

322 - Jesus Sits on Colt
(Matthew 21:7, Mark 11:7, Luke 19:35, John 12:14-15)

Matthew 21:7 - They brought the donkey and the colt and placed their clothes (*outer cloaks*) on them for Jesus to sit on.

Mark 11:7 - After the disciples brought the colt to Jesus and threw their clothes (*outer cloaks*) over it, he sat on it.

Luke 19:35 - They brought the colt to Jesus, threw some of their clothes (*outer cloaks*) on it, and put Jesus on it.

John 12:14-15 - (14) Jesus found a young donkey and sat on it, just as it is written in Zechariah 9:9, (15) "Fear not, daughter of Zion. Behold, your king is coming. He is sitting on the colt of a donkey."

323 - Jesus Enters Jerusalem as Victorious King
(Matthew 21:8-11, Mark 11:8-10, Luke 19:36-38, John 12:12-13,16-19)

Matthew 21:8-11 - (8) A very large crowd of people spread their clothes (*outer cloaks*) on the road leading down the Mount of Olives to Jerusalem, while others cut branches from the trees and spread them on the road. (9) The crowds that went in front of Jesus, and those who followed him, shouted Psalm 118:26, "Hosanna to the Son of David! Blessed is he who comes in the name of the Lord! Hosanna in the highest!" (10) When Jesus entered Jerusalem, the whole city was full of excitement and people asked one another, "Who is this?" (11) The people yelled, "This is Jesus, the prophet from Nazareth in Galilee!"

Mark 11:8-10 - Many people spread their outer clothes on the road, while others spread out branches they had cut in the fields. (9) Those who went ahead and those who followed shouted Psalm 118:26, "Hosanna! Blessed is he who comes in the name of the Lord! (10) Blessed is the coming kingdom of our father David! Hosanna in the highest heaven!"

Luke 19:36-38 - (36) As Jesus rode along on the colt, people spread their clothes on the road. (37) When Jesus came near the place where the road descends the Mount of Olives to Jerusalem, the whole crowd of disciples began to rejoice and praise God in loud voices for all the miracles they had seen. (38) They shouted, "Blessed is the king who comes in the name of the Lord! Peace in heaven and glory in the highest!"

John 12:12-13,16-19 - (12) The next day the large crowd of people that had come to celebrate Passover heard that Jesus was coming into Jerusalem. (13) So they took palm branches and went out to meet him, shouting Psalm 118:26, "Hosanna! Blessed is he who comes in the name of the Lord! Blessed is the king of Israel!" (16) At first Jesus' disciples did not understand what was going on. Only after Jesus was glorified did they remember that these things had been written about him and that these things had been done to him. (17) Now the crowd of people that were eyewitnesses when Jesus raised Lazarus from the dead never stopped telling others about him. (18) Many people went out to meet Jesus because they had heard that he had raised Lazarus from the dead. (19) So the Pharisees said to one another, "We are accomplishing nothing. Look! The whole world is following Jesus!"

324 - Religious Leaders Confront Jesus
(Luke 19:39-40)

Luke 19:39-40 - (39) Some of the Pharisees in the crowd said to Jesus, "Teacher, command your disciples to stop shouting these things!" (40) Jesus said to them, "I tell you the truth: If my disciples keep quiet, the rocks on the ground will cry out!"

325 - Jesus Prophecies the Roman Destruction of Jerusalem
(Luke 19:41-44)

Luke 19:41-44 - (41) When Jesus approached Jerusalem and saw the city, he wept over it (42) and said, "If you had only known on this day what would bring you peace—but now it is hidden from your eyes. (43) The days will come upon you when your enemies (*the Romans*) will set up an embankment against you, encircle you on every side, and you will not be able to escape. (44) They will tear Jerusalem down to the ground, with you and your children within its walls. They will not leave one stone upon another, because you did not recognize the time of God's visitation." (*Jesus predicted that the Romans would destroy Jerusalem and the temple, which was fulfilled between AD 66 and AD 70*).

326 - Jesus Visits Jerusalem Temple and Returns to Bethany
(Mark 11:11)

Mark 11:11 - Jesus entered Jerusalem and went into the temple courts. He looked around at everything, but because it was already late in the evening, he went with the Twelve Apostles to spend the night in Bethany on the Mount of Olives.

327 - Jesus Curses an Unfruitful Fig Tree
(Matthew 21:18-22, Mark 11:12-14, 20-26)

Matthew 21:18-22 - (18) Early in the morning, as Jesus was walking back to Jerusalem, he became hungry. (19) Seeing a fig tree by the road, he went over to it but found only leaves and no figs. Then he said to it, "You will never produce figs again!" Immediately the tree dried up and died (*possibly a symbolic judgment against Israel*). (20) When the disciples saw this, they were amazed and asked, "How did the fig tree die so quickly?" (21) Jesus said to them, "I tell you the truth: If you have faith and do not doubt, you will not only be able to do what I did to this fig tree, but you can also tell this mountain, 'Go, throw yourself into the sea,' and it will happen. (22) If you believe, you will receive whatever you ask for in prayer."

Mark 11:12-14 - (12) When they left Bethany the next morning, Jesus became hungry. (13) Seeing in the distance a fig tree with leaves, he went to find out if it had any figs. When he came to the tree it had leaves but no figs, because it was not the season for figs. (14) Then the disciples heard Jesus say to the tree, "No one will ever eat figs from you again." (*possibly representing a symbolic judgment on Israel*).

Mark 11:20-26 - (20) As they were walking the next morning, the disciples saw that the fig tree was dead, withered to its roots. (21) Peter remembered and said to Jesus, "Teacher (*Rabbi*), look! The fig tree you cursed is withered and dead!" (22) Jesus said, "Have faith in God! (23) For I tell you the truth: Whoever says to this mountain, 'Go, throw yourself into the sea,' and does not doubt in their heart but believes that what they say will happen, it will be done for them. (24) Therefore I tell you the truth: Whatever you ask for in prayer, believe that you have received it, and it will be yours. (25-26) And whenever you stand praying, if you hold anything against anyone, forgive them, so that your Father in heaven will forgive you your sins."

328 - Jesus Clears Out the Jerusalem Temple
(Matthew 21:12-13, Mark 11:15-19, Luke 19:45-46)

Matthew 21:12-13 - (12) Jesus entered the temple courts (*probably refers to the court of the non-Jews*) and drove out all those who were buying and selling there. He turned over the tables of the money changers and the benches of those selling doves for sacrifices. (13) Jesus said to them, "It is written in Isaiah 56:7, 'My house will be called a house of prayer,' but as it is written in Jeremiah 7:11, 'You are making it a den of robbers.' "

Mark 11:15-17 - (15) When Jesus and his disciples entered Jerusalem, they went into the temple courts (*probably refers to the outermost court of the non-Jews*). And Jesus began driving out those who were buying and selling things there. He turned over the tables of the money changers and the benches of those selling sacrificial doves, (16) and would not allow anyone to carry merchandise through the temple courts. (17) And as he was teaching them, he declared, "It is written in Isaiah 56:7, 'My house will be called a house of prayer for all nations,' but as Jeremiah 7:11 says, you have made it 'a den of robbers.' "

Luke 19:45-46 - (45) When Jesus entered the temple courts (*probably refers to the court of the non-Jews*), he began to drive out those who were selling sacrifices. (46) He said to them, "It is written in Isaiah 56:7, 'My house will be a house of prayer,' but as it is written in Jeremiah 7:11, 'You have made it a den of robbers.' "

329 - Jesus' Ministry in the Temple
(Matthew 21:14, Luke 19:47)

Matthew 21:14 - The blind and lame came to Jesus at the temple, and he healed them.

Luke 19:47 - Jesus taught every day in the temple...

330 - Religious Leaders Plan to Kill Jesus
(Mark 11:18, Luke 19:47-48)

Mark 11:18 - The Jewish chief priests and teachers of the law of Moses heard this and began looking for a way to kill Jesus, for they feared him, because all the people were so amazed at his teaching.

Luke 19:47-48 - (47) ... while the Jewish chief priests, teachers of the law of Moses, and the leaders among the people were seeking to kill him. (48) But they could not find any way to kill Jesus, because all the people were listening intently to every word he spoke.

331- Religious Leaders Angry About the Praise of Children
(Matthew 21:15-16)

Matthew 21:15-16 - (15) But the Jewish chief priests and teachers of the law of Moses were furious when they saw the wonderful things that he did and the children shouting in the temple courts, "Hosanna to the Son of David." (16) They asked Jesus, "Don't you hear what these children are shouting?" Jesus said to them, "Yes, haven't you ever read Psalm 8:2? It says, 'From the lips of children and infants you, Lord, have called forth your praise.' "

332 - Non-Jews Want to Meet Jesus
(John 12:20-23)

John 12:20-23 - (20) Now there were some Greeks among the people who went up to worship at the Passover Festival. (21) They went to Philip, who was from Bethsaida in Galilee, and said to him, "Sir, we want to meet Jesus." (22) Philip went and told Andrew; so Andrew and Philip went and told Jesus. (23) Jesus said to them, "The time has come for the Son of Man (*see Daniel 7:13-14*) to be glorified."

333 - Life Through Death
(John 12:24-26)

John 12:24-26 - Jesus said, (24) "I tell you the truth: Unless a grain of wheat falls to the ground and dies, it remains a single seed. But if it dies, it produces many seeds. (25) Whoever loves their life will lose it, but whoever hates their life in this world will keep it for eternal life. (26) Whoever serves me must follow me; and where I am, my servant also will be. My Father will honor the one who serves me."

334 - Jesus Predicts His Death
(John 12:27-33)

John 12:27-33 - Jesus said, (27) "Now my soul is greatly troubled, but what should I ask for? Father, deliver me from this time of suffering. No, it was for this very reason that I came to this hour. (28) Father, glorify your name!" Then a voice came from heaven and said, "I have glorified it, and I will glorify it again." (29) A crowd of people that was there heard the voice and said it sounded like thunder. Others said, "An angel spoke to him!" (30) Jesus said, "This voice was for your good, not mine. (31) Now is the time for judgment to come on this world. And now, Satan—the ruler of this world—will be cast out. (32) And I, when I am lifted up from the earth, will draw all people to myself!" (33) Jesus said this to tell the people the kind of death he was going to die (*crucifixion*).

335 - Who is the Son of Man?
(John 12:34-36)

John 12:34-36 - (34) The crowd of people said, "We have heard from the law of Moses that the Messiah (*Christ*) will stay in this world forever. So how can you say, 'The Son of Man (*see Daniel 7:13-14*) must be lifted up'? Who is this 'Son of Man'?" (35) Then Jesus said to them, "The light is with you for a little while longer. Walk while you have the light, before darkness overcomes you. Whoever walks in the dark does not know where he is going. (36) Believe in the light while you have light, so that you will become children of light." When Jesus finished teaching, he left and hid himself from them.

336 - Jesus Returns to Bethany
(Matthew 21:17, Mark 11:19)

Matthew 21:17 - And Jesus left Jerusalem and walked back to the village of Bethany on the Mount of Olives, where he spent the night.

Mark 11:19 - When evening came, Jesus and his disciples left Jerusalem.

337 - Jesus on Faith in God
(Mark 11:20-26)

Mark 11:20-26 - (20) As they were walking the next morning, the disciples saw that the fig tree was dead, withered to its roots. (21) Peter remembered and said to Jesus, "Teacher (*Rabbi*), look! The fig tree you cursed is withered and dead!" (22) Jesus said, "Have faith in God! (23) For I tell you the truth: Whoever says to this mountain, 'Go, throw yourself into the sea,' and does not doubt in their heart but believes that what they say will happen, it will be done for them. (24) Therefore I tell you the truth: Whatever you ask for in prayer, believe that you have received it, and it will be yours. (25-26) And whenever you stand praying, if you hold anything against anyone, forgive them, so that your Father in heaven will forgive you your sins."

338 - Jesus' Authority Is Questioned
(Matthew 21:23-27, Mark 11:27-33, Luke 20:1-8)

Matthew 21:23-27 - (23) Jesus entered the temple courts, and, while he was teaching, the Jewish chief priests and elders came and asked him, "By what authority are you doing these things? Who gave you this authority?" (24) Jesus said to them, "I will also ask you a question. If you answer me, I will tell you by what authority I do these things." (25) Jesus asked, "Was the baptism of John from heaven or was it from man?" The religious leaders talked with each other and said, "If we say, 'From heaven,' he will ask, 'Then why did you not believe John?' (26) But if we say, 'It was from man,' we are afraid of what the people might do because they believe that John was a prophet." (27) So they answered Jesus, "We do not know." Then Jesus said to them, "Neither will I tell you by what authority I do these things."

Mark 11:27-33 - (27) Jesus and the disciples entered Jerusalem, and while Jesus was walking in the temple courts, the Jewish chief priests, teachers of the law of Moses, and elders came to him. (28) They asked him, "By what authority are you doing these things? And who gave you your authority to do this?" (29) Jesus said to them, "I will ask you a question, and if you answer me then I will tell you by what authority I do these things. (30) Tell me, was John's baptism from heaven, or was it from man?" (31) The religious leaders discussed this question among themselves and said, "If we say, 'From heaven,' he will ask, 'Then why didn't you believe him?' (32) But if we say, 'It originated on the earth'—then we fear the people, because everyone believes that John was a prophet." (33) So they said to Jesus, "We do not know." Jesus said, "Neither will I tell you by what authority I am doing these things."

Luke 20:1-8 - (1) One day as Jesus was teaching the people in the temple courts and proclaiming the gospel (good news), the Jewish chief priests, teachers of the law of Moses, and elders, walked up to him and said, (2) "Tell us by what authority you do these things. Tell us who gave you this authority." (3) Jesus said to them, "I ask you this question: (4) Tell me, was the baptism of John from heaven or from man?" (5) They discussed this question with one another and said, "If we say, 'From heaven,' he will say, 'Why didn't you believe him?' (6) But if we say, 'From man,' all the people will throw rocks at us, because they believe that John was a prophet." (7) So they said to Jesus, "We don't know where John's baptism came from." (8) Jesus said, "Then I will not tell you by what authority I am doing these things."

339 - The Parable of Two Sons
(Matthew 21:28-32)

Matthew 21:28-32 - (28) Jesus asked the Jewish religious leaders, "What do you think about this parable (*story*)? There was a man who had two sons. He went to the first and said, 'Son, go and work today in the vineyard.' (29) The son answered, 'No, I will not go,' but later he changed his mind and went into the vineyard to work. (30) Then the father went to his second son and said the same thing, 'Go work today in the vineyard.' He answered, 'Yes, I will, father,' but he did not go into the vineyard to work." (31) Jesus asked them, "Tell me, which of the two sons did the will of their father?" The religious leaders answered, "The first son." Jesus said to them, "I tell you the truth: The tax collectors and the prostitutes are entering the kingdom of God before you! (32) For John came to show you the way of righteousness, and you refused to believe him, but tax collectors and prostitutes did believe him. And even after you saw this with your own eyes, you still would not repent and believe him."

- -

- -

- -

- -

- -

340 - The Parable of a Landowner
(Matthew 21:33-44, Mark 12:1-11, Luke 20:9-18)

Matthew 21:33-44 - (33) Jesus said, "Listen to another parable (*story*): There was a landowner who planted a vineyard. He built a wall around it, dug a hole for a winepress, and built a watchtower. Then he rented his vineyard to some farmers and moved to another place. (34) When it was time for the harvest, the landowner sent his servants to the farmers to collect his fruit. (35) They grabbed his servants, beat one, threw rocks at one, and killed another. (36) Then he sent a larger number of servants to the farmers, but they did the same thing to them. (37) Last of all, he sent his son to them. The landowner thought, 'They will respect my son.' (38) But when the farmers saw the son coming, they said, 'This is the inheritor of the vineyard; come, let's kill him and take his inheritance.' (39) So they took the son and threw him out of the vineyard and killed him." (40) Jesus asked the religious leaders, "Therefore, when the vineyard's owner comes, what will he do to those farmers?" (41) They replied, "He will destroy those evil men, and he will rent his vineyard to other farmers, who will give him his share of the crops at harvest time." (42) Jesus said to them, "Haven't you ever read Psalm 118:22-23? 'The stone the builders rejected has become the cornerstone; the Lord has done this, and it is marvelous in our eyes.' (43) Therefore I tell you the truth: The kingdom of God will be taken away from you and given to people who will produce its fruit. (44) Whoever falls on this stone will be broken to pieces, and the one on whom the stone falls will be crushed into powder."

Mark 12:1-11 - (1) Then Jesus began to tell the religious leaders this parable (*story*): "There was a landowner who planted a vineyard. He built a wall around it, dug a hole for a winepress, and built a watchtower. Then he rented his vineyard to some farmers and travelled to another place. (2) "When it was time for the harvest, the landowner sent a servant to the farmers to collect from them some of the fruit of his vineyard. (3) But they grabbed him, beat him, and sent him away without any fruit. (4) Then the landowner sent another servant to them, but they hit him on the head and treated him with great shame. (5) The landowner sent still another servant to them, and the farmers killed him. The landowner sent many others; some of them they beat, others they killed. (6) The landowner's son, whom he loved, was the only one left to send. Finally, he sent his son, saying to himself, 'They will respect my son.' (7) But when the farmers saw the son coming, they said to one another, 'This is the heir of the vineyard; come, let us kill him and his inheritance will be ours.' (8) So they killed the son, and threw him out of the vineyard." (9) Jesus asked the Jewish religious leaders, "Therefore, what will the vineyard owner do? He will come and kill the farmers and give the vineyard to others. (10) Haven't you read Psalm 118:22-23? 'The stone the builders rejected has become the cornerstone; (11) the Lord has done this, and it is marvelous in our eyes.'"

Luke 20:9-18 - (9) Jesus told the people this parable (story): "A man planted a vineyard and rented it to some farmers and went away on a long journey. (10) At harvest time he sent a servant to the farmers to receive his share of the vineyard's fruit. But the farmers beat him and sent him away with nothing. (11) The owner sent another servant, but that servant was beaten, mistreated terribly, and was sent away with nothing. (12) The owner sent a third servant, and they hurt him and threw him out of the vineyard. (13) Then the owner of the vineyard said, 'What should I do? I will send my son, whom I love; surely the farmers will respect him.' (14) But when the farmers saw the son coming, they discussed what they should do. They said 'This is the son who will inherit the vineyard. Let's kill him, and his inheritance will be ours.' (15) So they threw the son out of the vineyard and killed him." Jesus asked them, "What will the owner of the vineyard do to these evil men? (16) He will come and kill these farmers and give the vineyard to other people." When the people heard this, they said, "God forbid! May this never be!" (17) Jesus looked directly at them and asked, "Then what is the meaning of that which is written in Psalm 118:22-23, 'The stone the builders rejected has become the cornerstone'? (18) Whoever falls on that stone will be broken to pieces, and on whoever it falls will be crushed."

- -

- -

- -

- -

- -

341 - Religious Leaders Try to Arrest Jesus
(Matthew 21:45-46, Mark 12:12, Luke 20:19)

Matthew 21:45-46 - (45) When the Jewish chief priests and Pharisees heard Jesus' parables, they knew that he was talking about them. (46) So they looked for a way to arrest him, but they were afraid of the people because they believed that Jesus was a prophet.

Mark 12:12 - Then the Jewish chief priests, teachers of the law of Moses, and elders began to look for a way to arrest Jesus because they knew he had spoken this parable against them. But they were afraid of the crowd of people; so they left him and went away.

Luke 20:19 - The teachers of the law of Moses and the chief priests looked for a way to arrest Jesus right then, because they knew that his parable was against them. But they couldn't, because they were afraid of the people.

---

342 - The Parable of a Wedding Banquet
(Matthew 22:1-14, Luke 14:16-24)

Matthew 22:1-14 - (1) Jesus told them another parable (story): (2) "The kingdom of heaven (*God*) is like a king who prepared a wedding banquet for his son. (3) He sent his servants to those who had been invited to the banquet to tell them to come, but those who were invited refused to come. (4) Then the king sent out more servants and told them, 'Tell those who have been invited that I have prepared my dinner: My oxen and cattle have been butchered and everything is ready to eat. Come to the wedding banquet!' (5) But the invited guests ignored them and left—one went to his field and another went to his business. (6) The others grabbed the king's servants, mistreated them, and killed them. (7) The king was full of anger. He sent out his soldiers and destroyed those murderers, and burned their city. (8) Then the king told his servants, 'The wedding banquet of my son is ready, but those that I have invited do not deserve to come. (9) Therefore go to the street corners and invite anyone you can find to the banquet.' (10) So the servants went out into the streets and gathered all the people they could find—the good and the bad—and the wedding hall was filled with guests. (11) "But when the king came in to see the guests, he noticed a man there who was not dressed in wedding clothes. (12) He asked him, 'Friend, how did you get in here without wedding clothes?' The man was speechless. (13) Then the king told the servants, 'Tie this man hand and foot, and throw him outside into the outer darkness, where people will be weeping and grinding their teeth.'" (14) Jesus said, "For many people are called (*invited*) but only a few are chosen."

Luke 14:16-24 - (16) Jesus told this parable (*story*): "A man was preparing a great banquet and invited many guests. (17) At the time of the banquet he sent his servant to tell everyone who had been invited, 'Come, for everything is now ready!' (18) But they all made excuses. The first person said, 'I have just bought land and I must go see it. Please excuse me.' (19) Another person said, 'I have just bought five teams of oxen and I'm on my way to try them out. Please excuse me.' (20) Still another person said, 'I have just got married, so I can't come.' (21) The servant returned and told his master about all the excuses that those who were invited had made. Then the owner of the house became angry and ordered his servant, 'Go out quickly into the streets and alleys of the town and bring in the poor, crippled, blind, and lame.' (22) The servant said, 'Sir, what you asked us to do, we have already done, but there is still room in the banquet room.' (23) Then the master told his servant, 'Go out to the roads and country paths and persuade people to come in, so that my house will be full. (24) For I tell you the truth: Not one of these people who were invited will eat at my banquet.' "

- -

- -

- -

- -

- -

343 - Paying Taxes to the Roman Emperor
(Matthew 22:15-22, Mark 12:13-17, Luke 20:20-26)

Matthew 22:15-22 - (15) Then the Pharisees left the temple courts and made plans to trap Jesus in what he taught. (16) They sent their disciples to Jesus along with some Herodians (*members of a Jewish political party that supported the Herodian rulers*). They said to him, "Teacher, we know that you are a man of integrity and that you teach the true way of God. You aren't swayed by others, because you pay no attention to who they are. (17) Tell us then, do you think it is right to pay the imperial tax to the Roman emperor Caesar or not?" (18) But Jesus knew the evil intent of their hearts, and said to them, "You are religious hypocrites! Why are you trying to trap me in what I say?" (19) Then Jesus said, "Bring me a coin (*a denarius, a common Roman coin*) used for paying the imperial tax." They brought him one, (20) and he asked them, "Whose image and inscription is on the coin?" (*on one side of the coin was the image of Emperor Tiberius, with the Latin inscription: "Tiberius Caesar, son of the divine Augustus"*) (21) They said, "It is Caesar's." Jesus said to them, "So give to Caesar what is Caesar's, and give to God what is God's." (22) When they heard this, they were amazed and left Jesus and walked away.

Mark 12:13-17 - (13) Later the Jewish religious leaders sent some Pharisees and Herodians (*a Jewish political party supporting the Herodian rulers*) to trap Jesus in what he was teaching. (14) They came to him and said, "Teacher, we know that you speak the truth and that you aren't swayed by others, because you do not worry about who they are; instead you teach the true way of God. Tell us what you think: Is it right to pay the imperial tax to the Roman emperor Caesar or not? (15) Should we pay it or not?" But Jesus knew that they were religious hypocrites, and so he said to them, "Why are you trying to trap me? Bring me the denarius coin (*a day's wages for a laborer*) used for paying the imperial tax, and let me look at it." (16) They brought the coin, and Jesus asked them, "Whose image and inscription is stamped on this coin?" (*On one side of the coin was the image of Emperor Tiberius, with the Latin inscription: "Tiberius Caesar, son of the divine Augustus"*). They said to him, "Caesar's." (17) Then Jesus said to them, "So give to Caesar the things that are Caesar's, and give to God the things that are God's." And they were amazed at how Jesus answered them.

Luke 20:20-26 - (20) The Jewish religious leaders were keeping a very close watch on Jesus, and they sent spies, who pretended to be friendly to him. They hoped to catch Jesus in what he said, so that they could hand him over to the power and authority of the Roman governor. (21) So the spies asked Jesus, "Teacher, we know what you speak and teach is right. You show no favoritism but teach the way of God in accordance with the truth. (22) Tell us, is it lawful for us to pay taxes to the Roman emperor Caesar or not?" (23) But Jesus knew their deception and said to them, (24) "Show me a Roman coin. Whose image and inscription are stamped on it?" They said, "Tiberius Caesar's." (*On one side of the coin was the image of Emperor Tiberius, with the Latin inscription: "Tiberius Caesar, son of the divine Augustus"*). (25) Jesus said to them, "Then give back to Caesar what belongs to Caesar, and give to God what belongs to God." (26) The spies failed to trap Jesus in what he said in public. And they were amazed by his answer, so they no longer asked Jesus any more questions.

---

344 - Marriage After the Resurrection
(Matthew 22:23-33, Mark 12:18-27, Luke 20:27-40)

Matthew 22:23-33 - (23) That same day some Sadducees—who deny the resurrection from the dead—came to Jesus and asked him this question, (24) "Teacher, Moses told us that if a man dies without having children, his brother must marry the widow and have children for him. (25) Now there were seven brothers among us. The first one married and died without children, so he left his wife to his brother. (26) The same thing happened to all seven brothers. (27) Finally, the woman died. (28) Now tell us, which one of the seven brothers will the woman be married to at the resurrection from the dead, since she had married all the brothers?" (29) Jesus said, "You are wrong because you do not know the Bible or the power of God. (30) For at the resurrection of the dead, people will not marry nor be given in marriage; they will be like the angels in heaven. (31) Why do you not believe in the resurrection of the dead? Haven't you read Exodus 3:6, (32) 'I am the God of Abraham, the God of Isaac, and the God of Jacob.' So God is not the God of the dead but of the living." (33) When the crowds of people heard Jesus speak, they were amazed at his teaching.

Mark 12:18-27 - (18) Then some Sadducees—who teach that there is no resurrection from the dead—came to Jesus with a question. (19) They said, "Teacher, Moses wrote to us that if a man's brother dies leaving behind a wife without children, his brother must marry the widow and have children for his brother. (20) Now there were seven brothers. The first one married and died without leaving any children. (21) The second brother married the widow, but he also died having no children. It was the same with the third brother. (22) In fact, none of the seven brothers left any children. And then finally the widow died too. (23) In the resurrection, whose wife will she be, because she was married to all seven brothers?" (24) Jesus said to them, "You are wrong because you do not know the Bible or the power of God. (25) When the dead are resurrected to life, people will not marry nor be given in marriage, but they will be like the angels in heaven. (26) "Now about the resurrection of the dead—have you not read the words of Moses in Exodus 3:6 when God spoke to him at the burning bush? God said to him, 'I am the God of Abraham, the God of Isaac, and the God of Jacob.' (27) So God is the God of the living, not of the dead. You are very wrong!"

Luke 20:27-40 - (27) Some of the Sadducees—who did not believe in the resurrection of the dead—came to Jesus and asked him, (28) "Teacher, Moses wrote that if a man's brother dies and leaves a wife without children, the man must marry his brother's widow and produce children for his brother. (29) Now there were seven brothers. The first brother married a woman and died without children. (30) The second brother (31) and then the third brother married her, and then all seven died, leaving behind no children. (32) Finally, the woman died too. (33) Now tell us, since the woman was married to seven men, who will be her husband at the resurrection of the dead?" (34) Jesus said to them, "The people of this world (*age*) get married and are given in marriage. (35) But the worthy who enter the age to come and the resurrection of the dead will not get married or be given in marriage. (36) They will not die, for they will be like the angels. They are God's children, since they are children of the resurrection. (37) For even Moses believed in the resurrection of the dead. As it is written in Exodus 3:6, when he met God at the burning bush he called the Lord 'the God of Abraham, and the God of Isaac, and the God of Jacob.' (38) So God is not the God of the dead, but is the God of the living!" (39) Then some teachers of the law of Moses (*who believed in the resurrection of the dead*) said to Jesus, "Teacher, very good!" (40) From then on, no one dared to ask Jesus any more questions.

345 - The Greatest Commandments
(Matthew 22:34-40, Mark 12:28-34, Luke 10:25-28)

Matthew 22:34-40 - (34) When the Pharisees heard that Jesus had silenced the Sadducees, they met together. (35) One of the Pharisees, an expert in the law of Moses, tried to test Jesus by asking him this question, (36) "Teacher, which is the greatest commandment in the law of Moses?" (37) Jesus said to him, "Deuteronomy 6:5, 'Love the Lord your God with all your heart and with all your soul and with all your mind.' (38) This is the first and greatest commandment. (39) And the second greatest commandment is Leviticus 19:18, 'Love your neighbor as you love yourself.' (40) For the whole truth of the law of Moses and the prophets (*the entire Old Testament*) are contained in these two commandments."

Mark 12:28-34 - (28) A teacher of the law of Moses came and heard them debating with one another. He noticed that Jesus had given them a good answer and he asked him, "Of all of God's commandments, which one is the most important?" (29) Jesus said, "The most important commandment is Deuteronomy 6:4-5, 'Hear, O Israel, the Lord is our God, the Lord is one. (30) Love the Lord your God with all your heart and with all your soul and with all your mind and with all your strength.' (31) The second greatest commandment is Leviticus 19:18, 'Love your neighbor as yourself.' There is no commandment greater than these two." (32) The man said, "Teacher, well said. You are right in saying that God is one and there is no other but him. (33) To love him with all your heart, with all your understanding, and with all your strength, and to love your neighbor as yourself is much more important than all burnt offerings and sacrifices." (34) When Jesus heard that he had answered him wisely, he said to him, "You are not far from the kingdom of God." And from that time on, no one dared ask him any more questions.

Luke 10:25-28 - (25) On one occasion an expert in the law of Moses stood up to test Jesus. He asked him, "Teacher, what must I do to inherit eternal life?" (26) Jesus said to him, "What is written in the law of Moses? How do you understand what it says?" (27) He said, "It is written in Deuteronomy 6:5, 'Love the Lord your God with all your heart and with all your soul and with all your strength and with all your mind,' and in Leviticus 19:18, 'Love your neighbor as yourself.' " (28) Jesus said, "Very good, your answer is correct; do this and you will live."

346 - Is the Messiah the Son of David?
(Matthew 22:41-46, Mark 12:35-37, Luke 20:41-44)

Matthew 22:41-46 - (41) While the Pharisees were gathered together, Jesus asked them, (42) "What do you think about the Messiah (*Christ*)? Whose son is he?" They said, "The son of David." (43) Jesus asked them, "Why is it then that David, speaking by the Holy Spirit, calls him 'Lord' in Psalm 110:1? For it reads, (44) 'The Lord said to my Lord, "Sit at my right hand until I put your enemies under your feet." ' (45) If then David calls him 'Lord,' how then can the Messiah (Christ) be his son?" (46) The Pharisees had no answer for Jesus, and from that day on no one dared to ask him any more questions.

Mark 12:35-37 - (35) While Jesus was teaching in the temple courts, he asked, "Why do the teachers of the law of Moses say that the Messiah (*Christ*) is the son of David? (36) For David speaking by the Holy Spirit in Psalm 110:1 declared, 'The Lord said to my Lord, "Sit at my right hand until I put your enemies under your feet." ' (37) Therefore, David calls him 'Lord.' So how then can he be his son?" The large crowd of people were listening to Jesus with excitement.

Luke 20:41-44 - (41) Then Jesus said to the Jewish religious leaders, "Why do you teach that the Messiah (*Christ*) is the son of David? (42) For David himself declares in Psalm 110:1, 'The Lord said to my Lord, sit at my right hand (43) until I make your enemies a footstool for your feet.' (44) If David calls him 'Lord', how then can he be called his son?"

347 - Jesus Condemns the Religious Leaders
(Matthew 23:1-36, Mark 12:38-40, Luke 20:45-47)

Matthew 23:1-36 - (1) Then Jesus said to his disciples and the crowds of people, (2) "The Pharisees and teachers of the law sit in the seat of Moses (*seats of special authority in the synagogue*). (3) So be careful to obey what they teach, but do not live as they live, because they do not practice what they preach. (4) They tie heavy religious burdens and put them on the shoulders of people, but they themselves are not willing to lift a finger to move them. (5) Everything they do is done so that they will be seen by other people: They make their phylacteries (*leather boxes containing Bible verses, worn on a man's left arm and forehead*) wide, and their tassels that they wear on their garments (*worn on the four corners of a man's outer garment, the cloak*) long; (6) they love to sit at places of honor at banquets (*on either side of the host*) and in the most important seats in the synagogues; (7) they love to be greeted with respect in the public market and to be called 'Rabbi' (teacher) by others. (8) But you should not be called 'Rabbi,' because you have only one Teacher, and you are all fellow believers. (9) And do not call anyone on earth 'father,' because you have only one Father in heaven. (10) Also you are not to be called 'teacher,' because you only have one Teacher, the Messiah (*Christ*). (11) The greatest among you will be your servant. (12) For whoever exalts themselves in pride will be humbled, and whoever humbles themselves will be exalted by God. (13) How terrible for you, teachers of the law of Moses and Pharisees! You are religious hypocrites! You slam the door of the kingdom of heaven (*God*) in people's faces. And you yourselves do not even enter it, nor will you let those enter who are trying to. (14-15) How terrible for you, teachers of the law of Moses and Pharisees! You are religious hypocrites! You travel over land and sea to win a single convert, and when they convert, you make them twice the child of hell (*gehenna*) as you are. (16) How terrible for you, blind leaders! You say, 'Whoever makes a promise by the temple, it means nothing; but whoever promises by the gold of the temple is bound to keep his oath.' (17) You are blind fools! Which is greater—the gold, or the temple that makes the gold holy? (18) You also say, 'Whoever makes a promise by the altar, it means nothing; but whoever promises by the gift that is on the altar is bound to keep his oath.' (19) You are blind men! Which is greater—the gift, or the altar that makes the gift holy? (20) Therefore, whoever makes a promise by the altar swears an oath by it and by all the offerings on it. (21) And whoever makes a promise by the temple swears an oath by it and by God who dwells in it. (22) And whoever makes a promise by heaven swears an oath by God's throne and by the one who sits on it. (23) How terrible for you, teachers of the law of Moses and Pharisees! You are religious hypocrites! You give to God a tenth (*tithe*) of your spices—mint, dill, and cumin—but you neglect the more important matters of the law—justice, mercy, and faithfulness. You should have practiced these, without neglecting the former things. (24) You are blind leaders! You remove insects from your drinks, but you swallow a camel. (25) How terrible for you, teachers of the law of Moses and Pharisees! You are religious hypocrites! You clean the outside of the cup and dish you use, but your hearts are full of greed and self-indulgence. (26) You blind Pharisees! First clean the inside of the cup and dish, and then the outside will also be clean. (27) How terrible for you, teachers of the law of Moses and Pharisees! You are religious hypocrites! You are like tombs that are painted white and beautiful on the outside, but on the inside they are full of dead, rotting bones and everything unclean. (28) In the same way, on the outside you appear to people as righteous, but on the inside you are full of hypocrisy and wickedness. (29) How terrible for you, teachers of the law of Moses and Pharisees! You are religious hypocrites! You build tombs for the prophets and decorate the graves of the righteous. (30) And you say, 'If we lived in the days of our ancestors, we would not have helped kill the prophets.' (31) In saying this, you testify against yourselves that you are the children of those who murdered the prophets. (32) Go ahead, then, and finish what your ancestors started! (33) You are snakes! You are the children of snakes! Why do you think you will escape being condemned to hell *(gehenna)*? (34) Therefore I am sending you prophets, wise men, and teachers. Some of them you will kill and crucify; others you will flog in your synagogues and chase them from town to town. (35) And so upon you will come all the righteous blood that has been shed on earth, from the righteous blood of Abel to the righteous blood of Zechariah, son of Berekiah, whom you murdered between the temple and the altar. (36) I tell you the truth: This will all come on this generation of Israel."

Mark 12:38-40 - (38) Jesus continued to teach in the temple courts, saying, "Watch out for the teachers of the law of Moses, because they like to walk around in flowing robes and desire to be greeted with respect in the public market, (39) and sit in the seats of importance in the synagogues and in the places of honor at banquets. (40) They devour widows' houses and for a show make long prayers before people. These men will receive the most severe judgment of God."

Luke 20:45-47 - (45) While the people were listening, Jesus said to his disciples, (46) "Beware of the teachers of the law of Moses. They like to walk around in flowing robes and love to be greeted with respect in the public markets and have the most important seats in the synagogues and the places of honor at banquets. (47) They defraud widows' houses and put on a public show with their long prayers. But you can be assured, they will receive a severe judgment from God!"

348 - Jesus Condemns the Religious Leaders
(Luke 11:37-54)

Luke 11:37-54 - (37) When Jesus had finished speaking, a Pharisee invited him to eat with him; so Jesus went into his house and sat at the table. (38) But the Pharisee was surprised when he saw that Jesus did not wash his hands before eating. (39) Then Jesus said to him, "Now you Pharisees clean the outside of the cup and dish, but your hearts are full of greed and wickedness. (40) You are religious fools! Did not the one who made the outside make the inside also? (41) But now as to what is in your heart—be generous to the poor, and everything will be clean for you.(42) How terrible for you Pharisees! For you give God a tenth (*tithe*) of your mint, rue, and all other kinds of garden herbs, but you neglect justice and the love of God. You should give your offering to God without neglecting the justice and love of God. (43) How terrible for you Pharisees! For you love the most important seats in the synagogues and to be greeted with honor in the public market. (44) How terrible for you Pharisees! You are like unmarked graves, which people do not see and walk over without knowing it." (45) Then one of the experts of the law of Moses said to Jesus, "Teacher, when you say these things, you insult us also." (46) Jesus said to him, "And you experts of the law of Moses, how terrible for you! For you load people down with heavy burdens that they struggle to carry, and you will not lift a finger to help them. (47) How terrible for you! For you build tombs for the prophets, and it was your ancestors who killed them. (48) So you testify that you approve of what your ancestors did; they killed the prophets, and you build their tombs. (49) Because of this, God in his wisdom said, 'I will send them prophets and apostles, some they will persecute and others they will kill.' (50) Therefore this generation of Israel will be held guilty for the blood of all the prophets that has been shed since the beginning of the world, (51) from the blood of Abel to the blood of Zechariah, who was killed between the altar and the sanctuary. Yes, I tell you the truth: This generation of Israel will be guilty for it all. (52) How terrible for you experts in the law of Moses! For you have taken away the key to knowledge. You have not entered, and you hinder others from entering." (53) When Jesus went outside, the Pharisees and teachers of the law of Moses began to viciously oppose him and bombard him with hostile questions, (54) because they wanted to condemn him for something he might say.

349 - Jesus Condemns Jerusalem
(Matthew 23:37-39, Luke 13:34-35)

Matthew 23:37-39 - Jesus declared, (37) "Jerusalem, Jerusalem, you who kill God's prophets and throw rocks at those sent to you, how often I have longed to gather your children together, as a mother bird gathers her chicks under her wings, but you were not willing! (38) Look! Your house has been forsaken by God and left desolate. (39) I tell you the truth: You will not see me again until you shout Psalm 118:26, 'Blessed is he who comes in the name of the Lord.'"

Luke 13:34-35 - Jesus declared, (34) "Jerusalem, Jerusalem, you who kill the prophets and stone to death those sent to you! How often I have longed to gather your children together, as a hen gathers her chicks under her wings, but you were not willing! (35) Look! Your house is now forsaken and desolate! I tell you the truth: You will not see me again until you declare Psalm 118:26, 'Blessed is he who comes in the name of the Lord.'"

350 - Jesus on True Giving
(Mark 12:41-44, Luke 21:1-4)

Mark 12:41-44 - (41) Jesus sat down opposite the place where the offerings were given in the temple and watched the crowd putting their money into the temple treasury. He saw many rich people throw in large amounts of money. (42) But a poor widow came and put in two very small copper coins, worth only a few cents. (43) Calling his disciples, Jesus said to them, "I tell you the truth: This poor widow has put more into the temple treasury than all the other people. (44) They all gave out of their wealth, but she gave out of her poverty—she gave everything she had to live on."

Luke 21:1-4 - (1) When Jesus looked up, he saw rich people putting their gifts into the temple treasury. (2) He also saw a poor widow put in two small copper coins. (3) Jesus said, "I tell you the truth: This poor widow has put in more than all of the rich people. (4) For the rich gave out of their abundant wealth, but she gave out of her poverty. She gave all she had to live on."

351 - The Disciples Praise the Jerusalem Temple
(Matthew 24:1, Mark 13:1, Luke 21:5)

Matthew 24:1 - Jesus left the temple courts and was walking away when his disciples came to him and told him to look at the temple buildings.

Mark 13:1 - As Jesus was leaving the Jerusalem temple courts, one of his disciples said to him, "Teacher, look at the massive stones and magnificent buildings of the temple complex!

Luke 21:5 - Some of his disciples were talking about how the temple was decorated with beautiful stones and with gifts dedicated to God.

(Herod the Great had rebuilt the Jewish temple with these massive stones and magnificent buildings).

352 - Jesus Prophecies the Destruction of the Jerusalem Temple
(Matthew 24:2, Mark 13:2, Luke 21:6)

Matthew 24:2 - Jesus said to them, "Do you see all these buildings? I tell you the truth: A time is coming when these temple buildings will be destroyed and not one stone will be left on another—every stone will be thrown down."

Mark 13:2 - Jesus said to him, "Do you see all these great buildings? Not one stone will be left on another; every one will be thrown down."

Luke 21:6- - But Jesus said to them, "Now concerning all the things you see here, the time is coming when not one stone will be left upon another; they will all be thrown down."

(Jesus predicted the Romans' destruction of Jerusalem and the temple, between AD 66 and AD 70).

353 - The Disciples Question Jesus
(Matthew 24:3: Mark 13:3-4; Luke 21:7)

Matthew 24:3 - As Jesus was sitting on the Mount of Olives his disciples came to him in private and asked, "Tell us, when will all these things happen? And what will be the sign of your coming and of the end of this age?"

Mark 13:3-4 - (3) Jesus sat on the Mount of Olives opposite the temple. Peter, James, John, and Andrew asked him in private, (4) "Jesus, tell us, when will these things happen? And what will be the sign that they are all about to be fulfilled?"

Luke 21:7 - The disciples asked Jesus, "Teacher, when will this happen? And what will be the sign that these things are about to take place?"

354 - False Messiahs, Wars, Earthquakes, and Famines
(Matthew 24:4-8, Mark 13:5-8, Luke 21:8-11)

Matthew 24:4-8 - (4) Jesus answered, "Watch out for those who will try to deceive you, (5) because many will come in my name, claiming, 'I am the Messiah (*Christ*),' and they will lead astray many people. (6) You will hear of wars and rumors of wars, but do not be afraid, for these things must take place, but the end is still to come. (7) For nation will rise up and fight against nation and kingdom will rise up and fight against kingdom, and there will be famines and earthquakes in various places. (8) But all of these things are only the beginning of the pains of childbirth."

Mark 13:5-8 - (5) Jesus said to them, "Watch out that no one deceives you. (6) Many people will come in my name, saying, 'I am the Messiah (*Christ*),' and will deceive many. (7) But when you hear of wars and rumors of wars, do not be afraid. For these things must happen, but the end of the world is still to come. (8) Nation will rise up and fight against nation, and kingdom will rise up and fight against kingdom. There will be earthquakes and famines in various places. But these things are only the beginning of the pains of childbirth."

Luke 21:8-11 - (8) Jesus said to his disciples, "Stay alert so that you will not be deceived and led astray, because many will come in my name claiming that they are the Messiah (*Christ*) and that the time is near. Do not follow them! (9) When you hear of wars and uprisings, do not be afraid. These things must happen first, but the end of the world will not come right away." (10) Then Jesus said, "Nation will rise up and fight against nation, and kingdom will rise up and fight against kingdom. (11) There will be great earthquakes, famines and plagues in various places, and there will be terrifying sights and great signs from heaven."

355 - Global Mission and Persecution
(Matthew 24:9-14, Mark 13:9-13, Luke 21:12-18)

Matthew 24:9-14 - (9) Jesus said, "Then you will be arrested and handed over to be punished and killed. People from all over the world will hate you because you believe in me. (10) At that time many believers will turn away from the faith and will betray and hate each other. (11) Many false prophets will appear and lead many people to believe in things that are false. (12) Because of the increase of wickedness, the love of many people will grow cold, (13) but those who stand strong (*endure*) to the end will be saved. (14) And this gospel (*good news*) of the kingdom of God will be proclaimed throughout the whole world as a witness to all nations, and then the end will come."

Mark 13:9-13 - (9) Jesus said, "But you must be on your guard; watch out for yourselves. For you will be handed over to the Jewish local councils and flogged in the synagogues. Because you are my disciples, you will stand before governors and kings as witnesses to them. (10) And the gospel (*good news*) must first be proclaimed to all nations. (11) Whenever you are arrested and brought to trial, do not worry beforehand about what you will say. Just say whatever words that are given to you at that time, because it will be the Holy Spirit within you speaking, and not you. (12) Brother will betray brother to death, and a father will have his child put to death. Children will rebel against their parents and have them put to death. (13) Everyone will hate you because you are my disciples, but those who stand strong (*endure*) to the end will be saved."

Luke 21:12-18 - Jesus said, (12) "But before all these things happen, they will arrest you and persecute you. They will hand you over to synagogues and put you in prison, and you will be brought before kings and governors, because you are my disciples. (13) And so you will be my witnesses before them. (14) But determine in your minds not to worry beforehand about how you will defend yourselves, (15) because I will give you words and wisdom that none of your enemies will be able to oppose or argue against. (16) You will be betrayed even by parents, brothers, sisters, relatives, and friends, and they will put some of you to death. (17) Everyone will hate you because you are my disciples, (18) but not a hair of your head will perish.

356 - Jesus Prophesies the Roman Destruction of Jerusalem
(Matthew 24:15-22, Mark 13:14-20, Luke 21:20-24)

Matthew 24:15-22 - (15) Jesus said, "So when you see standing in the holy place 'the abomination that causes destruction,' as it is written in Daniel 9:27 (let the reader understand), (16) then let those who are living in Judea flee to the mountains for refuge. (17) Those who are on their rooftops (*houses had flat roofs*) should not go down to take anything out of their houses, (18) and those working in their fields (*normally working in their tunics, their inner clothes*) should not go back to their homes to get their clothes (*outer cloaks*). (19) Those days will be horrifying for pregnant women and nursing mothers. (20) Pray that your flight will not take place in winter or on the Sabbath. (21) For then there will be great distress, unequaled from the beginning of the world until now—and never to be equaled again. (22) If those terrible days had not been cut short, no one would survive, but for the sake of the chosen those days will be kept short."

Mark 13:14-20 - (14) Jesus said, "But as it is written in Daniel 9:27, when you see 'the abomination that causes destruction' standing where it does not belong (*let the reader understand*) (14) then let those who are in Judea flee to the mountains. (15) Let no one on a housetop (*houses had a flat roofs*) go down or enter the house to take anything out of it. (16) Let no one working in the field (*they often worked in their inner clothes, tunic*) go back to get their clothes (*outer cloak*). (17) Those days will be terrible for pregnant women and nursing mothers! (18) Pray that this will not take place in the winter (19) because those will be days full of suffering unequaled since God's creation of the world, until now—and will never be equaled again. (20) If the Lord had not cut short these terrible days, no one would survive. But for the sake of the elect, whom he has chosen, he has shortened them."

Luke 21:20-24 - (20) Jesus said, "When you see Jerusalem being surrounded by Roman armies, you will know that its destruction is near. (21) Then let those who are in Judea flee to the mountains, let those in the city leave, and let those in the country not enter the city. (22) For this is the time of punishment in fulfillment of all that has been written (*in the Old Testament*). (23) How terrible it will be in those days for pregnant women and nursing mothers! There will be great trouble in the land and wrath against this people. (24) They will die by the sword and will be taken as prisoners to all the nations. Jerusalem will be trampled on by the Romans until the times of the non-Jews are fulfilled.

(*Jesus predicted the Romans' destruction of Jerusalem and the temple, between AD 66 and AD 70*).

357 - False Christs and Prophets
(Matthew 24:23-26, Mark 13:21-23, Luke 21:8)

Matthew 24:23-26 - Jesus said, (23) "At that time whoever declares to you, 'Look, here is the Messiah (*Christ*)!' or, 'There is the Messiah (*Christ*)!' do not believe them. (24) For false messiahs (*Christs*) and prophets will appear and do great miraculous signs and wonders to deceive, if possible, even the chosen. (25) I am telling you these things before they happen. (26) So if anyone declares, 'The Messiah (*Christ*) is out in the wilderness,' do not go out there; or, 'Here is the Messiah (Christ) in the inner rooms,' do not believe them."

Mark 13:21-23 - Jesus said, (21) "At that time if anyone says to you, 'Look, here is the Messiah (Christ)!' or 'Look, there is the Messiah (*Christ*)!' do not believe them. (22) For false messiahs and false prophets will appear and do miraculous signs and wonders (*miracles*) to deceive, if possible, even the chosen. (23) So be on your guard, because I have told you everything before it happens."

Luke 21:8 - Jesus said to his disciples, "Stay alert so that you will not be deceived and led astray, because many will come in my name claiming that they are the Messiah (*Christ*) and that the time is near. Do not follow them!

358 - The Second Coming of Jesus Christ
(Matthew 24:27-44, Mark 13:24-37, Luke 21:25-36)

Matthew 24:27-44 - Jesus said, (27) "The coming of the Son of Man (*see Daniel 7:13-14*) will be like lightning that flashes in the sky from the east to the west. (28) There will be no surprises, just as we know that wherever there are dead bodies, there will be vultures to eat them. (29) As it is written in Joel 2:10, 'Immediately after the trouble of those days, the sun will be darkened, and the moon will not give off light; the stars will fall from the sky, and the heavenly bodies will be shaken.' (30) Then will appear the sign of the Son of Man in the sky. And then all the peoples of the earth will mourn when they see the Son of Man coming on the clouds, with power and great glory. (31) And he will send out his angels with a loud trumpet call, and they will gather his chosen from the four winds of the earth—from one end of the heavens to the other. (32) Now learn this lesson from the fig tree: As soon as its twigs get tender and its leaves come out, you know that summer is near. (33) So when you see all these things, you will know that the time is near, right at the door. (34) I tell you the truth: This generation will not pass away until all these things have happened. (35) Heaven and earth will pass away, but my words will never pass away. (36) But about the day or hour of the coming of the Son of Man no one knows, not even the angels of heaven, nor the Son, but only the Father. (37) As it was in the days of Noah, so it will be at the coming of the Son of Man. (38) For in those days before the great flood, people were living normal lives—eating and drinking, marrying and giving in marriage—up to the day Noah entered the ark; (39) and they did not know what would happen until the great flood came and washed them. That is how it will be at the coming of the Son of Man. (40) Two men will be working in the field; one will be taken away and the other one will be left. (41) Two women will be grinding grain with a hand mill; one will be taken away and the other one will be left. (42) Therefore stay alert, because you do not know on what day your Lord will come. (43) But understand this: If the house's owner had known at what time of night a thief was coming, he would have kept watch and would not have let the thief break into his house. (44) So you also must be ready, because the Son of Man will come at an hour when you do not expect him."

Mark 13:24-37 - Jesus said, (24) "But in those days, following the time of great distress (*tribulation*), what is written in Isaiah 13:10 will come true, 'The sun will be darkened, and the moon will not give forth its light; (25) the stars will fall from the sky, and the powers in heaven will be shaken.' (26) At that time people will see the Son of Man (*see Daniel 7:13-14*) coming in clouds with great power and glory. (27) And he will send out his angels to gather his chosen ones from the four winds—from the ends of the earth to the ends of the heavens. (28) Now learn this lesson from the fig tree: As soon as its twigs get tender and its leaves come out, you know that summer is near. (29) So also when you see these things happening, you know that it is very near, right at the door. (30) I tell you the truth: This generation of Israel will certainly not pass away until all these things have happened. (31) Heaven and earth will pass away, but my words will never pass away. (32) But about the day or hour no one knows, not even the angels in heaven, nor the Son, but only the Father. (33) Be on your guard! Be alert! Pay close attention for yourself! For you do not know when that time will come. (34) It's like a man who goes away on a trip: He leaves his servants in charge of his house and gives each one a job, and tells the one at the door to keep watch. (35) Therefore keep watch because you do not know when the owner of the house will return—it could be in the evening, or at midnight, or at dawn when the rooster crows. (36) If he comes suddenly, do not let him find you sleeping. (37) What I say to you, I declare to everyone: Keep watch!"

Luke 21:25-36 - Jesus said, (25) "There will be signs in the sun, moon, and stars. On the earth, nations will experience great turmoil and anguish at the roaring and tossing of the sea. (26) People will faint from overwhelming fear at what is coming on this world, for the elements of the heavens will be shaken. (27) At that time they will see the Son of Man (*see Daniel 7:13-14*) coming in a cloud with great power and brilliant glory. (28) When these things begin to take place, stand up and lift up your heads, because your salvation is coming soon." (29) Jesus told the people this parable (*story*), "Look at the fig tree and all of the trees. (30) As soon as they sprout leaves, you know that summer is near. (31) In the same way, when you see these things happening, you will know that the kingdom of God is coming. (32) I tell you the truth: This generation in Israel will see all these things happen. (33) Heaven and earth will pass away, but my words will never pass away. (34) Be careful, or your hearts will be weighted down by partying, drunkenness, and the worries of this life, and the day of the Lord will come upon you suddenly like a trap. (35) For the day of the Lord will come on everyone living on the whole earth. (36) Be always alert, and pray that you will have the strength to escape all that is about to happen, and that you will be able to stand before the Son of Man."

_____

_____

_____

_____

_____

359 - The Parable of a Faithful Servant
(Matthew 24:45-51, Luke 12:41-48)

Matthew 24:45-51 - (45) Jesus told this parable (*story*): "Who then is the faithful and wise servant, whom the master has put in charge of his household servants to give them their food at the proper time? (46) It will be good for that servant whose master finds him doing so when he returns. (47) I tell you the truth, he will put him in charge of all his possessions. (48) But if that servant is wicked and says to himself, 'My master is staying away a long time,' (49) and so he begins to beat his fellow servants and to eat and drink with drunkards, (50) the master of that servant will come on a day when he does not expect him and at a time he is not aware of. (51) He will cut him to pieces and put him in a place with the hypocrites—where people will be weeping and grinding their teeth."

Luke 12:41-48 - (41) Peter asked Jesus, "Lord, are you telling this parable (*story*) to us, or to the people?" (42) The Lord said to him, "Who then is the faithful and wise manager, whom the master puts in charge of his servants to give them their food to eat at the proper time? (43) Blessed is that servant whom the master finds faithfully doing what he was told to do. (44) I tell you the truth: He will put him in charge over everything he owns. (45) But if the servant says to himself, 'My master is taking a long time in coming,' and so he starts to beat the male and female servants and to eat and drink and get drunk, (46) the master of that servant will come at a time when he does not expect him and at an hour he is not aware of. The master will cut that servant into pieces and send him to the place with the unbelievers. (47) The servant who knows the master's will but does not get ready or does not do what the master wants will receive a severe beating. (48) But the servant who does not know the master's will and does things deserving punishment will receive only a few blows. From everyone who has been given much, much will be demanded of them; and from the one who has been entrusted with much, much more will be required of them."

360 - The Parable of Ten Young Girls
(Matthew 25:1-13)

Matthew 25:1-12 - Jesus told this parable (*story*): (1) "At that time the kingdom of heaven (*God*) will be like ten young girls (*virgins*) who took their lamps and went out to meet the bridegroom. (2) Now five of the young girls were foolish, and five were wise. (3) The foolish girls took their lamps but did not take any oil with them. (4) However, the wise girls took oil in jars along with their lamps. (5) The bridegroom was delayed a long time in coming, so they all became tired and fell asleep. (6) At midnight the cry rang out, 'Here comes the bridegroom! Come out to meet him!' (7) Then all the young girls woke up and lit their lamps. (8) The foolish girls said to the wise girls, 'Give us some of your oil because our lamps are going out.' (9) The wise girls said, 'No! There is not enough oil for both of us. Go and buy your own oil.' (10) But while they were going to buy oil, the bridegroom arrived. The wise girls went in with him to the wedding banquet. And the door was shut. (11) Later the foolish young girls came and said, 'Sir! Sir! Open the door for us!' (12) But he replied, 'I tell you the truth: I don't know you.' (13) Therefore keep watch, because you do not know the day or the hour of the coming of the Son of Man (*see Daniel 7:13-14*)."

361 - The Parable of Faithful Stewardship
(Matthew 25:14-30; Luke 19:11-27)

Matthew 25:14-30 - (14) Jesus told this parable (*story*): "Again, the kingdom of God will be like a man going on a journey, who called his servants and entrusted his riches to them. (15) To one servant he gave five bags of money (*a talent was a unit of money not a coin, weighing around 75 lb. and worth around $240,000*), to another two bags of money, and to another one bag of money, each according to his ability. Then the man went on his journey. (16) The servant who received five bags of money immediately went and invested the money and earned another five bags of money. (17) So also, the servant with the two bags of money earned another two bags. (18) But the servant who was given one bag of money went and dug a hole in the ground and buried it. (19) After a long time the master of the servants returned and settled the accounts with them. (20) The servant who had been given five bags of money brought the other five bags that he earned. He said, 'Master, you gave me five bags of money, and I now have five more bags of money to give you.' (21) His master said, 'Well done, good and faithful servant! You have been faithful with a few things; so I will put you in charge of many things. Come and share your master's happiness.' (22) The servant who was given two bags of money also came and said, 'Master, you gave me two bags of money, and now I have two more bags of money to give you.' (23) His master said, 'Well done, good and faithful servant! You have been faithful with a few things; so I will put you in charge of many things. Come and share in your master's happiness!' (24) Then the servant who was given one bag of money came and said, 'Master, because I knew that you are a hard man—harvesting where you have not planted, and gathering where you have not thrown seed—(25) I was afraid and went out and buried the bag of money in the ground. So, here is the bag of money that you gave me.' (26) His master said, 'You wicked and lazy servant! Since you know that I harvest where I have not planted, and gather where I have not thrown seed, (27) you should have put my bag of money in the bank, so that when I returned I would have received it back with interest. (28) So take the one bag of money from him and give it to the servant who had ten bags of money. (29) For whoever has will be given more, and they will have an abundance. Whoever has very little, even what they have will be taken away from them. (30) And throw that worthless servant outside into the darkness—where people will be weeping and grinding their teeth.'

   Luke 19:11-27 - (11) While they were listening to Jesus, he told them a parable (*story*) because he was near Jerusalem and the people expected the kingdom of God to appear immediately. (12) He said, "A man of royal birth traveled to a far country to have himself appointed king and then to return. (13) So he called 10 of his servants and gave them 10 valuable coins (*a mina coin was about three months' wages*), saying, 'Invest this money until I come back.' (14) But his citizens hated him and sent messengers after him to the far country, saying, 'We don't want this man to be our king.' (15) But the man was made king and came back home. Then he sent for the servants to whom he had given his money to invest. He wanted to find out how much money they had earned for him. (16) The first servant came and said, 'Sir, your coin has earned 10 more coins.' (17) The king said, 'Well done, my good servant! Because you have been faithful in little, I will give you charge of 10 cities.' (18) The second servant came and said, 'Sir, your coin has earned five more coins.' (19) The king said, 'You take charge of five cities.' (20) Then another servant came and said, 'Sir, here is your coin; I have kept it safe by wrapping it in a piece of cloth. (21) I was afraid of you, because you are a very hard man. You take out what you did not put in and harvest what you did not plant.' (22) The king said harshly, 'I will judge you by your own words, you wicked servant! You knew that I am a hard man, taking out what I do not put in and harvesting what I did not plant. (23) Why then didn't you put my money in the bank, so that I could have collected some interest when I returned?' (24) Then the king said to those standing by, 'Take his coin away from him and give it to the one who has 10 coins.' (25) They said, 'Sir, he already has 10 coins!' (26) The king said, 'I tell you that to whoever has much, more will be given, but whoever has little, even what he has will be taken away. (27) And bring my enemies who did not want me to be king over them—bring them in front of me and kill them.'

362 - God's Final Judgment
(Matthew 25:31-46)

Matthew 25:31-46 - Jesus said, (31) "When the Son of Man (*see Daniel 7:13-14*) comes in his glory along with all the angels, he will sit on his glorious throne. (32) All the nations will be gathered before him, and he will separate the people from one another as a shepherd separates the sheep from the goats. (33) He will put the sheep on his right side and the goats on his left. (34) Then the King will say to those on his right, 'Come, you who are blessed by my Father; receive your inheritance, the kingdom prepared for you since the creation of the universe. (35) For I was hungry and you gave me something to eat; I was thirsty and you gave me something to drink, I was a stranger and you invited me in, (36) I needed clothes and you clothed me, I was sick and you took care of me, and I was in prison and you came to visit me.' (37) Then the righteous will ask him, 'Lord, when did we see you hungry and feed you, or thirsty and give you something to drink? (38) When did we see you as a stranger and invite you in, or needing clothes and clothe you? (39) When did we see you sick or in prison and go visit you?' (40) The King will reply, 'I tell you the truth: Whatever you did for one of the least of my followers, you did for me.' (41) Then the King will say to those on his left, 'Depart from me, you who are cursed, into the eternal fire prepared for the devil and his demons. (42) For I was hungry and you gave me nothing to eat, I was thirsty and you gave me nothing to drink, (43) I was a stranger and you did not invite me in, I needed clothes and you did not clothe me; I was sick and in prison and you did not take care of me.' (44) They also will ask, 'Lord, when did we see you hungry or thirsty or a stranger or needing clothes or sick or in prison, and did not help you?' (45) The Lord will say 'I tell you the truth: Whatever you did not do for the least of my followers, you did not do for me.' (46) Then the wicked will go away to eternal punishment, and the righteous to eternal life."

363 - Jesus Predicts His Crucifixion
(Matthew 26:1-2)

Matthew 26:1-2 - (1) When Jesus finished teaching all these things, he said to his disciples, (2) "As you know, the Passover Festival is only two days away—and the Son of Man (*see Daniel 7:13-14*) will be handed over to the Romans to be crucified."

364 - The Plan to Kill Jesus
(Matthew 26:3-5, Mark 14:1-2, Luke 22:1-2, John 11:45-53)

Matthew 26:3-5 - (3) Then the Jewish chief priests and elders of the people met together in the palace of Caiaphas the high priest, (4) and they made plans to arrest Jesus in private and kill him. (5) But they said to one another, "We can't kill him during the Passover because the people will riot."

Mark 14:1-2 - (1) Now the Passover and the feast of Unleavened Bread were only two days away, and the Jewish chief priests and teachers of the law of Moses were making devious plans to arrest Jesus secretly and kill him. (2) But they said to each other, "We cannot arrest Jesus during the feast, or the people might riot."

Luke 22:1-2 - (1) Now the time of the Passover—the feast of Unleavened Bread—was coming soon (2) and the Jewish chief priests and teachers of the law of Moses were scheming how to kill Jesus, but they were afraid of the people.

John 11:45-53 - (45) Therefore many of the Jews who had come to visit Mary believed in Jesus after they saw him raise Lazarus from the dead. (46) But some other Jews went and told the Pharisees what Jesus had done. (47) So the chief priests and Pharisees called a meeting of the Jewish governing council (*the Sanhedrin*). They asked, "What are we going to do? For this man Jesus is doing many miraculous signs (*miracles*). (48) If we do not stop him, everyone will believe in him, and then the Romans will come and destroy our temple and our nation." (49) Then one of them, named Caiaphas, who was the high priest that year, said, "You know nothing at all! (50) You don't realize that it is better for you that one man die for the people than that the whole nation be destroyed." (51) Caiaphas did not say this in his own ability, but as high priest that year he prophesied that Jesus would die for the Jewish nation, (52) and not only for the nation, but also to gather together as one the children of God who were scattered abroad (*the Jewish diaspora*). (53) So from that day on the Jewish religious leaders made plans to kill Jesus.

365 - Judas' Plan to Betray Jesus
(Matthew 26:14-16, Mark 14:10-11, Luke 22:3-6)

Matthew 26:14-16 - (14) Then Judas Iscariot—one of Jesus' Twelve Apostles—went to the Jewish chief priests (15) and (*Judas*) asked them, "How much money will you give me to turn Jesus over to you?" And they paid him 30 silver coins (*worth around $5,000*). (16) From then on Judas looked for an opportunity to betray Jesus.

Mark 14:10-11 - (10) Then Judas Iscariot—one of the Twelve Apostles—went to the Jewish chief priests to betray Jesus to them. (11) The religious leaders were thrilled to hear this and promised to give him money. So Judas watched for an opportune time to betray Jesus and deliver him over to them.

Luke 22:3-6 - (3) Then Satan entered the heart of Judas Iscariot, one of Jesus' Twelve Apostles. (4) And Judas went and discussed with the Jewish chief priests and officers of the temple guard how he could betray Jesus. (5) They were thrilled and agreed to give Judas money. (6) He agreed and looked for an opportunity to have Jesus arrested when the people were not present.

366 - Jesus Teaches in the Jerusalem Temple
(Luke 21:37-38)

Luke 21:37-38 - (37) Jesus taught every day in the temple courts, but spent the night in Bethany, on the Mount of Olives. (38) And all the people came early every morning to hear him teach at the temple.

367 - Belief and Unbelief
(John 12:37-43)

John 12:37-43 - (37) Even after Jesus had performed many miraculous signs (*miracles*) in their presence, they still refused to believe in him. (38) This fulfilled the words of Isaiah 53:1, "Lord, who has believed our message and to whom has the arm of the Lord been revealed?" (39) For this is why they did not believe, because, as it is written in Isaiah 6:10, (40) "He has blinded their eyes and hardened their hearts, so they cannot see with their eyes, nor understand with their hearts, nor turn to God—and I would heal them." (41) The prophet Isaiah said this because he saw Jesus' glory and spoke about him. (42) Yet at the same time, many even among the Jewish religious leaders believed in Jesus. But because of the Pharisees they did not openly tell others about their faith for they were afraid that they would be put out of the synagogue, (43) because they loved to receive human praise more than praise from God.

--- (lines for notes) ---

368 - Jesus is the Light of the World
(John 12:44-50)

John 12:44-50 - (44) Then Jesus shouted out, "Whoever believes in me also believes in the one who sent me into this world. (45) Whoever sees me, sees the one who sent me into this world. (46) I came into this world as a light, so that whoever believes in me will not remain in darkness. (47) If anyone hears my teaching but does not practice it, I do not judge that person. For I did not come to judge this world, but to save this world. (48) There is a judge for the person who rejects me and does not believe in my teaching; because the very words I have spoken will condemn them at the last day. (49) For I do not speak on my own, but the Father who sent me commanded me to say all that I have spoken. (50) I know that his commandment leads to eternal life. So whatever I say is just what the Father told me to say."

--- (lines for notes) ---

369 - Apostles Prepare the Passover Meal
(Matthew 26:17-19, Mark 14:12-16, Luke 22:7-13)

Matthew 26:17-19 - (17) On the first day of the festival of Unleavened Bread, the disciples (*Peter and John; see Luke 22:8*) came to Jesus and asked him, "Where do you want us to prepare the Passover meal for you?" (18) Jesus said, "Go into Jerusalem to a certain man and tell him, 'The Teacher says: My appointed time is near. I will celebrate the Passover meal at your house with my disciples.' " (19) So the disciples did as Jesus told them, and they prepared the Passover meal.

Mark 14:12-16 - (12) On the first day of the festival of Unleavened Bread, when it was customary to sacrifice the Passover lamb, Jesus' disciples asked him, "Where do you want us to go and prepare the Passover meal for you to eat?" (13) So Jesus sent two of his disciples (*Peter and John*), telling them, "Go into Jerusalem, and a man carrying a jar of water will meet you. Follow him. (14) Tell the owner of the house he enters, 'The Teacher asks: Where is my guest room, where I can eat the Passover meal with my disciples?' (15) He will show you a large furnished guest room upstairs in his house. Make preparations for us there." (16) The disciples went into the city and they found everything happened as Jesus had told them. So they prepared the Passover meal in the upper room.

Luke 22:7-13 - (7) Then came the day of Unleavened Bread on which the Passover lamb was to be sacrificed. (8) So Jesus told Peter and John, "Go and make preparations for the Passover meal for us, so that we can eat together." (9) They asked, "Where do you want us to prepare it?" (10) Jesus said to them, "As you enter Jerusalem, a man carrying a jar of water will meet you. Follow him to a house that he enters, (11) and tell the owner of the house, 'The Teacher asks, "Where is the guest room, where I can eat the Passover meal with my disciples?" ' (12) He will show you a large room upstairs that is furnished. It is in this guest room that you are to make preparations for our Passover meal." (13) Peter and John left and found things just as Jesus had told them. So they prepared the Passover meal.

(The location of Jesus' last Passover meal with his apostles—the Last Supper—was an upper guest room in a private home in Jerusalem. It has became known as the "Upper Room." Based on the early chapters of the book of Acts, it is possible that the apostles used the Upper Room as a temporary residence or regular gathering place. According to church tradition, the Upper Room was located in the southern part of the old city of Jerusalem, on Mount Zion.)

370 - The Passover Meal
(Matthew 26:20, Mark 14:17, Luke 22:14-16, John 13:1)

Matthew 26:20 - When it was evening, Jesus reclined at the table with his Twelve Apostles.

Mark 14:17 - When evening came, Jesus arrived with the Twelve Apostles.

Luke 22:14-16 - (14) When the time had come, Jesus and his Twelve Apostles sat at the table to eat the Passover together. (15) And Jesus said to them, "I have been very eager to eat this Passover with you before I suffer. (16) For I tell you the truth: I will not eat it again until it is fulfilled in the kingdom of God."

John 13:1 - It was near the time of the Passover feast, and Jesus knew the time had come for him to leave this world and return to the Father. Having loved his disciples who were in this world, he loved them to the end.

371 - The Lord's Supper
(Matthew 26:26-30, Mark 14:22-25, Luke 22:19-20)

Matthew 26:26-29 - (26) While they were eating, Jesus took bread and gave thanks, then he broke the bread and gave the pieces to his disciples, saying, "Take and eat, because this is my body." (27) Then he took the cup of wine, gave thanks, and he gave it to them, saying, "Drink from it, all of you, (28) because this is my blood of the new covenant, which is poured out for the forgiveness of sins of many. (29) I tell you the truth: I will not drink wine again until that day when I drink it with you in my Father's kingdom."

Mark 14:22-25 - (22) While they were eating, Jesus took bread, gave thanks to God, and then he broke it and gave the pieces to his disciples and said, "Take and eat, for this is my body." (23) Then Jesus took the cup of wine. And after he gave thanks to God, he gave it to his disciples, and they all drank from it. (24) Jesus said to them, "This is my blood of the new covenant, which is poured out for many people. (25) I tell you the truth: I will not drink again from the fruit of the vine until that day when I drink it new in the kingdom of God."

Luke 22:19-20 - (16) Then Jesus took bread, gave thanks to God, and broke it. He gave the pieces of bread to the Twelve and said, "This is my body given for you; eat it in remembrance of me." (17) Jesus took the cup of wine, gave thanks to God, and said, "Take this cup of wine, and share it among you. (18) For I tell you the truth: I will not drink wine again until the kingdom of God comes." (20) Jesus took the cup of wine after the meal and said, "This cup is the new covenant in my blood, which is poured out for you.

372 - Jesus on Servanthood
(Luke 22:21-27)

Luke 22:21-27 - Jesus said, (21) "But the one who will betray me is here with me at the table. (22) For what will happen to the Son of Man (*see Daniel 7:13-14*) will happen as it has been determined by God, but how terrible for the one who betrays him!" (23) The apostles began to ask each other which of them would be the one who betrayed Jesus. (24) Then the Twelve Apostles began to argue among themselves about which one of them was considered the greatest. (25) Jesus said to them, "Non-Jewish kings exercise power over the people, and those who rule with authority over them call themselves Benefactors. (26) But you are not to be like them. Instead, the greatest among you will be like the youngest, and a leader will be one who serves others. (27) For you know that in this world the master who eats at the table is greater than the one who serves. But I live among you as the one who serves."

373 - Jesus Washes the Disciples' Feet
(John 13:4-11)

John 13:4-11 - (4) So Jesus got up from the table, removed his outer clothing (*cloak*), and wrapped a towel around his waist. He then filled a bowl with water, (5) and began to wash his disciples' feet, and dried them with the towel wrapped around him. (6) Jesus came to Simon Peter, who said to him, "Lord, are you going to wash my feet?" (7) Jesus said, "You do not know now what I am doing, but later on you will understand." (8) But Peter said, "No! You will never wash my feet!" Jesus said, "You will never be my disciple unless I wash your feet." (9) Simon Peter cried out, "Lord! Then wash not just my feet but my hands and my head as well!" (10) Jesus said, "Whoever has taken a bath needs only to wash their feet; their whole body has been bathed. And you are clean, although not all of you." (11) For Jesus knew that Judas Iscariot was going to betray him; that is why he said not every one was clean.

374 - Follow Jesus' Example of Servanthood
(John 13:12-17)

John 13:12-17 - (12) After washing his disciples' feet, Jesus put on his outer clothing (*cloak*) and returned to his place at the table. He said to his disciples, (13) "Do you understand what I have done for you? You call me your 'Teacher' and 'Lord,' and you are right. For that is what I am. (14) Now that I—your Lord and Teacher—have washed your feet, you also should wash one another's feet. (15) I washed your feet to give you an example to follow. (16) I tell you the truth: A slave is not greater than his master, and a messenger is not greater than the one who sent him. (17) Now that you know my teaching, you will be blessed if you do it."

375 - Judas the Betrayer of Jesus
(Matthew 26:21-25, Mark 14:18-21, John 13:2-30)

Matthew 26:21-25 - (21) And while they were eating, he said to them, "I tell you the truth: One of you will betray me." (22) They were all very troubled and asked, "Lord, is it me?" (23) Jesus said, "The one who has dipped his hand into the bowl with me will betray me. (24) The Son of Man (*see Daniel 7:13-14*) will suffer just as it is written about him in God's word, but how terrible for the one who betrays the Son of Man! It would be much better for him if he had not been born." (25) Then Judas Iscariot, who would betray him, asked, "Teacher (*Rabbi*), surely it isn't me?" Jesus replied, "Yes, it is you."

Mark 14:18-21 - (18) While they were eating at the table, Jesus said, "I tell you the truth: One of you eating with me will betray me." (19) All the disciples were very troubled, and one by one they said to Jesus, "Surely you don't mean me?" (20) Jesus said, "It is one of the Twelve; the one who dips bread into the bowl with me. (21) The Son of Man (*see Daniel 7:13-14*) will go just as it is written about him in the Bible (*Old Testament*). But how terrible it is for the man who betrays the Son of Man! It would be much better for him if he had never been born."

John 13:2-30 - (2) The evening Passover meal was in progress, and the devil had already put into the heart of Judas Iscariot, Simon's son, to betray Jesus. (3) Jesus knew that the Father had put everything under his power, and that he had come from God, and that he was going back to God. (18) Jesus said, "I am not speaking about all of you, because I know those I have chosen. But this is to fulfill Psalm 41:9, 'He who ate my bread has gone against me." (19) I am telling you now before it happens, so that when it does happen you will believe that I am who I am. (20) I tell you the truth: Whoever receives anyone I send receives me; and whoever receives me receives the one who sent me into this world." (21) After Jesus had said this, his heart was troubled in spirit and he told his disciples, "I tell you the truth: One of you is going to betray me." (22) His disciples stared at one another, because they were confused about what he was saying. (23) One of them, the disciple Jesus loved (*the apostle John*), was reclining next to him at the table. (24) Simon Peter motioned to him and said, "Ask Jesus which one of us he is talking about." (25) The disciple leaned against Jesus and asked him, "Lord, which one of us is going to betray you?" (26) Jesus said, "It is the one to whom I will give this piece of bread after I dip it in the dish." Then Jesus dipped the piece of bread into the dish and gave it to Judas, son of Simon Iscariot. (27) As soon as Judas took the piece of bread, Satan entered his heart. So Jesus told Judas, "What you are about to do, do quickly!" (28) But the disciples did not understand why Jesus had said this to Judas. (29) Because Judas was in charge of the money bag, some of the disciples thought Jesus was telling him to buy what was needed for the Passover feast, or to give some money to the poor. (30) As soon as Judas had taken the bread, he left. And it was night.

---

376 - Love One Another
(John 13:31-35)

John 13:31-35 - (31) When Judas was gone Jesus said to his disciples, "Now the Son of Man (*see Daniel 7:13-14*) is glorified and God is glorified in him. (32) If God is glorified in him, God will also glorify the Son in himself, and he will glorify him at once. (33) My dear children, I will be living with you only a little longer. You will look for me, but as I told the Jews so I tell you, where I am going, you cannot come. (34) I give you this new command: Love one another. As I have loved you, so you must love one another. (35) By your love everyone will know that you are my disciples, if you love one another."

377 - Jesus Predicts Peter's Denial
(Luke 22:31-34, John 13:36-38)

Luke 22:31-34 - Jesus said, (31) "Simon (*Peter*), Simon, listen to me. Satan has asked to sift you like wheat. (32) But I have prayed for you, Simon, so that your faith will not fail. And when you repent and return again, be sure to strengthen your fellow brothers." (33) But Simon said to Jesus, "Lord, I am ready to go with you to prison and even to death!" (34) Jesus said, "I tell you the truth: Peter, before the rooster crows today, you will deny that you know me three times."

John 13:36-38 - (36) Simon Peter asked Jesus, "Lord, where are you going?" Jesus said, "Where I am going, you cannot follow now, but you will follow me later." (37) Peter said, "Lord, why can't I follow you now? I will die for you!" (38) Then Jesus said to him, "Will you really die for me? I tell you the truth: Before the rooster crows, you will deny me three times."

378 - Jesus is the Way, the Truth, and the Life
(John 14:1-15)

John 14:1-15 - Jesus said to his disciples, (1) "Do not allow your hearts to be troubled, but believe in God and believe also in me. (2) For my Father's house has many rooms. If this was not true, I would not have told you so, because I am going to prepare a place for you. (3) And if I go to prepare a place for you, I will return and take you to be with me, so that you will be where I am. (4) You know the way to the place where I am going." (5) Thomas said to him, "Lord, we don't know where you are going, so how can you say we know the way?" (6) Jesus said, "I am the way and the truth and the life! No one comes to the Father except through me. (7) If you really know me, you will also know the Father. From now on, you do know him and have seen him." (8) Philip said to Jesus, "Lord, all we ask is that you show us the Father, and that will satisfy us." (9) Jesus said,

"Philip, I have been with you a long time, and you still do not know me? Whoever has seen me has seen the Father. So why do you ask me to show you the Father? (10) Don't you believe that I am in the Father, and the Father is in me? The words that I speak to you are not on my own authority, but the Father who lives in me and does his work through me. (11) Believe me when I tell you that I am in the Father and the Father is in me; or at least believe on the evidence of the miraculous works (*miracles*) themselves. (12) I tell you the truth: Whoever believes in me will also do the works I do, and they will do even greater works than I do, because I am going to the Father. (13) And I will do whatever you ask in my name, so that the Father will be glorified in the Son. (14) You can ask me anything in my name, and I will do it. (15) If you love me, you will obey my teaching."

379 - Jesus Promises the Holy Spirit
(John 14:16-31)

John 14:16-31 - Jesus said, (16) "I will ask the Father, and he will send you the Holy Spirit of truth, who is another Advocate (*Counselor*) to help you and be with you forever.(17) This world cannot receive the Holy Spirit of truth, because it does not see him or know him. But you know him, because he lives with you and will be in you. (18) I will never leave you as orphans, but I will come back for you. (19) Soon, this world will not see me anymore, but you will see me. Because I live, you also will live. (20) On that day you will know that I am in my Father, and you are in me, and I am in you. (21) Whoever has and obeys my teaching is the one who loves me. The one who loves me will be loved by my Father, and I too will love them and reveal myself to them." (22) Then Judas (*not Judas Iscariot*) said, "But, Lord, why are you going to reveal yourself to us but not to this world?" (23) Jesus said, "Whoever loves me will obey my teaching. My Father will love them, and we will come to them and make our home with them. (24) Whoever does not love me will not obey my teaching. My teaching is not my own, it belongs to the Father who sent me into this world. (25) I tell you all these things while I am still living among you. (26) But the Holy Spirit—the Advocate (*Helper or Counselor*)—whom the Father will send in my name will teach you everything and will remind you of everything I have told you. (27) I leave you my peace; my peace I give you! I do not give to you the passing peace that this world gives. Do not allow your hearts to be troubled and do not be afraid. (28) You have heard me say to you, 'I am leaving you, but I am coming back for you.' If you loved me, you should rejoice that I am going to the Father, because the Father is greater than me. (29) I tell you now before I leave you, so that when I leave you, you will believe. (30) I will not tell you much more, because Satan—the ruler of this world— is coming. He has no power over me, (31) but he comes so that this world will learn that I love the Father and do exactly what my Father has told me to do."

380 - Jesus Prepares His Twelve Apostles
(Luke 22:35-38)

Luke 22:35-38 - (35) Then Jesus asked his Twelve Apostles, "When I sent you on your mission journey without a moneybag, backpack, or sandals, did you need anything?" They said, "No." (36) Jesus then said to them, "But now if you have a moneybag, take it, and also a backpack, and if you don't have a sword, sell some clothes (*outer cloaks*) and buy one. (37) For it is written in Isaiah 53:12, 'And he was counted with the rebels.' I tell you the truth: This passage must be fulfilled in me. Yes, what is written about me (*in the Old Testament*) is about to be fulfilled." (38) Jesus' disciples said, "Look, Lord, here are two swords." And Jesus said, "That is enough!"

381 - Jesus Lead the Apostles to the Mount of Olives
(Matthew 26:30, Mark 14:26, Luke 22:39, John 14:31)

Matthew 26:30 - After they sang a song, they left the house for the Mount of Olives.

Mark 14:26 - After they had sung a song, they left and went out to the Mount of Olives.

Luke 22:39 - As was his custom, Jesus went out to the Mount of Olives, and his disciples followed him.

John 14:31 - "Stand up, let us leave this place."

382 - All the Apostles Will Fall Away
(Matthew 26:31-32, Mark 14:27-28)

Matthew 26:31-32 - (31) Then Jesus told his disciples, "This very night you will all fall away from me as it is written in Zechariah 13:7, 'I will strike the shepherd, and the sheep of the flock will be scattered.' (32) But after I have risen from the dead, I will go ahead of you into Galilee."

Mark 14:27-28 - (27) Jesus said to his Twelve Apostles, "You will all fall away from me, because it is written in Zechariah 13:7, 'I will strike the shepherd, and the sheep will be scattered.' (28) But after I rise from the dead, I will go ahead of you into Galilee."

383 - Jesus Predicts Peter's Denial
(Matthew 26:33-35, Mark 14:29-31)

Matthew 26:33-35 - (33) Peter said to Jesus, "Even if everyone else leaves you, I will never leave you." (34) Jesus answered, "I tell you the truth: You will deny me three times this very night before the rooster crows." (35) But Peter declared, "Even if I must die with you, I will never deny you!" And all of the apostles said the same thing.

Mark 14:29-31 - (29) Peter declared, "Even if everyone else falls aways, I will never fall away!" (30) Jesus said to him, "I tell you the truth: Tonight—yes, tonight—before the rooster crows twice, you will deny me three times." (31) But Peter insisted strongly, "Even if I have to die with you, I will never deny you!" And all the other apostles said the same thing.

384 - Jesus is the Vine
John 15:1-8)

John 15:1-8 - Jesus said, (1) "I am the true vine, and my Father is the gardener. (2) He cuts off every branch in me that doesn't produce fruit, and he prunes every branch that does produce fruit, so that it will produce even more fruit. (3) You are already clean because of the teaching I have spoken to you. (4) Live in me, as I also live in you, because no branch can produce fruit separate from the vine. Just as the branch must remain in the vine, so neither can you produce fruit unless you remain in me. (5) I am the vine, and you are the branches. If you live in me and I live in you, you will produce much fruit, but apart from me you can do nothing. (6) If you do not live in me, you are like a branch that is thrown away and dries up. And dried branches are then gathered and thrown into the fire and burned up. (7) If you live in me and my words live in you, ask me for whatever you desire, and it will be done for you. (8) The Father is glorified when you produce much fruit, proving that you are my disciples."

385 - Live in the Love of Jesus
(John 15:9-17)

John 15:9-17 - Jesus said, (9) "As the Father has loved me, so I have loved you. Now live in my love! (10) If you obey my teaching, you will live in my love, just as I have obeyed my Father's teaching and live in his love. (11) I tell you these things so that my joy will be in you and that you will have abundant joy. (12) This is my commandment: Love one another as I have loved you. (13) The greatest act of love is this: To lay down your life for your friends. (14) You are my friends if you obey my teaching. (15) I no longer call you servants, because a servant does not know what his master is doing. Instead, I call you friends, because everything I have learned from my Father I have made known to you. (16) You did not choose me, but I chose you and appointed you, so that you will go and produce fruit—fruit that will remain—and so that whatever you ask in my name the Father will give you. (17) This is my command: Love one another!"

386 - Jesus' Disciples Will Be Persecuted
(John 15:18-21)

John 15:18-21 - Jesus said, (18) "If the world hates you, remember that it hated me first. (19) If you belonged to this world, it would love you as one of its own. But you do not belong to this world, because I have brought you out of this world. That is why the world hates you. (20) Remember what I taught you: 'A servant is not greater than his master.' If they persecuted me, they will persecute you also. If they obeyed my teaching, they will obey your teaching also. (21) They will treat you this way because of my name, because they do not know the one who sent me into this world."

387 - The Holy Spirit of Truth
(John 15:22-27)

John 15:22-27 - Jesus said, (22) "If I had not come into this world and spoken to them, they would not be guilty of sin; but now they have no excuse for their sin. (23) Whoever hates me, hates my Father also. (24) If I had not done among them the miraculous works (*miracles*) no one else did, they would not be guilty of sin. But they have seen my miraculous works, and yet they still hated both me and my Father. (25) This happened to fulfill Psalm 35:19, 'They hated me for no reason.' (26) When the Holy Spirit of truth comes, whom I will send to you from the Father—the Advocate who proceeds from the Father—he will bear witness of me. (27) And you, my disciples, also must bear witness of me, because you have been with me from the beginning."

388 - Future Persecution
(John 16:1-4)

John 16:1-4 - Jesus said, (1) "I tell you all these things so you will not fall away from the faith. (2) For the Jewish religious leaders will excommunicate you from the synagogue. In fact, the time is coming when those who kill you will think they are murdering you in the service of God. (3) They will do these things to you because they have not known the Father or me. (4) I have told you these things so that when their time comes you will remember that I warned you about them. I did not tell you these things from the beginning, because I was with you."

389 - The Ministry of the Holy Spirit
(John 16:5-15)

John 16:5-15 - Jesus said, (5) "But now I am going to him who sent me into this world. Now you don't need to ask me, 'Where are you going?' (6) But because I have said that I am leaving you, your hearts are filled with sadness. (7) I tell you the truth: It is for your good that I am going away. Unless I go away, the Holy Spirit—the Advocate—will not come to you; but if I go, I will send him to you. (8) When the Holy Spirit comes, he will convict this world concerning sin and righteousness and judgment: (9) Concerning sin, because people do not believe in me; (10) concerning righteousness, because I am going to the Father and you will see me no longer; (11) and concerning judgment, because Satan—the ruler of this world—is already condemned. (12) I have much more to teach you, but you are not ready to accept it now. (13) But when the Holy Spirit of truth comes, he will guide you into all of God's truth. He will not speak on his own authority, but he will speak only what he hears. He will tell you what is yet to come. (14) He will glorify me because it is from me that he will receive what he will tell you. (15) All that belongs to the Father is mine. That is why I said the Holy Spirit will receive from me what he will tell you."

390 - Jesus Speaks About His Ascension to Heaven
(John 16:16-24)

John 16:16-24 - (16) Jesus went on to say, "In a little while I will leave and you will see me no more, but then after a little while you will see me again." (17) Confused, some of his disciples said to one another, "What is he talking about when he says, 'In a little while you will see me no more, but then after a little while you will see me again?' and 'Because I am going to the Father'?" (18) The disciples kept asking, "What does he mean by 'a little while'? We don't understand what he is saying." (19) Jesus knew that his disciples wanted to ask him about what he was saying, so he said to them, "Are you asking one another what I meant when I said, 'In a little while you will see me no more, but then after a little while you will see me again'? (20) I tell you the truth: When I leave, you will cry and mourn, but this world will rejoice. You will mourn, but your sorrow will become joy. (21) A woman giving birth has great pain at the time she is giving birth, but right after she gives birth she forgets her pain because of her great joy for her new baby born into the world. (22) In the same way, your hearts will be filled with sadness when I leave, but when I come again your hearts will be filled with joy, and no one will be able to take this joy away from you. (23) In the day that I come again, you will no longer ask me any questions. I tell you the truth: My Father will give you whatever you ask in my name. (24) Until now you have not asked for anything in my name. Ask and you will receive, and you will have abundant joy."

391 - Jesus Has Overcome the World
(John 16:25-33)

John 16:25-33 - Jesus said, (25) "Although I have been teaching you using figures of speech, the time is coming when I will no longer speak to you in figures of speech, but I will tell you plainly about my Father. (26) At that time you will ask in my name. I am not saying that I will ask the Father on your behalf. (27) No, for the Father loves you because you have loved me and have believed that I came from God. (28) I came into this world from the Father, and now I am leaving this world and returning to the Father." (29) Then Jesus' disciples said, "Now you are speaking in plain language and not in figures of speech. (30) Now we can see that you know all things and that you do not even need to have anyone ask you questions. This is why we believe that you came from God." (31) Jesus said, "Do you now believe? (32) Well, I tell you that a time is coming, and in fact has now come, when you will be scattered. You will leave me alone and go to your own home. But I will not be alone, because my Father will be with me. (33) I tell you these things so that in me you will have my peace. In this world you will have trouble. But take heart, be strong! For I have overcome this world!"

392 - Jesus Prays for Himself
(John 17:1-5)

John 17:1-5 - (1) After Jesus taught his disciples, he looked up to heaven and prayed "Father, my time has come. Glorify your Son, that your Son can glorify you. (2) For you have given him authority over all people, so that he can give eternal life to whoever you have given him. (3) Now this is eternal life: That they know you, the only true God, and Jesus Christ, whom you have sent into this world. (4) I have brought you glory on earth by finishing the work you gave me to do. (5) And now Father, glorify me in your presence with the glory I had with you before the creation of the universe."

393 - Jesus Prays for His Disciples
(John 17:6-19)

John 17:6-19 - Jesus prayed, (6) "I have revealed your name to the people you gave me out of this world. They were yours, but you gave them to me and they have obeyed your word. (7) Now they know that everything you have given me comes from you. (8) For I taught them the words you gave me and they believed. They believe with certainty that I came from you, and they believed that you sent me into this world. (9) I pray for them. I am not praying for the world, but for those you have given me, because they are yours. (10) All I have is yours, and everything you have is mine. And I am glorified in them. (11) I am leaving this world, but my disciples are still in this world, and I am coming to you. Holy Father, protect my disciples by the power of your name—the name you gave me, so that they will be one as we are one. (12) While I was living with them I protected them and kept them safe by the name you gave me. None of them has been lost except the one (*Judas Iscariot*) destined to destruction, so that God's Word would be fulfilled. (13) I am now coming to you, but I say these things while I am still living in this world, so that they will have the fullness of my joy within them. (14) I taught my disciples your word and the world has hated them, because they are not of this world any more than I am of this world. (15) My prayer is not that you take them out of this world but that you protect them from Satan, the evil one. (16) They do not belong to this world, even as I am not of this world. (17) Make them holy by the truth, for your word is truth. (18) As you sent me into this world, I have sent my disciples into this world. (19) And for them I sanctify myself, so that they too will be holy in truth."

394 - Jesus Prays for His Future Disciples
(John 17:20-26)

John 17:20-26 - Jesus said, (20) "I pray not for my disciples alone. I pray also for whoever will believe in me through their message, (21) so that they all will be one, Father, just as you are in me and I am in you. May they also be one in us so that this world will believe that you sent me into this world. (22) I have given them the glory that you gave me, so that they will be one as we are one—(23) I in them and you in me—so that they will be brought to complete unity. Then the world will know that you sent me into this world, and that you have loved them even as you have loved me. (24) Father, I want those you have given me to be with me where I am, so that they can see my glory—the glory you gave me because you loved me before the creation of the universe. (25) Righteous Father, although this world does not know you, I know you, and my disciples know that you have sent me into this world. (26) I have revealed your name to them, and I will continue to make it known, so that the love you have loved me with will be in them, and I will live in them."

395 - The Garden of Gethsemane
(Matthew 26:36, Mark 14:32, Luke 22:39, John 18:1)

Matthew 26:36 - Then Jesus walked with his apostles to a garden of olive trees called Gethsemane.

Mark 14:32 - Jesus and his disciples walked to a garden of olive trees called Gethsemane.

Luke 22:39 - As was his custom, Jesus went out to the Mount of Olives, and his disciples followed him.

John 18:1 - When Jesus finished saying these things, he walked with his disciples across the Kidron Valley to a garden of olive trees called Gethsemane.

(The garden of Gethsemane is located at the bottom of the slope of the Mount of Olives opposite the Temple Mount).

396 - Jesus Prays in Gethsemane
(Matthew 26:36-46, Mark 14:32-42, Luke 22:40-46)

Matthew 26:36-46 - (36) He said to his disciples, "Sit here while I go over there and pray." (37) Jesus took Peter, James, and John along with him, and he began to become deeply grieved and troubled. (38) Then he said to them, "My soul is so overcome with sorrow I feel as if I am going to die. Stay here and keep watch with me." (39) Going a little farther, Jesus fell with his face to the ground and prayed, "My Father, if it is possible, take this cup of suffering from me; yet not as I will, but as you will. I want to do your will!" (40) Then he went back to his disciples and found them sleeping. Jesus asked Peter, "Couldn't you stay awake with me for one hour? (41) Watch and pray so that you will not fall into temptation, for the spirit is willing, but the flesh is weak." (42) Jesus went away a second time and prayed, "My Father, if it is not possible for this cup of suffering to be taken away unless I drink it, I want to do your will!" (43) When he went back to his disciples, he found them sleeping, for they were tired. (44) So he left them and went away again and prayed a third time, saying the same words. (45) Then he went back to his disciples and said to them, "Are you still sleeping and resting? Look, the time has come, and the Son of Man (*see Daniel 7:13-14*) is delivered into the hands of sinners. (46) Get up! Let's go! Here comes my betrayer!"

Mark 14:32-42 - (32) Jesus said to his disciples, "Sit here while I go and pray." (33) He took Peter, James, and John along with him, and he began to be deeply grieved and troubled. (34) Jesus said to them, "My soul is overcome with sorrow to the point of death. Stay here and keep watch." (35) Going a little farther, Jesus fell to the ground and prayed that if possible this time of suffering would pass from him. (36) Jesus prayed, "Abba (*"Father" in Aramaic*), Father, everything is possible for you. Take this cup of suffering from me. Yet not what I want, but only your will be done!" Mark 14:37-38 - (37) Then Jesus returned to his disciples and found them sleeping. He said, "Simon (*Peter*), are you sleeping? Couldn't you keep watch for one hour? (38) Watch and pray so that you will not fall into temptation, because the spirit is willing, but the body (*flesh*) is weak." (39) Jesus went away a second time and prayed the same prayer as before. (40) When he returned, he again found his disciples sleeping, because they were tired. They did not know what to say to Jesus. (41) Returning the third time, Jesus said to them, "Are you still sleeping and resting? Enough! The time has come. Look, the Son of Man (*see Daniel 7:13-14*) is delivered into the hands of sinners. (42) Get up! Let us go! Here comes my betrayer!"

Luke 22:40-46 - (40) When they arrived at the garden of olive trees called Gethsemane, he said to them, "Pray that you will not fall into temptation." (41) Jesus went a short distance from his disciples, got down on his knees, and prayed, (42) "Father, if you are willing, take this cup of suffering from me, but not my will, but yours be done!" (43) An angel from heaven appeared to Jesus and gave him strength. (44) And experiencing deep agony, he prayed with greater energy, so that his sweat became like drops of blood falling down to the ground. (45) When Jesus stood up from praying, he walked back to his disciples and found them sleeping, because they were tired from sorrow. (46) Jesus said to them, "Why are you sleeping? Get up and pray so that you will not fall into temptation."

397 - Jesus Arrested in Gethsemane
(Matthew 26:47-56, Mark 14:43-49, Luke 22:47-53, John 18:2-11)

Matthew 26:47-56 - (47) While Jesus was still speaking, Judas Iscariot, one of his Twelve Apostles, arrived leading a large number of people carrying swords and clubs. They were sent by the Jewish chief priests and elders. (48) Judas the betrayer had arranged a signal with them, saying, "The one I kiss (*on the cheeks*) is Jesus, arrest him." (49) Judas went to Jesus and said, "Greetings, Teacher (*Rabbi*)!" and kissed him. (50) Jesus replied, "My friend, do what you came to do." Then the men stepped forward and grabbed Jesus and arrested him. (51) Seeing this, Peter took out his sword and cut off the ear of the high priest's servant. (52) Jesus shouted, "Put your sword away! All who fight with the sword will die by the sword. (53) You know I could call on my Father, and he would immediately send me more than 12 armies of angels. (54) But if I did, how then would God's word be fulfilled that says it must all happen this way?" (55) At that time, Jesus said to the crowd, "Am I leading a rebellion that you have come out with swords and clubs to arrest me? Every day I sat teaching the people in the temple courts, but you did not arrest me. (56) But this has all happened so the words of the (*Old Testament*) prophets would come true."

Mark 14:43-49 - (43) While Jesus was still speaking, Judas Iscariot, one of the Twelve Apostles, brought a crowd of people armed with swords and clubs, sent from the Jewish chief priests, teachers of the law of Moses, and elders. (44) Now Judas, the betrayer, had given them this signal: "The one I kiss (*on the cheeks*) is Jesus; arrest him and lead him away with the guards." (45) Going immediately to Jesus, Judas said, "Teacher (*Rabbi*)!" and kissed him (*on the cheeks*). (46) The men grabbed Jesus and arrested him. (47) Then one (*Peter*) who was standing nearby drew his sword and cut off the ear of the high priest's servant. (48) Jesus said, "Am I leading a rebellion that you have come with swords and clubs to arrest me? (49) I taught every day in the temple courts, and you did not arrest me. But now the Bible (*Old Testament*) must be fulfilled."

Luke 22:47-53 - (47) While Jesus was still speaking, a crowd of people led by Judas Iscariot, one of the Twelve Apostles, came up to him. Judas approached Jesus to give him a kiss (*on the cheeks*), (48) but Jesus asked him, "Judas, are you betraying the Son of Man (*see Daniel 7:13-14*) with a kiss?" (49) When Jesus' disciples saw what was about to happen, they said, "Lord! Should we attack them with our swords?" (50) One of his disciples (*Peter*) took his sword and cut off the right ear of the high priest's servant. (51) But Jesus yelled, "Stop!" He touched the man's ear and healed him. (52) Then Jesus said to the Jewish chief priests, officers of the temple guard, and elders who had come to arrest him, "Are you arresting me with swords and clubs as if I am leading a rebellion? (53) I taught daily in the temple courts, and you did not arrest me. But this is now your time—a time when the authority of darkness has come."

John 18:2-11 - (2) Now Judas Iscariot, who betrayed Jesus, knew where Gethsemane was because Jesus had often met there with his disciples. (3) So Judas led a group of soldiers, some officials from the Jewish chief priests and the Pharisees there. They carried torches, lanterns, and weapons. (4) Jesus knew what was going to happen to him, and he went out and asked them, "Who are you looking for?" (5) They said, "Jesus of Nazareth." (6) Jesus said, "I AM!" (*Jesus probably used the name of God "I AM WHO I AM," as written in Exodus 3:14.*) Judas Iscariot was standing with them, and when Jesus said, "I AM," they stepped back and fell to the ground. (7) Jesus asked them again, "Who are you looking for?" They said, "Jesus of Nazareth." (8) Jesus said, "I told you that I am the one you are looking for. If you are looking for me, then let my disciples go." (9) This happened so that the words he had spoken would be fulfilled: "I have not lost any of those you gave me." (10) Then Simon Peter drew his sword and cut off the right ear of Malchus, the servant of the high priest. (11) Jesus shouted to Peter, "Put your sword away! I must drink the cup of suffering that the Father has given me."

398 - All the Disciples Desert Jesus
(Matthew 26:56, Mark 14:50-52)

Matthew 26:56 - Then all the disciples deserted Jesus and ran away.

Mark 14:50-52 - (50) Then everyone ran away and deserted Jesus. (51) A young man who was wearing only a linen garment was following Jesus. When they grabbed him, he fled naked, (52) leaving his garment behind.

399 - Jesus Taken to High Priest Annas
(John 18:12-14)

John 18:12-14 - (12) Then the group of soldiers with their commander and the Jewish religious leaders arrested and bound Jesus. (13) They first took him to Annas, who was the father-in-law of Caiaphas, the high priest that year. (14) Caiaphas was the one who had told the Jewish religious leaders that it would be good if one man died for the people *(see John 11:49-52)*.

(Although Caiaphas held the official position of high priest, Annas was considered the patriarch of the high priestly family. They possibly lived in different wings of the same palace, with a common courtyard, located on the eastern slope of Mount Zion).

400 - Peter's First Denial of Jesus
(John 18:15-17)

John 18:15-17 - (15) Simon Peter and another disciple followed Jesus. Because the other disciple was known to the high priest, he went with Jesus into the high priest's courtyard, (16) but Peter stayed outside the gate of the courtyard. The other disciple, who was known to the high priest, came back, spoke to the servant girl on guard there, and brought Peter inside the courtyard. (17) The servant girl asked Peter, "Aren't you one of Jesus' disciples?" Peter said, "No, I am not!"

401 - Jesus Questioned by High Priest Annas
(John 18:19-23)

John 18:19-23 - (19) Meanwhile, the high priest Annas questioned Jesus about his disciples and his teaching. (20) Jesus said, "I continually taught in the synagogues and in the temple courts, where the Jews gather together. I taught you nothing in secret. (21) Why are you questioning me? Ask the people who heard my teaching. Surely they know what I taught." (22) When Jesus said this, one of the officials hit him in the face. He demanded, "Stop speaking to the high priest that way!" (23) Jesus said, "Tell me what I said wrong. But if I spoke the truth, why did you hit me?"

--- --- --- --- --- --- --- --- --- --- --- --- --- --- --- --- --- --- --- ---

--- --- --- --- --- --- --- --- --- --- --- --- --- --- --- --- --- --- --- ---

--- --- --- --- --- --- --- --- --- --- --- --- --- --- --- --- --- --- --- ---

--- --- --- --- --- --- --- --- --- --- --- --- --- --- --- --- --- --- --- ---

--- --- --- --- --- --- --- --- --- --- --- --- --- --- --- --- --- --- --- ---

402 - Jesus Taken to High Priest Caiaphas
(Matthew 26:57-58, Mark 14:53-54, Luke 22:54, John 18:18, 24)

Matthew 26:57-58 - (57) Those who had arrested Jesus took him to Caiaphas the high priest, where the teachers of the law of Moses and the elders had already gathered. (58) But Peter followed Jesus at a distance to the courtyard of the high priest. He went inside and sat down with the guards to see what would happen.

Mark 14:53-54 - (53) After arresting Jesus, they led him away to Caiaphas the high priest. And all the Jewish chief priests, elders, and teachers of the law of Moses met together. (54) Peter followed him from a distance, right into the courtyard of the high priest. There he sat with the guards and warmed himself by the fire.

Luke 22:54 - They arrested Jesus and took him away to the palace of the high priest.

John 18:24 - Then Annas sent Jesus, bound, to Caiaphas the high priest.

John 18:18 - It was cold, and the servants and officials stood around a fire they had made to keep warm. Peter also was standing with them to keep warm.

(*Caiaphas, possibly located on the eastern slope of Mount Zion*).

--- --- --- --- --- --- --- --- --- --- --- --- --- --- --- --- --- --- --- ---

--- --- --- --- --- --- --- --- --- --- --- --- --- --- --- --- --- --- --- ---

--- --- --- --- --- --- --- --- --- --- --- --- --- --- --- --- --- --- --- ---

--- --- --- --- --- --- --- --- --- --- --- --- --- --- --- --- --- --- --- ---

--- --- --- --- --- --- --- --- --- --- --- --- --- --- --- --- --- --- --- ---

403 - Peter's Second Denial of Jesus
(Matthew 26:69-72, Mark 14:66-70, Luke 22:55-58, John 18:25)

Matthew 26:69-72 - (69) Now Peter sat in the courtyard of the high priest, and a servant girl said to him, "You also were with Jesus of Galilee." (70) But Peter denied it before them all, saying, "I don't know what you're talking about." (71) Then Peter went to the gate, where another servant girl saw him and said to everyone there, "This man is a follower of Jesus of Nazareth." (72) But Peter denied it again, with an oath, "I don't know this man Jesus!"

Mark 14:66-70 - (66) While Peter was below in the courtyard, one of the servant girls of the high priest walked by. (67) When she saw Peter warming himself by the fire, she looked him in the face and said, "You were with Jesus the Nazarene." (68) But Peter denied it, saying, "I do not know what you're talking about." He went out into the entryway and the rooster crowed. (69) When the servant girl saw him there, she said again to those standing around, "This man is one of the followers of Jesus." (70) But again Peter denied it.

Luke 22:55-58 - (55) When they arrived, they started a fire in the middle of the courtyard and sat down together, and Peter sat down with them. (56) Then a servant girl saw Peter sitting by the fire and looking closely at his face said, "This man was with Jesus." (57) But Peter said, "Woman, I do not know Jesus!" (58) A little later someone else saw Peter and said, "You are one of the followers of Jesus." Peter said, "Man, I do not know Jesus!"

John 18:25 - Meanwhile, Simon Peter was still warming himself by the fire. Those around him asked him, "Aren't you one of Jesus' disciples?" Peter said, "No! I am not."

404 - Jesus Questioned by High Priest Caiaphas
(Matthew 26:59-66, Mark 14:55-60, Luke 22:63-64)

Matthew 26:59-66 - (59) The chief priests and the Jewish governing council (*the Sanhedrin*) were looking for false evidence against Jesus so that they could put him to death. (60) But they could not find anything wrong about Jesus, although many false witnesses came forward. Finally two came forward (61) and declared, "Jesus said, 'I will destroy God's temple and rebuild it in three days.' " But Jesus remained silent and did not say anything. Again the high priest asked him, "Are you the Messiah (*Christ*), the Son of the Blessed One?" (62) Then the high priest stood up and said to Jesus, "Are you not going to answer these charges? What are you going to say against the testimony of these men?" (63) But Jesus did not say anything. The high priest said to him, "I charge you under oath by the living God, tell us if you are the Messiah (*Christ*), the Son of God!" (64) Jesus said, "Yes, as you have said so, but I say to all of you as it is written in Psalm 110:1, from now on you will see the Son of Man (*Daniel 7:13-14*) enthroned in authority at the right hand of the Mighty God, and coming on the clouds of heaven." (65) Then the high priest tore his clothes and said, "He speaks blasphemy against God! Why do we need any more witnesses? Everyone has heard him speak blasphemy." The high priest asked, (66) "What do you think we should do?" The Jewish religious leaders said, "He is guilty and must be put to death."

Mark 14:55-60 - (55) The chief priests and the whole Jewish governing council (*the Sanhedrin*) were seeking for evidence against Jesus so that they could put him to death, but they did not find any. (56) They had many false witnesses, but their statements did not agree. (57) Then some people stood up and told lies about Jesus, saying, (58) "We heard him say, 'I will destroy our temple made with human hands and in three days I will build another one, not made with hands.'" (59) But even then their testimonies did not agree with each other. (60) Then the high priest stood up before them and asked Jesus, "Aren't you going to answer these charges? What about this testimony that these men are bringing against you?"

Luke 22:63-64 - (63) Then the high priest tore his clothes and yelled, "We do not need any more witnesses! (64) You have heard him blaspheme. What should we do?" The religious leaders condemned him and said that he deserved to die.

405 - Jesus is Mocked and Beat
(Matthew 26:67-68, Mark 14:65, Luke 22:63-65)

Matthew 26:67-68 - (67) Then they spit in his face and hit him with their fists. Others slapped him, (68) saying, "Prophesy to us, Messiah (*Christ*)! Who hit you?"

Mark 14:65 - Then some began to spit on him; they blindfolded him and hit him with their fists, saying, "Prophesy!" And the guards took him and beat him.

Luke 22:63-65 - (63) The men who were guarding Jesus began mocking and beating him. (64) They blindfolded him and said, "Prophesy! Who hit you?" (65) They said many insulting things to him.

406 - Peter's Third Denial of Jesus
(Matthew 26:73-75, Mark 14:70-72, Luke 22:59-62, John 18:26-27)

Matthew 26:73-75 - (73) After a little while, those standing there went up to Peter and said, "Yes, you are a follower of Jesus; you speak with the accent of a Galilean." (74) Then Peter began to call down curses, and he swore to them, "I don't know this man Jesus!" Immediately a rooster crowed. (75) Then Peter remembered what Jesus had said: "Before the rooster crows, you will deny me three times." And he went outside and cried bitterly.

Mark 14:70-72 - (70) After a short time, those standing nearby said to Peter, "Yes, you are one of the followers of Jesus, for you are a Galilean (*based on his accent*)." (71) Peter began to call down curses on himself, and he swore to them, "I don't know this man Jesus that you're talking about!" (72) Immediately the rooster crowed the second time. Then Peter remembered what Jesus had told him: "Before the rooster crows two times, you will deny me three times." And Peter broke down and cried.

Luke 22:59-62 - (59) About an hour later another person insisted, "Certainly this man is a follower of Jesus; he is from Galilee (*probably based on his accent*)." (60) Peter said, "Man, I don't know what you are talking about!" While he was speaking, a rooster crowed. (61) The Lord turned and looked straight in Peter's eyes, and then he remembered what Jesus had told him, "Before the rooster crows today, you will deny me three times." (62) And Peter went outside and cried bitterly.

John 18:26-27 - (26) One of the high priest's servants who was standing alongside Peter, a relative of the man whose ear Peter had cut off, said to him, "Didn't I see you in the garden of Gethsemane with Jesus?" (27) Again Peter denied it and at that moment a rooster began to crow.

407 - The Jewish Sanhedrin Condemns Jesus
(Matthew 27:1, Mark 15:1, Luke 22:66-71)

Matthew 27:1 - Early in the morning (*around 6 a.m.*), all the Jewish chief priests and elders of the people made their plans to have Jesus put to death.

Mark 15:1 - Very early in the morning (*around 6 a.m.*), the chief priests, with the elders, the teachers of the law of Moses, and the whole Jewish governing council (*the Sanhedrin*) made their plans.

Luke 22:66-71 - (66) At daybreak (*around 6 a.m.*), the Jewish council (*the Sanhedrin*) of the elders of the people—both the chief priests and teachers of the law of Moses—met together, and had Jesus brought before them. 67) They said to him, "Tell us, are you the Messiah (*Christ*)?" Jesus said, "Even if I tell you, you will not believe me, (68) and if I asked you, you would not answer. (69) But from now on, the Son of Man (*see Daniel 7:13-14*) will be enthroned in authority at the right hand of the power of God." (70) They asked Jesus, "So, are you claiming to be the Son of God?" Jesus said, "Yes, as you say that I am." (71) Then they said, "We do not need any more evidence. We have heard him say it."

408 - Judas Commits Suicide
(Matthew 27:3-10)

Matthew 27:3-10 - (3) When Judas Iscariot, the betrayer, saw that Jesus was being condemned, he was overcome with remorse and gave the 30 silver coins back to the Jewish chief priests and elders. (4) Judas said, "I have sinned, for I have betrayed innocent blood." The religious leaders replied, "We do not care what you did, that's your problem." (5) So Judas threw the money into the temple and left. Then he went away and hanged himself. (6) The chief priests picked up the coins and said, "It is against the Jewish law to put this blood money into the temple treasury." (7) So they used the money to buy the field of the potter to serve as a burial place for foreigners. (8) That is why it is called the "Field of Blood" today. (9) This fulfilled what was spoken by the prophet Jeremiah, "They took the 30 silver coins, the price set on him by the people of Israel, (10) and they used the coins to buy the potter's field, as the Lord commanded me" (*written in Zechariah 11:11-12 and Jeremiah 19:1-13*).

409 - Jesus Sent to Pontius Pilate
(Matthew 27:1-2, Mark 15:1, Luke 23:1, John 18:28)

Matthew 27:1-2 - (1) Then the whole assembly of Jewish religious leaders rose and led Jesus to Pontius Pilate, the Roman governor of Judea. (2) So they bound him and led him away and handed him over to Pontius Pilate, the governor of Judea.

Mark 15:1 - So they bound Jesus, led him away, and handed him over to Pontius Pilate, the Roman governor of Judea.

Luke 23:1 - Then the whole assembly of Jewish religious leaders rose and led Jesus to Pontius Pilate, the Roman governor of Judea.

John 18:28 - Then, early the next morning (*before 6 a.m.*), the Jewish religious leaders took Jesus from the house of Caiaphas to the palace of Pontius Pilate, the Roman governor of Judea. But the

Jews would not go inside the palace because it was non-Jewish. By now it was early in the morning, and to avoid ceremonial uncleanness they did not enter the palace, because they wanted to be able to eat the the Passover meal.

(There are two possible locations for the trial of Jesus before Pontius Pilate. The first is the Antonia Fortress built by Herod the Great, located at the northwestern corner of the Temple Mount. It is here that the traditional "Way of the Cross" begins. The second location is the palace of Herod the Great, located in the northwestern corner of the city walls of the upper city of Jerusalem).

410 - Pilate Hears the Charges Against Jesus
(Luke 23:2, John 18:29-32)

Luke 23:2 - Once there, they began accusing Jesus before Pilate, saying, "We found this man misleading the nation of Israel, and refusing to pay taxes to Caesar the Roman Emperor. He claims that he is the Messiah (*Christ*), a king!"

John 18:29-32 - (29) So Pilate went outside his palace to meet them and asked, "What charges do you bring against this man?" (30) They said, "We would not have brought him to you if he was not a criminal." (31) Pilate said to them, "Take him and judge him by your own law." But the religious leaders said, "But you know that it is not lawful for us to put anyone to death." (32) This happened to fulfill what Jesus had said about the kind of death he was going to die.

411 - Pilate Questions Jesus the First Time
(Matthew 27:11, Mark 15:2, Luke 23:3, John 18:33-38)

Matthew 27:11 - Meanwhile Jesus stood before governor Pontius Pilate, and the governor asked him, "Are you the king of the Jews?" Jesus said to him, "Yes, as you have said so."

Mark 15:2 - Pilate asked Jesus, "Are you the king of the Jews?" Jesus said, "You have said so."

Luke 23:3 - So Pilate asked Jesus, "Are you the king of the Jews?" Jesus said to him, "You have said so."

John 18:33-38 - (33) Pilate then went back inside his palace. He brought Jesus in and asked him, "Are you the king of the Jews?" (34) Jesus said, "Is this what you believe, or did others tell you this about me?" (35) Pilate said, "I am not a Jew. It is your own people and chief priests that handed you over to me. What did you do?" (36) Jesus said, "My kingdom is not of this world. If my kingdom were of this world, my disciples would have fought against my arrest by the Jewish leaders. But my kingdom is from another world." (37) Pilate said, "So you are a king!" Jesus said, "You say that I am a king. But the reason I was born and came into this world is to tell people the truth. Whoever belongs to the truth listens to my teaching." (38) Pilate said, "What is truth?"

412 - Pilate Speaks to the Jews
(Luke 23:4, John 18:38)

Luke 23:4 - Then Pilate announced to the Jewish chief priests and the crowd of people, "I do not find this man guilty of a crime."

John 18:38 - Then he went outside his palace again to talk to the Jews gathered there and said to them, "I don't find this man guilty of the charge you brought against him."

413 - Pilate Questions Jesus the Second Time
(Matthew 27:12-14, Mark 15:3-5)

Matthew 27:12-14 - (12) When Jesus was accused by the Jewish chief priests and elders, he gave no answer. (13) Then Pilate asked him, "Don't you hear the charges they are bringing against you?" (14) But Jesus did not reply, not even to a single charge. Pontius Pilate was totally amazed.

Mark 15:3-5 - (3) The Jewish chief priests accused Jesus of many things. (4) So again Pilate asked Jesus, "Aren't you going to give me an answer? They are accusing you of many things." (5) Pilate was amazed that Jesus still did not say anything.

414 - Pilate Sends Jesus to Herod Antipas
(Luke 23:5-7)

Luke 23:5-7 - (5) But they insisted, "Jesus stirs up the people all over Judea with his teaching. He started in Galilee and has now come to Jerusalem." (6) When Pilate heard this, he asked if Jesus was from Galilee. (7) When Pilate learned that Jesus was from Galilee—a region under the leadership of the governor Herod Antipas—he sent Jesus to Herod, who was in Jerusalem at that time.

(Herod Antipas was a son of Herod the Great and governed Galilee and Perea. He was also the one who ordered the imprisonment and beheading of John).

415 - Herod Antipas Questions Jesus
(Luke 23:8-10)

Luke 23:8-10 - (8) When Herod Antipas saw Jesus, he was very pleased, because he had wanted to meet him for a long time. From everything that he had heard about Jesus, he hoped to see him do a miracle of some sort. (9) Although Herod asked Jesus many questions, he did not answer him. (10) The Jewish chief priests and teachers of the law of Moses were standing there, viciously accusing Jesus before Herod.

416 - Jesus is Mocked and Sent Back to Pilate
(Luke 23:11-12)

Luke 23:11-12 - (11) Then Herod Antipas and his soldiers ridiculed Jesus and mocked him. They dressed him in a royal robe and sent him back to Pontius Pilate. (12) Although they had previously been enemies, Herod Antipas and Pontius Pilate became friends during this time.

417 - Pilate's Wife Pleads for Jesus' Freedom
(Matthew 27:19)

Matthew 27:19 - While Pilate was sitting on the judge's seat, his wife sent him this message: "Don't have anything to do with the innocent man, because I have suffered a great amount in a dream today because of him."

- -

- -

- -

- -

- -

418 - Pilate Finds Jesus Innocent
(Luke 23:13-17)

Luke 23:13-17 - (13) Pontius Pilate called together the Jewish chief priests, rulers, and the people, (14) and said to them, "You brought Jesus to me as one who was inciting a rebellion among the people. I have examined him before you, and I have not found him guilty of the criminal charges that have been brought against him. (15) Neither has Herod Antipas, for he has sent Jesus back to us. He has done nothing to deserve death. (16-17) Therefore, I will punish him and then let him go free."

- -

- -

- -

- -

- -

419 - Jews Chose Barabbas Over Jesus
(Matthew 27:15-21, Mark 15:6-11, John 18:39-40)

Matthew 27:15-21 - (15) Now it was the governor's custom at the Jewish Passover to release a prisoner chosen by the people. (16) At that time the Romans had a well-known prisoner named Barabbas. (17) So when the crowd of people had gathered, Pilate asked them, "Which prisoner do you want me to release to you: Jesus Barabbas, or Jesus who is called the Messiah (*Christ*)?" (18) For Pilate knew it was out of jealously that the Jews had delivered Jesus over to him. (20) But the Jewish chief priests and the elders persuaded the crowd of people to ask for Barabbas and to have Jesus put to death. (21) Pilate asked again, "Which of the two prisoners do you want me to release to you?" The people yelled, ""Barabbas!"

Mark 15:6-11 - (6) Now it was the governor's custom at the Passover to release a Jewish prisoner whom the people chose. (7) There was a man named Barabbas bound in prison with the insurrectionists who had committed murder during an uprising against Rome. (8) The crowd came up and asked Pilate to release a prisoner just as he would always do. (9) Pilate asked them, "Do you want me to release to you the king of the Jews?" (10) Pilate knew that it was out of jealousy that the chief priests had handed Jesus over to him. (11) But the chief priests incited the crowd to ask Pilate to release Barabbas instead of Jesus.

John 18:39-40 - (39) But since it is your custom for me to free one prisoner every Passover, do you want me to free 'the king of the Jews'?" (40) They shouted, "No! Do not free Jesus! We want you to free Barabbas!" Now Barabbas had taken part in an insurrection against the Romans.

420 - The Jews Demanded That Jesus Be Crucified
(Matthew 27:22-23, Mark 15:12-14, Luke 23:18-24)

Matthew 27:22-23 - (22) Pilate said to them, "What should I do with Jesus who is called the Messiah (*Christ*)?" They shouted, "Crucify him!" (23) Pilate asked them, "Why? What crime is he guilty of?" But the crowd shouted louder, "Crucify him!"

Mark 15:12-14 - (12) Then Pilate asked them, "What do you want me to do with the one you call the king of the Jews?" (13) But the people yelled, "Crucify him!" (14) Pilate asked, "Why? What crime has he committed?" But they shouted even louder, "Crucify him!"

Luke 23:18-24 - (18) But the whole crowd shouted, "Away with Jesus! Release Barabbas to us!" (19) (*Barabbas was in prison for starting an insurrection in Jerusalem, and for murder*). (20) Wanting to release Jesus, Pilate appealed to the crowd again. (21) But they kept shouting, "Crucify Jesus! Crucify Jesus!" (22) Pilate said to them the third time, "Why? What crime has he committed? I do not find him guilty of any crimes deserving death. Therefore I will punish him and let him go." (23) But the crowd yelled louder and insisted that Jesus be crucified. Finally the loud shouting of the chief priests and the people prevailed (24) and Pilate gave in to what they demanded.

421 - Pilate Sentences Jesus to Crucifixion
(Matthew 27:26, Mark 15:15, Luke 23:25, John 19:1,16)

Matthew 27:26 - So Pilate released Barabbas to them, but he had Jesus flogged and gave him to the soldiers to be crucified.

Mark 15:15 - Pilate wanted to please the Jewish crowd, so he released Barabbas to them. He had Jesus flogged and handed him over to the Roman soldiers to be crucified.

Luke 23:25 - He released Barabbas, who had been thrown in prison for insurrection and murder and sentenced Jesus to crucifixion, as they wanted.

John 19:1,16 - (1) Then Pontius Pilate ordered the Roman soldiers to flog Jesus. (16) Finally Pilate handed Jesus over to them to be crucified. So the Roman soldiers took control of Jesus.

(Flogging or scourging was a legal preliminary to Roman execution or crucifixion for men only. They usually used a short whip with leather straps of different lengths, in which pieces of metal, small iron balls, or sharp pieces of sheep bones were tied at intervals. A man was stripped of his clothing and his hands were tied to an upright post, and then the soldiers would whip his exposed back, backside, and legs—cutting and slashing his skin and muscles. The purpose of flogging was to weaken a man to a state just short of collapse or death. After the flogging, soldiers would often mock and make fun of the man.)

422 - Roman Soldiers Mock and Beat Jesus
(Matthew 27:27-31, Mark 15:16-20, Luke 22:63-65, John 19:2-3)

Matthew 27:27-31 - (27) Then the Roman soldiers took Jesus into the governor's palace (*the Praetorium, headquarters*) and gathered the whole company of soldiers (*a cohort, around 600 men*) around him. (28) They took off his clothes and put a scarlet robe on him (29) and then twisted together a crown of thorns and pushed it down onto his head. They put a staff in his right hand. Then they knelt in front of him and mocked him, shouting, "Hail, king of the Jews!" (30) They spit on him and took the staff and hit him on the head again and again. (31) After they had mocked him, they took off his robe and put his own clothes back on him.

Mark 15:16-20 - (16) Then the Roman soldiers took Jesus into the governor's palace (*the Praetorium, headquarters*) and gathered the whole company of soldiers (*a cohort, around 600 men*) around him. (17) They clothed Jesus in a purple robe and then they twisted together a wreath crown of thorns and pushed it down on his head. (18) And they began to call out to him, "Hail, King of the Jews!" (19) Falling to their knees, the soldiers pretended that they were worshiping him and spit on him. Again and again they hit him on the head with a staff. (20) And after they had mocked him, they took off the purple robe and put his own clothes back on him. Then the Roman soldiers led Jesus out to be crucified.

Luke 22:63-65 - (63) The men who were guarding Jesus began mocking and beating him. (64) They blindfolded him and said, "Prophesy! Who hit you?" (65) They said many insulting things to him.

John 19:2-3 - (2) The Roman soldiers twisted together a crown of thorn branches and pushed it on Jesus' head. They put a purple robe on him (3) and went up to him again and again, saying, "Hail, long live the king of the Jews!" And they slapped him in the face.

---

423 - Pilate Presents Jesus to the Jews the First Time
(John 19:4-8)

John 19:4-8 - (4) Once again Pontius Pilate went outside his palace and said to the Jews gathered there, "Look, I am bringing Jesus out to you so that you will know that I find no legal basis for the charge you have brought against him." (5) When Jesus came outside wearing the crown of thorns and the purple robe, Pilate said to the Jews, "Here is the man!" (6) As soon as the chief priests and their officials saw him, they shouted, "Crucify him! Crucify him!" But Pilate said, "You take him and crucify him, because I do not find a legal basis for a charge against him." (7) The Jewish religious leaders said, "Our law says that he must die, because he claimed to be the Son of God." (8) When Pontius Pilate heard this, he became even more afraid.

---

424 - Pilate Questions Jesus the Third Time
(John 19:9-11)

John 19:9-11 - (9) He went back inside his palace again, and asked Jesus, "Where did you come from?" But Jesus did not answer him. (10) Pilate said, "Do you refuse to answer me! Don't you know that I have power to free you or to crucify you?" (11) Jesus said, "You would have no power over me if it were not given to you from God above. Therefore the one who handed me over to you is guilty of a greater sin."

425 - Pilate Presents Jesus to the Jews the Second Time
(John 19:12-15)

John 19:12-15 - (12) From then on, Pilate tried to let Jesus go free, but the Jewish religious leaders kept shouting, "If you let Jesus go free, you are no friend of the Roman emperor Caesar. Whoever claims to be a king is against Caesar!" (13) When Pilate heard this, he brought Jesus out and sat down on the judge's seat at a place called the Stone Pavement, which in Aramaic is Gabbatha. (14) It was about noon on Friday, the day of Preparation of the Passover (*the Sabbath*). Pontius Pilate shouted to the Jews, "Look, here is your king!" (15) But the Jews shouted back, "Take him away! Take him away! Crucify him!" Pontius Pilate said, "Should I crucify your king?" The chief priests said, "We have no king but the Roman emperor Caesar!"

426 - Pilate Washes His Hands
(Matthew 27:24-25)

Matthew 27:24-25 - (24) When Pilate saw that he was getting nowhere, and that the people were getting out of control, he took water and washed his hands in front of the people. He declared, "I am innocent of this man's blood, it is now your responsibility!" (25) And the crowd shouted, "Let his blood be on us and on our children!"

427 - Simon Carries Jesus' Cross
(Matthew 27:32, Mark 15:21, Luke 23:26)

Matthew 27:32 - As the soldiers were taking Jesus to be crucified, they met a man from the city of Cyrene (*in modern Libya, North Africa*), named Simon, and they forced him to carry Jesus' cross.

Mark 15:21 - Then Simon, a man from the city of Cyrene (*located in modern Libya, North Africa*), the father of Alexander and Rufus, was walking into Jerusalem from the country, and the Roman soldiers forced him to carry Jesus' cross.

Luke 23:26 - As the Roman soldiers led Jesus away to be crucified, they grabbed Simon from the city of Cyrene (*in modern Libya, North Africa*), who was walking into Jerusalem from the country, and put the cross on him and forced him to carry the cross behind Jesus.

428 - Women Weep
(Luke 23:27-31)

Luke 23:27-31 - (27) A large crowd of people followed him, including women who were mourning and crying for him. (28) Jesus turned to the women and said, "Daughters of Jerusalem, do not weep for me; weep for yourselves and for your children. (29) For the time is coming when you will say, 'Blessed are the childless women, the wombs that never gave birth, and the breasts that never nursed!' (30) Then 'they will say to the mountains, "Fall on us!" and to the hills, "Cover us!" ' (31) For if people do these things when the tree is green, what will happen when it is dry?"

429 - Golgatha, the Place of the Skull
(Matthew 27:33, Mark 15:22, Luke 23:33, John 19:17)

Matthew 27:33 - They stopped at a place called Golgotha (*outside of the walls of Jerusalem*), which means "Place of the Skull."

Mark 15:22 - They brought Jesus to the place called Golgotha (*outside the walls of Jerusalem*), which means "Place of the Skull."

Luke 23:33 - When they came to a place called the Place of the Skull (*which in Aramaic is called Golgotha; the common designation "Calvary" comes from the Latin word for skull*),

John 19:17 - Jesus carried his own cross to the Place of the Skull (*outside the walls of Jerusalem*), which in Aramaic is called Golgotha.

(The common designation "Calvary" comes from the Latin word for skull). (There are two traditional sites for the crucifixion of Jesus Christ. The first is within the area now occupied by the Church of the Holy Sepulchre, in the Christian quarter of the old city of Jerusalem. This site was confirmed by early Christian tradition and queen Helena, Constantine's mother, who made a pilgrimage to Jerusalem in AD 326. The second location is a rocky hill called "Gordon's Calvary" just north of Jerusalem's old city. Because Golgotha was called "The Place of the Skull," people

claim that one can see the shape of a human skull in the cliff face of Gordon's Calvary. However the idea that the name of Golgotha was based on appearance is a modern one. Golgotha was most likely named The Place of the Skull because it was a place of execution and crucifixion, with skulls and bones scattered around the area. Also, Gordon's Calvary was probably not a hill at the time of Jesus, but is the product of modern quarrying operations.)

430 - Roman Soldiers Mock Jesus and Offer Him Mixed Wine
(Matthew 27:34, Mark 15:23, Luke 23:36-37)

Matthew 27:34 - There they offered Jesus wine mixed with bitter juice to drink to numb his senses, but after tasting it Jesus refused to drink it.

Mark 15:23 - Then the soldiers offered Jesus wine mixed with myrrh (*a sap-like oil that is extracted from trees for use in medicines*) for his pain, but he would not take it.

Luke 23:36-37 - (36) The Roman soldiers also came and mocked him, offering him wine vinegar, (37) and said, "If you are the king of the Jews, save yourself!"

431 - Jesus was Crucified at 9 a.m.
(Matthew 27:35, Mark 15:24-25)

Matthew 27:35 - When they had crucified him...

Mark 15:24-25 - (24) And they crucified him... (25) They crucified Jesus at 9 a.m. (*the third hour*)...

432 - Roman Soldiers Divide Jesus' Clothes
(Matthew 27:35-36, Mark 15:24, Luke 23:34, John 19:23-24)

Matthew 27:35-36 - (35) ...the soldiers divided up his clothes by throwing dice (*lots*). (36) And sitting down, they kept watch over him.

Mark 15:24 - Dividing up his clothes, they threw dice (*lots*) to see which part of clothing each one would get.

Luke 23:34 - And the Roman soldiers divided up his clothes by throwing dice (*lots*).

John 19:23-24 - (23) When the Roman soldiers crucified Jesus, they took his outer clothes (*cloak*) and divided them into four parts, one part for each of them, while Jesus' undergarment remained. The undergarment was seamless, woven in one piece from top to bottom. (24) The soldiers said to one another, "Let's not tear it, but let's throw dice (*lots*) to decide who will get it." This happened to fulfill Psalm 22:18, "They divided my clothes among them and cast dice (*lots*) for my clothing." So this is what the Roman soldiers did.

433 - Jesus' Prayer of Forgiveness
(Luke 23:34)

Luke 23:34 - Jesus prayed, "Father, forgive them, for they do not know what they are doing."

434 - Written Charge: The King of the Jews
(Matthew 27:37, Mark 15:26, Luke 23:38. John 19:19-22)

Matthew 27:37 - Above Jesus' head they nailed a sign with the charge against him; it read, "THIS IS JESUS, THE KING OF THE JEWS."

Mark 15:26 - ...and they attached a sign to Jesus' cross with the written charge against him, "THE KING OF THE JEWS."

Luke 23:38 - There was a sign nailed above Jesus on the cross, which read, "THIS IS THE KING OF THE JEWS."

John 19:19-22 - (19) Pontius Pilate had a sign prepared and nailed to Jesus' cross that read, "JESUS OF NAZARETH. THE KING OF THE JEWS." (20) Many of the Jews read this sign, because the place where Jesus was crucified was near the city of Jerusalem, and the sign was written in Aramaic, Latin, and Greek. (21) The Jewish chief priests protested to Pilate. They said, "Do not write

'The king of the Jews!' Write that Jesus claimed to be 'the king of the Jews.' " (22) Pilate said, "What I have written, I have written."

----

435 - The Two Thieves
(Matthew 27:38, Mark 15:27-28, Luke 23:33, John 19:18)

Matthew 27:38 - Two thieves were crucified with Jesus, one of them on a cross at his right side and one on a cross at his left side.

Mark 15:27-28 - (27-28) They also crucified two thieves with Jesus, one on his right and one on his left.

Luke 23:33 - ...they crucified Jesus and the two criminals there—one criminal was hung on a cross to his right, and the other criminal was hung on a cross to his left.

John 19:18 - There they crucified Jesus, and with him were crucified two other men—one on a cross on one side and another on his other side.

----

436 - The People Yell Insults at Jesus
(Matthew 27:39-40, Mark 15:29-30, Luke 23:35)

Matthew 27:39-40 - (39) The people walking by Jesus yelled words of shame at him. Shaking their heads in disgust, (40) they shouted, "You were going to destroy the temple and build it again in three days, save yourself! If you are the Son of God come down off the cross!"

Mark 15:29-30 - (29) The people who walked by Jesus yelled insults at him, shaking their heads in disgust and said, "So! You who were going to destroy our temple and build it in three days, (30) come down from the cross and save yourself!"

Luke 23:35 - The people stood by watching, and the rulers sneered at Jesus. They said, "He saved other people; let him save himself if he is God's Messiah (*Christ*), the Chosen One."

----

437 - The Religious Leaders Yell Insults at Jesus
(Matthew 27:41-43, Mark 15:31-32)

Matthew 27:41-43 - (41) In the same way the Jewish chief priests, teachers of the law of Moses, and elders made fun of him, (42) shouting, "He saved others, but he can't save himself! If he is the king of Israel, let him come down from the cross, and then we will believe in him. (43) He trusts in God, so let God rescue him if he wants him, for he said, 'I am the Son of God.' "

Mark 15:31-32 - (31) In the same way the Jewish chief priests and the teachers of the law of Moses mocked him among themselves, saying, "He saved others, but he can't save himself! (32) Let this Messiah (*Christ*)—this king of Israel—come down now from the cross, so that we will see and believe in him."

438 - The Thieves Yell Insults at Jesus
(Matthew 27:44, Mark 15:32, Luke 23:39)

Matthew 27:44 - In the same way the thieves who were crucified with Jesus also shouted insults at him.

Mark 15:32 - Even the two men crucified alongside Jesus shouted insults at him.

Luke 23:39 - One of the criminals who hung next to Jesus shouted insults at him, "Aren't you the Messiah (*Christ*)? Save yourself and us!"

439 - Thief Receives Forgiveness
(Luke 23:40-43)

Luke 23:40-43 - (40) But the other criminal rebuked the man. He said, "Don't you fear God, since you are under the same sentence of crucifixion? (41) We are being punished justly, because we are getting what we deserve, but he did nothing wrong." (42) Then he said, "Jesus, remember me when you come into your kingdom." (43) Jesus said to him, "I tell you the truth: Today you will be with me in paradise."

440 - Mary and the Women Disciples of Jesus
(John 19:25-27)

John 19:25-27 - (25) Near Jesus' cross stood his mother Mary, his mother's sister, Mary the wife of Clopas, and Mary Magdalene. (26) When Jesus looked down, he saw his mother, and the disciple whom he loved (*probably the apostle John*) standing nearby. He said to his mother, "Woman, here is your son," (27) and to the disciple he said, "Here is your mother." From that time on, this disciple took Mary into his home.

441 - Darkness From Noon to 3 p.m.
(Matthew 27:45, Mark 15:33, Luke 23:44-45)

Matthew 27:45 - Darkness came over all the land from noon to 3 p.m.

Mark 15:33 - Darkness came and covered the whole land from noon to 3 p.m.

Luke 23:44-45 - (44) It was now about noon, and darkness covered the land of Israel until 3 p.m, (45) because the sun stopped shining.

442 - Jesus Cries Out Psalm 22:1
(Matthew 27:46-49, Mark 15:34-36)

Matthew 27:46-49 - (46) Then Jesus cried out Psalm 22:1 in a loud voice, "Eloi, Eloi, lama sabachthani," which means, "My God, my God, why have you abandoned (*forsaken*) me?" (47) When some of those standing near heard this, they said, "He's calling for Elijah." (48) Immediately one of them ran and got a sponge that he filled with wine vinegar. He put the sponge on a stick and lifted it up to Jesus to drink. (49) The others said, "Leave him alone. Let's see if Elijah comes to save him."

Mark 15:34-36 - (34) Then at 3 p.m. Jesus cried out in a loud voice, "Eloi, Eloi, lama sabachthani?" which means, "My God, my God, why have you abandoned (*forsaken*) me?" (35) When some people standing nearby heard Jesus, they said, "Listen, he's calling Elijah." (36) Someone ran, filled a sponge with wine vinegar, put it on a staff, and lifted it up for Jesus to drink. He said, "Now leave him alone. Let's see if Elijah comes to take him down from the cross."

443 - It is Finished!
(John 19:28-30)

John 19:28-30 - (28) Later, knowing that everything had now been finished, so that God's word would be fulfilled, Jesus said, "I am thirsty." (29) They dipped a sponge into a jar of sour wine, put it on the end of a hyssop branch, and lifted it to Jesus' mouth.

(30) When Jesus tasted the sour wine, he cried out, "It is finished!"

444 - Jesus Gives Up His Spirit
(Matthew 27:50, Mark 15:47, Luke 23:46, John 19:30)

Matthew 27:50 - And when Jesus had cried out again in a loud voice, he gave up his spirit.

Mark 15:47 - With a loud cry, Jesus took his last breath.

Luke 23:46 - Then Jesus called out with a loud voice, "Father, I commit my spirit into your hands." Immediately after he said this, Jesus took his last breath.

John 19:30 - Then he bowed his head and gave up his spirit.

445 - Temple's Curtain Torn in Two
(Matthew 27:51, Mark 15:38, Luke 23:44)

Matthew 27:51 - At that moment the inner curtain of the temple—separating the Holy Place and the Most Holy Place—was torn in two from top to bottom.

Mark 15:38 - Immediately the inner curtain of the temple—separating the Holy Place and the Most Holy Place—was torn in two from top to bottom.

Luke 23:44 - At that time the temple's inner curtain—separating the Holy Place and the Most Holy Place—was torn in two.

446 - Earthquake and Tombs Open
(Matthew 27:51-52)

Matthew 27:51-52 - (51) The earth shook and the rocks split (52) and the tombs broke open.

447 - Roman Soldiers Praise Jesus
(Matthew 27:54, Mark 15:39, Luke 23:47)

Matthew 27:54 - When a high-ranking Roman solider (*centurion*) and the guards with him saw the earthquake and all that had happened, they were terrified, and proclaimed, "It is true, he was the Son of God!"

Mark 15:39 - And when the Roman soldier (*a centurion*), who had been standing in front of Jesus, saw how he had died, he said, "This man was truly the Son of God!"

Luke 23:47 - The high-ranking Roman soldier (*a centurion*), seeing what had happened, praised God and said, "Surely he was a righteous man."

448 - Women Disciples Watch Jesus' Crucifixion
(Matthew 27:55-56, Mark 15:40-41, Luke 23:48-49)

Matthew 27:55-56 - (55) Many women were there, watching from a distance. They had followed Jesus from Galilee to care for his needs. (56) Among them were Mary Magdalene, Mary the mother of James and Joseph, and the mother of James and John.

Mark 15:40-41 - (40) Some women were watching from a distance—among them were Mary Magdalene, Mary the mother of James the younger and Joseph, and Salome. (41) These women had followed Jesus when he was in Galilee and cared for his needs. There were also with them many other women who had followed Jesus from Galilee to Jerusalem.

Luke 23:48-49 - (48) When all the people who gathered to witness Jesus' crucifixion saw what had happened, they beat their chests in sorrow and went away. (49) But all those who knew Jesus, including the women who had followed him from Galilee, watched his crucifixion from a distance.

449 - Roman Soldier Pierces Jesus' Side
(John 19:31-34)

John 19:31-34 - (31) Now it was Friday—the day of Preparation—and the next day was to be a special Sabbath day. Because the Jewish religious leaders did not want dead bodies left on the crosses during the Sabbath day, they asked Pilate to have the legs broken of the crucified men (to hasten their deaths), and take their bodies down. (32) Therefore, the Roman soldiers came and broke the legs of the two men who were crucified with Jesus. (33) But when they came to Jesus and found that he was already dead, they did not break his legs. (34) Instead, a Roman soldier pierced Jesus' side with a spear, and a flow of blood and water poured from his side.

450 - The Testimony of the Apostle John
(John 19:35-37)

John 19:35-37 - (35) The man (*the apostle John, the writer of the Gospel of John*) who is an eye-witness of this has given testimony, and his testimony is true. He knows that he tells the truth, and he testifies so that you also will believe. (36) These things happened to fulfill what is written in Exodus 12:46, "Not one of his bones will be broken," (37) and what is written in Zechariah 12:10, "They will look on the one whom they have pierced."

451 - Joseph of Arimathea Takes Jesus' Body
(Matthew 27:57-58, Mark 15:42-45, Luke 23:50-51, John 19:38)

Matthew 27:57-58 - (57) When it was getting dark, a rich man from the Judean town of Arimathea, named Joseph, who was a disciple of Jesus, (58) went to Pilate and asked for Jesus' body. So Pilate ordered that it be given to him.

Mark 15:42-45 - (42) It was the Preparation Day, the day before the Sabbath day. (43) And Joseph from the Judean city of Arimathea, a prominent member of the Jewish governing council (*the Sanhedrin*) who was waiting for the kingdom of God to come, went to Pilate with boldness and asked for Jesus' body. (44) Pilate was surprised to hear that Jesus was already dead. He called for the Roman soldier (*a centurion*), and asked him if Jesus had already died. (45) The soldier said, "Yes." When Pilate learned from the soldier that he was dead, he gave the body to Joseph.

Luke 23:50-51 - (50) Now there was a good and righteous man named Joseph from the Judean town of Arimathea, who was a member of the Jewish governing council (*the Sanhedrin*). (51) He did not agree with the Sanhedrin's decision to crucify Jesus and was waiting for the coming of the kingdom of God. (52) Joseph went to Pontius Pilate and asked for Jesus' body.

John 19:38 - Later, after Jesus' death, Joseph of Arimathea (*a member of the Jewish governing council, the Sanhedrin*) asked Pontius Pilate for the body of Jesus. Now Joseph was a disciple of Jesus, but he kept it a secret because he was afraid of the Jewish religious leaders. With Pontius Pilate's permission, Joseph came and took Jesus' body away.

452 - Jesus' Body Wrapped in Linen and Oils
(Matthew 27:59, Mark 15:46, Luke 23:53, John 19:39-40)

Matthew 27:59 - Joseph took the body, wrapped it in a clean linen cloth...

Mark 15:46 - So Joseph bought some linen cloth, took Jesus' body down from the cross, wrapped it in the linen...

Luke 23:53 - Then he took Jesus' body down from the cross and wrapped it in linen cloth...

John 19:39-40 - (39) Pharisee Nicodemus (*also a member of the Jewish governing council, the Sanhedrin*) was with Joseph. Nicodemus had earlier talked with Jesus under the darkness of night (*see John 3:1-15*). He brought a mixture of oils (*myrrh and aloes*) that weighed about 75 lb. (40) In accordance with Jewish burial customs, they took Jesus' body and wrapped it in strips of linen covered with fragrant oils.

453 - Jesus' Body Put in a New Tomb
(Matthew 27:60, Mark 15:46, Luke 23:53, John 19:41-42)

Matthew 27:60 - ...and placed it in his own new tomb that he had cut out of the rock (*outside of the walls of Jerusalem*). He rolled a big stone in front of the tomb's entrance and went away.

Mark 15:46 - ...and placed it in a tomb cut out of rock (*outside of the walls of Jerusalem*). Then he rolled a large stone in front of the tomb's entrance.

Luke 23:53 - ...placing it in a new tomb cut into the rock—one that had never been used before located in a garden (*outside of the city walls of Jerusalem*).

John 19:41-42 - (41) Near the place where Jesus was crucified there was a garden, and in the garden was a new rock tomb that had never been used (*outside of the walls of Jerusalem*). (42) Because it was Friday—the Jewish day of Preparation for the Passover—and since the tomb was nearby they laid Jesus in this new tomb.

(There are two traditional locations for the tomb of Jesus Christ. The first is among the first-century rock-cut tombs in the area today occupied by the Church of the Holy Sepulchre, in the Christian quarter of the old city of Jerusalem, which upholds the fact that Jesus' tomb was a "new tomb." The second location is today called "The Garden Tomb." However, it is not a first-century tomb but was created around the 700s BC, so it couldn't have been the new tomb of Jesus).

454 - Women Disciples See Jesus' Tomb
(Matthew 27:61, Mark 15:47, Luke 23:54-56)

Matthew 27:61 - Mary Magdalene and the other Mary were sitting near the tomb.

Mark 15:47 - Mary Magdalene and Mary the mother of Joseph saw where Jesus' body was laid.

Luke 23:54-56 - (54) It was the day before the Sabbath—Preparation Day—and the Sabbath day was about to begin. (55) The women who had come with Jesus from Galilee followed Joseph and saw the tomb and how Jesus' body was laid in it. (56) Then these women went home and prepared fragrant spices and oils. But they rested on the Sabbath in obedience to the Jewish commandment.

455 - Roman Soldiers Guard Jesus' Tomb
(Matthew 27:62-66)

Matthew 27:62-66 - (62) The next day after the day of Preparation (*Sabbath*), the Jewish chief priests and the Pharisees went to Pontius Pilate (63) and said, "Sir, we remember that when the deceiver Jesus was alive, he said, 'After three days I will rise from the dead.' (64) So give the order for his tomb to be sealed for three days. Otherwise, his disciples will come and steal his body and tell the people that he has risen from the dead. This last lie will be a greater deception." (65) Pilate said to them, "Take a guard. Go, make the tomb as secure as you know how." (66) So the religious leaders went, secured the tomb's entrance stone, and had a guard stand in front of it.

456 - Women Disciples Go to Jesus' Tomb on Sunday Morning

(Matthew 28:1-8, Mark 16:1-8, Luke 24:1-8, John 20:1-2)

Matthew 28:1-8 - (1) At dawn on Sunday morning after the Sabbath day, Mary Magdalene and the other Mary went to look at Jesus' tomb. (2) There was a violent earthquake as an angel of the Lord came down from heaven and, going to the tomb, rolled back the entrance stone and sat on it. (3) The angel's appearance was like lightning, and his clothes were white as snow. (4) The guards were so afraid of him that they shook in fear and became like dead men. (5) The angel said to the women, "Do not be afraid! I know you are looking for Jesus, who was crucified. (6) He is not here; he has risen from the dead as he said he would. Come and see the place where his body once was. (7) Then go quickly and tell his disciples: 'He has risen from the dead and is going ahead of you into Galilee. There you will see him again.' Now I have told you." (8) So the women ran away from the tomb. As they ran to tell his disciples they were afraid but also filled with joy.

Mark 16:1-8 - (1) When the Sabbath day was over, Mary Magdalene, Mary the mother of James, and Salome bought fragrant oils so that they might go to anoint Jesus' body. (2) Very early on Sunday morning—just after sunrise—they went to the tomb (3) and they asked each other, "Who will roll the large stone away from the entrance of the tomb?" (4) But when they arrived at the tomb, they looked and saw that the large stone had already been rolled away. (5) As they entered the tomb, they saw a young man dressed in a white robe sitting on the right side, and they became very afraid. (6) But he said to them, "Do not be afraid! Jesus the Nazarene, who was crucified, has risen from the dead! He is not here. You can see the place where they laid him is empty." Mark 16:7 - But go and tell Peter and the disciples that Jesus is going ahead of you into Galilee. There you will see him, just as he told you." (8) Shaking and filled with amazement, the women went out and ran from the tomb. They said nothing to anyone, because they were very afraid.

Luke 24:1-8 - (1) Early on Sunday morning—the first day of the week—the women took the fragrant oils they had prepared and went to Jesus' tomb. (2) When they arrived, they found the large stone rolled away from the opening of the tomb (3) but when they went inside, they did not find the body of the Lord Jesus. (4) While they were confused about this, suddenly two men (*angels*) stood by them, wearing bright shining clothing that looked like lightning. (5) The women were filled with fear and bowed down with their faces to the ground, but the men said to them, "Why are you looking for the living among the dead? (6) Jesus is not here; he has risen from the dead! Remember how he told you when he was with you in Galilee, (7) 'The Son of Man (*see Daniel 7:13-14*) must be delivered into the hands of sinful men, be crucified, and raised from the dead on the third day.' " (8) Then the women remembered what Jesus had told them.

John 20:1-2 - (1) Very early Sunday morning—the first day of the week—Mary Magdalene went to Jesus' tomb when it was still dark, and saw that the stone had been moved away from the entrance of the tomb. (2) So Mary Magdalene ran to Simon Peter and the other disciple—the one Jesus loved (*probably the apostle John*)—and said to them, "They have taken the Lord's body out of the tomb, and we do not know where they have moved him!"

457 - Peter and John Go to Jesus' Tomb
(Luke 24:12, John 20:3-10)

Luke 24:12 - However, Peter got up and ran to the tomb. He bent over, looked inside the tomb, and saw the strips of linen clothes lying there, and so he went away, wondering to himself what had happened.

John 20:3-10 - (3) So Peter and the other disciple (*probably John*) ran toward the tomb. (4) Although both were running, the other disciple outran Peter and reached the tomb first. (5) He bent down and looked inside at the strips of linen lying there but he did not go into the tomb. (6) Then Simon Peter arrived and went immediately inside the tomb. He saw the strips of linen lying there, (7) and the cloth that had been wrapped around Jesus' head. The cloth was lying in its place, separate from the linen. (8) Then the other disciple, who had reached the tomb first, also went inside the tomb. He saw and believed. (9) But they still did not understand from God's word that Jesus had to rise from the dead. (10) Then the two disciples went back to where they were staying.

458 - Jesus Appears to Mary Magdalene
(Mark 16:9-10, John 20:11-17)

Mark 16:9-10 - (9) After Jesus rose from the dead early on Sunday morning—the first day of the week—he appeared first to Mary Magdalene, from whom he had cast out seven demons. (10) Mary Magdalene went and told those who had been with him and who were mourning and weeping.

John 20:11-17 - (11) Now Mary Magdalene stood outside the tomb crying. As she cried, she bent over to look inside the tomb (12) and saw two angels dressed in white, seated where Jesus' body had been laid. One was sitting where Jesus' head had rested, and the other was sitting where Jesus' feet had been. (13) They asked Mary Magdalene, "Woman, why are you crying?" She said, "They have taken my Lord's body, and I do not know where they have taken him." (14) Then Mary turned around and saw Jesus standing there, but she did not recognize him. (15) Jesus asked her, "Woman, why are you crying? Who are you looking for?" Thinking he was the gardener, she said, "Sir, if you have taken my Lord's body away, tell me where you have put him, and I will get him." (16) Jesus said to her, "Mary!" She turned to him and shouted out in Aramaic, "Rabboni!" (*which means Teacher*). (17) Jesus said, "Do not hold on to me, because I have not yet ascended to the Father. Go to my disciples and tell them, 'I am ascending to my Father and your Father, to my God and your God.'"

459 - Jesus Appears to Women Disciples
(Matthew 28:9-10)

Matthew 28:9-10 - (9) Suddenly Jesus met them (*the women*) and said, "Greetings!" They came to him, fell down and held his feet, worshiping him. (10) Then Jesus said to them, "Do not be afraid. Go and tell my brothers to go to Galilee; there they will see me."

460 - The Woman Disciples Tell the Apostles
(Mark 16:11, Luke 24:9-11, John 20:18)

Mark 16:11 - When Mary Magdalene told them that she had seen Jesus alive, they did not believe her. `

Luke 24:9-11 - (9) When the women left the tomb, they told what they saw to the Eleven Apostles and to all the others. (10) It was Mary Magdalene, Joanna, Mary the mother of James, and the other women with them who told everything to the apostles. (11) But they did not believe the women, because they thought what they said was nonsense.

John 20:18 - Mary Magdalene went to the disciples with the good news and said, "I have seen the Lord!" And she told them everything that Jesus had said to her.

461 - The Roman Guards' Falsew Report
(Matthew 28:11-15)

Matthew 28:11-15 - (11) While the women were leaving, some of the guards went into Jerusalem and told the Jewish chief priests everything that had happened. (12) When the chief priests had met with the elders and devised a plan, they gave the soldiers a large sum of money. (13) They told them, "You must lie and say, 'His disciples came during the night and took Jesus' body while we were sleeping.' (14) This lie will persuade the governor Pontius Pilate and will keep you out of trouble." (15) So the soldiers took the money and did as they were told. And this false story has been told many times among the Jews to this very day.

462 - Jesus Appears to Disciples Near Emmaus
(Mark 16:12-13, Luke 24:13-33, 35)

Mark 16:12-13 - (12) Afterward Jesus appeared in a different form to two disciples who were walking from Jerusalem into the country. (13) These two returned to Jerusalem and reported to the disciples, but they did not believe them either.

Luke 24:13-33, 35 - (13) Now that same Sunday, two disciples were walking to the village of Emmaus from Jerusalem, which was located about seven miles (11 km) from Jerusalem. (14) They were talking with each other about everything that had happened. (15) While they were talking, Jesus came up and walked along with them; (16) but they were kept from recognizing him. (17) Jesus asked them, "What are you talking about?" They stopped, and their faces were very sad. (18) Then one of them, named Cleopas, said, "Are you the only visitor to Jerusalem who does not know what has happened there?" (19) Jesus said, "What things?" They said to him, "About Jesus of Nazareth! He was a prophet, powerful in word and deed before God and all the people. (20) The Jewish chief priests and our rulers delivered him over to the Romans to be sentenced to death, and they crucified him. (21) We were hoping that he was the one who was going to redeem Israel. And it has been three days since all this took place. (22) Also, some of the women disciples surprised us. They went to Jesus' tomb early this morning, (23) but they didn't find his body. They came and told us that they had seen a vision of angels, who said that Jesus was raised from the dead and is alive! (24) Then some of the disciples went to the tomb and found it just as the women had said, but they did not see Jesus." (25) Jesus said to them, "You are foolish. Are you so slow of heart to believe all that the (*Old Testament*) prophets have written! (26) Didn't the

Messiah (*Christ*) have to suffer all these things and then enter his glory?" (27) And beginning with Moses and all the (*Old Testament*) prophets, Jesus interpreted for them what was said in the Bible concerning himself. (28) As they approached the village of Emmaus, Jesus acted like he was going to walk farther. (29) But they begged him, "Stay with us, for it is almost night." So Jesus stayed with them. (30) When Jesus was eating with them, he took bread, gave thanks to God, broke it and began to give it to them. (31) Then their eyes were opened and they recognized that it was Jesus—but then he immediately disappeared from their sight. (32) They said to each other, "Our hearts were burning within us while he talked to us on the road and explained the Bible (*Old Testament*) to us!"

(33) They immediately got up and went back up to Jerusalem. When they found the Eleven Apostles and the other disciples together. (35) Then the two men told them that Jesus had appeared to them on the road to Emmaus, and how they recognized him when he broke bread.

463 - Jesus Appears to Peter
(Luke 24:34)

Luke 24:34 - ... they were told, "It is true! The Lord has risen from the dead and has appeared to Simon (*Peter*)."

464 - Jesus Appears to the Apostles the First Time
(Mark 16:14-18, Luke 24:36-49, John 20:19-23)

Mark 16:14-18 - (14) Later Jesus appeared to the Eleven Apostles as they were eating. He rebuked them for their lack of faith and because they were so stubborn that they had refused to believe those who had seen him alive after he rose from the dead.(15) Jesus said to them, "Go into all the world and proclaim the gospel (*good news*) of God to all creation. (16) Whoever believes and is baptized will be saved, but whoever does not believe will be condemned. (17) And these signs will accompany those who believe: In my name they will cast out demons; they will speak in new languages (*tongues*); (18) they will pick up snakes with their hands; and if they drink deadly poison, it will not hurt them; and they will place their hands on sick people and they will be healed."

Luke 24:36-49 (36) While they were still talking about these things, Jesus stood among them and said to them, "Peace be with you!" (37) But they were all startled and terrified, because they thought they were seeing a ghost. (38) Jesus said to them, "Why are you troubled, and why do you have doubts in your minds? (39) Look at my hands and feet. It is me! Touch me and see; a ghost does not have flesh and bones as I do." (40) When he had said this, he showed them his hands and feet. (41) And although they still did not believe it because of their joy and amazement, he asked them, "Do you have anything here to eat?" (42) They gave him a piece of cooked fish, (43) and he took it and ate it in front of them. (44) Jesus said to them, "Remember, this is what I told you would happen when I was with you: Everything must be fulfilled that is written about me in the law of Moses, the Prophets, and the Psalms (*the entire Old Testament*)." (45) Then Jesus opened their minds so they could understand God's word. (46) He told them, "This is what is written: The Messiah (*Christ*) must suffer and be raised from the dead on the third day, (47) and repentance for the forgiveness of sins will be proclaimed in my name to all nations, beginning in Jerusalem. (48) You are all eyewitnesses of these things. (49) I am going to send you the Holy Spirit who my Father has promised; but stay in Jerusalem until you have been anointed with power from heaven."

John 20:19-23 (19) It was Sunday evening—the first day of the week—and the disciples were gathered together in a locked room of a private house in Jerusalem because they feared the Jewish religious leaders. Jesus came and stood among them and said, "Peace be with you!" (20) Then he showed them the marks on his hands and side. The disciples were filled with joy when they saw the Lord. (21) Again Jesus said, "Peace be with you! As the Father has sent me into this world, I am sending you." (22) And then Jesus breathed on them and said, "Receive the Holy Spirit! (23) If you forgive a person's sins, their sins are forgiven, but if you refuse to forgive a person's sins, they are not forgiven."

465 - Apostles Tell Thomas About Jesus' Resurrection
(John 20:24-25)

John 20:24-25 - (24) Now Thomas (*also called Didymus, the Twin*), one of the Twelve Apostles, was not with the disciples when Jesus first appeared to them. (25) So the other disciples told him, "We have seen the Lord!" But Thomas said to them, "Unless I see and touch the nail marks in his hands, and put my hand into his side, I will not believe."

466 - Jesus Appears to the Apostles the Second Time
(John 20:26-29)

John 20:26-29 - (26) Eight days later (*after Jesus' resurrection*), his disciples were gathered in the locked room again, and Thomas was with them. Jesus came and stood among them and said, "Peace be with you!" (27) Then he said to Thomas, "Touch the nail marks on my hands and put your hand into my side. Now stop doubting and believe." (28) Thomas shouted, "My Lord and my God!" (29) Then Jesus said to him, "You believe in me because you have seen me, but blessed are those who have not seen me and still believe."

467 - Jesus Appears to the Apostles in Galilee
(John 21:1-14)

John 21:1-14 - (1) Later Jesus appeared again to his disciples by Lake Galilee. It happened this way: (2) Simon Peter, Thomas (*called Didymus, the Twin*), Nathanael from Cana in Galilee, James and John the sons of Zebedee, and two other disciples were all together. (3) Simon Peter said to them, "I'm going fishing." The others said, "We're going with you." So they got into the boat and fished all night, but they did not catch any fish. (4) As the sun was rising early in the morning, Jesus stood on the shore of Lake Galilee, but the disciples did not recognize him. (5) Jesus shouted to them, "Friends, haven't you caught any fish?" They said, "No!" (6) Jesus said, "Throw your net to the right side of the boat and you will catch fish." When they did what Jesus said, they caught so many fish that they could not bring their net into the boat. (7) Then the disciple whom Jesus loved (*probably the apostle John*) said to Peter, "It is the Lord!" As soon as Simon Peter heard that it was the Lord, he wrapped his outer garment (*cloak*) around him (*for he had taken it off to fish*) and jumped into the water. (8) The other disciples followed in the boat, towing the net full of fish, because they were about 100 yards (*90 meters*) from the shore. (9) When they landed, they saw fish being cooked on a charcoal fire and some bread. (10) Jesus said to them, "Bring me some of the fish you have caught." (11) So Simon Peter climbed back into the boat and dragged the net onto the shore. The net was full of 153 large fish, but it did not tear. (12) Jesus said to them, "Come and eat breakfast." None of the disciples dared ask him, "Who are you?" For they knew it was the Lord. (13) Jesus took the bread and fish and gave it to them. (14) This was now the third time that Jesus appeared to his disciples after his resurrection from the dead.

468 - Jesus Speaks to Peter
(John 21:15-23)

John 21:15-19 - (15) After they had finished eating, Jesus asked Simon Peter, "Simon, son of John, do you love me more than the other disciples?" Peter said, "Yes, Lord, you know that I love you." Jesus said to Simon Peter, "Feed my young sheep." (16) Again Jesus asked, "Simon, son of John, do you love me?" Peter said, "Yes, Lord, you know that I love you." Jesus said, "Take care of my sheep." (17) Jesus asked Peter a third time, "Simon, son of John, do you love me?" Peter was sad because Jesus had asked him three times whether he loved him. He said, "Lord, you know everything; you know that I love you." Jesus said, "Feed my sheep. (18) I tell you the truth: When you were younger you dressed yourself and went where you wanted to go. But when you are old you will stretch out your hands for help, and other people will dress you and will take you where you do not want to go." (19) Jesus said this to reveal the kind of death (*crucifixion*) by which Peter would glorify God. Then he said to Peter, "Follow me!"

John 21:20-23 - (20) Peter turned and saw the disciple whom Jesus loved (*the apostle John*) was following them. This was the disciple who had leaned back against Jesus at the Passover meal and had said, "Lord, who is going to betray you?" (21) When Peter saw him, he asked Jesus, "Lord, what is going to happen to him?" (22) Jesus said, "What is it to you if I want him to stay alive until I come again? You just follow me!" (23) Because of Jesus' statement, a rumor spread among the believers that this disciple (*the apostle John*) would not die. But Jesus did not say that he would not die; he only said, "What is it to you if I want him to stay alive until I come again?"

- -

- -

- -

- -

- -

469 - Jesus Gives the Apostles the Great Commission
(Matthew 28:16-20)

Matthew 28:16-20 - Then the Eleven Apostles traveled to the Galilean mountainside (*probably in the hills west of Capernaum*) where Jesus had told them to meet him. (17) When they saw Jesus, they worshiped him; but some of them were not sure that it was him. (18) Then Jesus came and said to them, "All authority in heaven and on earth has been given to me. (19) Therefore go and make disciples of all nations, baptizing them in the name of the Father and of the Son and of the Holy Spirit, (20) and teaching them to obey everything that I have taught you. I tell you the truth: I am with you always, to the very the end of the world (*of this age*)!"

470 - Jesus Ascends to Heaven
(Mark 16:19, Luke 24:50-51)

Mark 16:19 - After the Lord Jesus had said these things to his disciples, he was taken up into heaven (*from Bethany on the Mount of Olives*) and enthroned in authority at God's right hand.

Luke 24:50-51 - (50) Jesus led them to the area of Bethany on the Mount of Olives. He raised his hands and blessed them. (51) While he was blessing them, he left them and was taken up into heaven.

471 - The Apostles Return to Jerusalem
(Luke 24:52)

Luke 24:52 - Then they worshiped Jesus and went back to Jerusalem with great joy. (53) And they continually met in the Jerusalem temple, praising God.

472 - Holy People Resurrected from the Tombs
(Matthew 27:52-53)

Matthew 27:52-53 - (52) The bodies of many holy people who had died were raised to life. (53) They came out of their tombs after Jesus' resurrection and went into the holy city of Jerusalem and appeared to many people.

473 - The Great Commission Begins
(Mark 16:20)

Mark 16:20 - Then the disciples went out to proclaim the gospel (*good news*) of God everywhere in the world, and the Lord helped them by confirming the salvation message with miraculous signs (*miracles*).

474 - The Miraculous Signs of Jesus
(John 20:30-31)

John 20:30-31 - (30) Jesus did many other miraculous signs (*miracles*) in the presence of his disciples that are not written about in this book. (31) But these are written that you will believe that Jesus is the Messiah (*Christ*), the Son of God, and that by believing you will have eternal life in his name.

475 - The Eyewitness Testimony of the Apostle John
(John 21:24-25)

John 21:24-25 - (24) This is the disciple (*the apostle John*) who testifies to all these things, and who has written them down. We know that his eyewitness testimony is true! (25) Jesus did many other things as well, but if every one of them were written down, I suppose that the whole world would not have room for the books that would be written.

Other books
by Dr. Andrew Jackson

The International English Bible

A New Testament Translation

A Guide Inside the Early Church of Asia Minor

300 Profiles

Istanbul

A Guide Inside the Early Church of Constantinople

The Lost Land of the Bible

Prayer Pilgrimages Through Turkey

The Way of Jesus

Living a Life of Grace and Hope Toward Others

Mormonism Examined

*Comparing the Teaching and Practices
of Latter-day Saints With Biblical Christianity (release 2018)*

Made in the USA
Lexington, KY
30 May 2018